Governance, Accountability, and Sustainable Development

A New Agenda for the 21st Century

Nick A. Shepherd, FCMC, CGA, FCCA

THOMSON

CARSWELL

Library and Archives Canada Cataloguing in Publication

Shepherd, Nick
Governance, accountability, and sustainable development:
a new agenda for the 21st century / Nick A. Shepherd.

Includes bibliographical references and index.
ISBN 0-459-28195-X

1. Corporate governance. 2. Social responsibility
of business. 3. Organizational change. I. Title.

HD2741.S44 2005   658.4'08   C2005-900964-0

Composition: Computer Composition of Canada Inc.

THOMSON
CARSWELL

One Corporate Plaza
2075 Kennedy Road
Toronto, Ontario
M1T 3V4

Customer Relations:
Toronto 1-416-609-3800
Elsewhere in Canada/U.S. 1-800-387-5164
Fax 1-416-298-5082
website: www.carswell.com
E-mail: carswell.orders@thomson.com

*For our children: that every generation may work
to create a better place than we inherited*

PREFACE

This book is not about Boards of directors or the legal aspects of organizational governance. It is about fixing a broken model that is becoming unworkable; it is about new thinking. Most importantly, it is about addressing the sacred trust and accountability of those who spend their lives using the resources that belong to others. Recognition of the current problems is key to changing the traditional model of accounting frameworks that present the value of an enterprise in a true and fair way.

As we enter the 21st century, we have started to confuse accounting with accountability. We are forgetting that organizations are, in essence, economic structures established to provide products and services and, in the process, to generate profits for those willing to take the risk as investors. The problem is that commerce today cannot be managed in a prudent way simply by looking back at results. To be effective, Boards of directors and others having accountability for legal persons need to ensure that the economic worth of their enterprise is being managed and nurtured in a way that ensures sustainability for the future. While accounting, audit, and financial reporting will continue to play a core role in ensuring financial viability, today's directors and managers need a framework that includes economic as well as historic financial measures. They need leading and lagging indicators along with external and internal performance validation.

This book is presented in five parts. Part 1 is a "background briefing" and introduces the history of the development of today's approaches to corporate governance and why they need to change. Part 1 also establishes a framework for thinking about governance as an *enterprise issue*, rather than one that deals purely with Boards and their relationships with investors and regulators.

Part 2 deals with work currently underway around the world that provides some of the building blocks for a new model. One of the challenges of any change management initiative is the ability to step back from the issues and place them in a "big picture" context. Much improvement of accountability has already been carried out internationally, starting with changes made as a result of the financial scandals of the 1980s and 1990s, at which time the focus was on enterprise risk management. Into this mix we stir such aspects as models for organizational excellence, international management standards, and global reporting models to light the way ahead.

Part 3 covers the critical components for building a new framework of enterprise governance. Elements of this framework are driven from a concept of sustainability of the economic value of the organization, broadening the framework from a focus on corporate assets and performance based on financial results. This includes dealing with issues from the Board right through to reporting, and the need for breadth and transparency.

Part 4 outlines how organizations might get started using an assessment approach and then moving forward to create an integrated and aligned model that incorporates an effective enterprise risk management framework.

Part 5 contains a series of templates, checklists, and references that readers may use to implement the design and development of these concepts within their own organizations.

The major benefit to readers of this book will be varied but overall it will provide a solid background of what changes are occurring and how these changes can be harnessed and implemented in a way that voluntary compliance and the evolution of business community best practice will replace the "shoot from the hip" legislated changes and new rules that politicians respond with. Custodians of community property (*i.e.*, belonging to the general public or to a group of investors) need to hear the message for improvement and to respond by building a better mousetrap.

TABLE OF CONTENTS

TABLE OF CONTENTS

TABLE OF CONTENTS

WHY READ THIS BOOK?

Writing any book on a subject that is changing and developing is a challenge. Not only do events keep occurring, requiring constant updates to manuscripts, but the potential audience can also change. Governance is no exception. Long thought by many to be an issue for investors, investment advisors, and Boards of directors, governance is changing and is impacting a wider audience. The desire of the author is that governance be seen by and understood by a broad constituency of society — the reality being that we are all impacted one way or another by governance.

If you are an owner and/or investor, you will want to read this book because it explains how the sustainability and health of your investment can no longer be assured by looking at historical or even current financial and accounting reports. Balance sheets no longer reflect many of the critical assets that an organization has developed and employs to carry out its work. In the future, your insight into the performance of those responsible for managing and using your investments must encompass aspects that have been hidden in the past — aspects that only become apparent after financial performance starts to decline and investors realize that management has been exploiting and plundering their investments in a manner where long-term sustainability has been eroded or destroyed. This problem necessitates corporate transparency and the full accountability of the Board and the CEO for a broad range of performance reporting. This book presents many of the current initiatives that address these concerns and brings them together in a possible framework for the future.

If you are a member of a Board of Directors, this book is definitely required reading. With the problems of the last 20 years, Boards and their members have come under much criticism for failing to do their job. In addition, investors are more often holding their Boards accountable for what is going on in their business and for acting in their best interests. The question is are Board members in the unenviable position of not knowing what they don't know? There are many legal books that deal with the new legislation affecting Boards, and university programs that are providing training for Board members in their need to meet statutory and mandatory requirements outlined by business and securities laws. This book provides directors with "the big picture" of corporate governance and outlines the breadth of an organization's "worth" and sustainability that directors have the "sacred trust" of protecting.

Second, it explains how the development of best practice worldwide is starting to hold organizations accountable for a wider range of performance criteria that deals with the overall sustainability of the enterprise. It provides examples and sources of where this type of practice can be reviewed, based on those who are already applying the ideas.

Third, it shows how management — held accountable for the actual running of the organization — has already developed a new range of performance management and reporting approaches that help them deal with the problem that directors are facing — the need for a wider range of information and greater performance transparency.

Fourth, the book exposes one of the key problems with today's approaches to corporate governance — the expectation that tightening up accounting rules and disclosures will actually help directors solve their problem of effective accountability. In short — it won't. Even the accounting profession agrees with this. Directors need something else and this book provides some ideas of what to look for.

Finally, this book is about integration — trying to bring together much of what is already evolving in many best practice organizations and integrate it into a path to the future. This includes building a framework that will help you as a director deal with enterprise risk management as well as with improved accountability and sustainability.

If you are the CEO? This book confirms that the CEO holds one of the most critical leadership roles in converting organizational intent into executable actions that deliver results. For those of you in the majority that are committed to running sustainable and effective organizations and balancing the needs of many stakeholders, this book will help you coordinate many of the initiatives that you already have in place. It also provides you with an integrated framework that brings together the need for effective governance "upward" with the initiatives that you have deployed to help you do your own job better. This book identifies how many individual performance improvement activities are part of an overall framework for improved accountability and effective governance. In addition, this book provides some of the pieces of the governance puzzle that may have been missing up to now — including the ability to verify your own approaches and strategies with some developing and proven best practices worldwide.

However, a few CEOs are resisting some of these changes. One aim of this book is to provide insight into emerging trends to greater accountability of public and private sector organizations, and this insight is provided in a societal context of the new economy that has been emerging for over twenty years. Many themes are drawn together to indicate that many aspects of society and governance are converging and changing expectations for corporate conduct. Also shown are examples of how many global organizations have already stepped up to the plate and have implemented transparency in their reporting and accountability, which would have been unthinkable in the past. This book illustrates how an effective CEO must be clearly aligned with the intent, values, and principles of the Board, and must act in a leadership role to communicate and demonstrate these ways of conducting organizational affairs in a clear and consistent manner. This includes taking seriously the sacred trust that is given a CEO to manage effectively assets and liabilities, both financial and non-financial, that have been entrusted to them by investors. The reader may draw their own conclusions. Some will continue to believe that today's introspection into corporate governance is a passing fad and at the end of the day only short-term financial performance matters. They may be right — but only time will tell.

How about an investment advisor? This book impacts you. The investment industry is implementing many new rules and procedures to ensure the integrity of advice provided by the profession as well as to improve requirements for those who list or place their securities to the general public. This book provides a context for the securities changes that are taking place but also goes much further. Considerable debate continues on the merits of rules-based systems as compared to principles-based approaches. Corporate behaviour will continue to be a problem for advisors to assess; this book touches on some of the approaches to broad-based performance accountability that some advisors, such as the globally leading pension funds, are putting in place. In addition, some of the new reporting frameworks that exist outside of those required by statute are outlined, providing key insight into the behaviour of an organization. New tools are becoming available that support ethical investing as well as provide insights into how organizations are managing their assets and liabilities for longer term sustainability and are meeting the changing public demands for enhanced transparency and accountability. These are aspects of research that *must* form part of a future advisory to investors. The ability of an organization to generate effective financial returns continues to be a balance — new tools are available that assess how some are actually working to "manage" this balance and enhance their future value.

Or the legal profession? Is this book for you? This is certainly not a book about the legal implications of corporate governance[1] however it does shed light on emerging trends that legal advisors should be aware of as they and their clients move into a new world where expectations of corporate governance go beyond meeting statutory requirements alone. This book provides a perspective on what questions effective Boards should be asking, in order that they can truly protect the broad base of their shareholders' interests. In addition, structuring organizations to take a more holistic view of governance will, it is suggested, add to the probability that systems will be in place to minimize corporate surprises that could lead to legal action, even class action by disgruntled investors who feel that the Board has not been representing them in accordance with the expectations outlined in the legislation. This, in today's economy, must surely stretch to protection of both financial and economic value. Society is taking a greater interest in the

---

1   *E.g.*, C. Hansell, *What Directors Need to Know* (Toronto: Carswell, 2003).

accountability of both directors and officers in their responsibility to protect those they represent. One only has to look at the Canadian Bill C45 as an example of how federal legislation is beginning to require directors and officers to act in a responsible way in order to avoid *criminal* prosecutions.

Accountants, auditors and financial professionals? It is hoped this book serves as a wake-up call to the profession. There are a number of reasons that financial professionals should heed the trends discussed here.

First, there is a growing recognition that accountability for corporate performance cannot be laid solely at the door of auditors. Directors need a broader complement of performance information to ensure that shareholder interests are being protected and value enhanced, and much of this moves outside the scope of accounting standards.

Second, the existing approach to recognizing intangible assets, mainly through the recognition of goodwill in the books of an acquiring entity, is based on a sound accounting principle — but a misleading one when applied to investors and the general public.

Third, the profession is failing to build many of the concepts developed to assist management in the field of management accounting into value-added components of Director, Board and shareholder reporting. In fact, both management and financial accounting (including auditing) are in the danger of becoming more and more irrelevant — indeed misleading — as the economy shifts from being a tangible asset-based economy, towards one that is knowledge-based.

Fourth, if the profession fails to fully embrace aspects of non-financial performance reporting through active involvement in areas such as sustainability accounting and global reporting initiatives (GRI) then the role of the profession in providing value-added information to investors and to those who rely on third-party advice, will gradually be given up to a new and emerging body of professionals more in tune with societal requirements.

This book helps financial professionals to look outside the traditional box and see how many initiatives, some of which they may already be involved in, are converging to create a renewed framework for corporate governance. Those who embrace the concepts will be able to play a positive aspect in renewing the profession for the future.

How about those who work in the public sector — is this a book for you? Yes! Governance as a concept applies to both the public and private sector. While stakeholders and organizational structures are considerably different, the issues of transparency and accountability based on shared information are very similar. In addition, the public is concerned about accountability of both public and private institutions. Both have failed to live up to a level of disclosure, performance, transparency, and accountability expected by society today. This book shows how the adoption of many private sector type tools for management are already providing a basis that will help in greater accountability. Good examples already exist of annual reports from public sector institutions that are using broad-based performance scorecards to show non-financial performance measures. However, a key issue that is shared by both public and private sector organizations is related to behaviour — the role of values and ethics in determining not "what" the organization does, but how it does it. Many public sector scandals have related equally to a failure in process as well as to a failure in behaviour of those entrusted with the public good. This book identifies how behaviour, including both a commitment to as well as a compliance with codes of conduct becomes equally as important as financial reporting.

What about the academic world — will this book help teach new ideas? Again — yes! The world of corporate governance and accountability is changing rapidly. Compliance with statutory legislation is no longer considered enough to satisfy the public's expectations, so progressive organizations are turning to new methods and approaches in an effort to voluntarily improve their public image and act responsibly. This is an exciting time to be raising new ideas and approaches that can position progressive managers and future professionals as leaders responding to a new set of expectations that meet the needs of an emerging 21st century knowledge-based economy. As the Wall Street crash became the harbinger of change for the approaches to accounting and governance that we have today — so did the risk management problems of the 1980s and the fiscal scandals of the late 1990s and early 21st century signal a sea change in corporate accountability.

Sustainability appears to be one of the key new approaches and this book expands the concept from a limited framework — seen by many to be overly focused on environmental issues — to one that deals with sustainability in a broad sense. This includes the "triple bottom line" concept of focusing on economic, societal, and environmental issues. But it does more than this. It weaves together these leading edge initiatives with many of the other organizational change initiatives that have been emerging over the last 20 years into an integrated and connected system that treats corporate governance as the overarching framework that embraces all of these new concepts.

This movement is not new. Many organizations have been moving towards additional voluntary disclosure for many years. Yet never before have so many individual initiatives started to move towards a common framework. Academic institutions who are positioning themselves to move beyond compliance to leading edge thinking on systems and frameworks for managing 21st century economies, and who are achieving once again the public trust through effective accountability frameworks will find this book a watershed experience and a text that will lead the way in these new ideas.

Lastly, this book is for members of society who want to influence accountability of both private and public sector organizations. You may be disillusioned with those in positions of power or you may no longer trust the behaviour of those whom you have relied on in the past. You may be one of the many who, up until now, accepted that "the system worked" but today are becoming more concerned about the behaviour and appearance of greed and insularity among leaders. Take heart — our institutions will continue to be important factors in our society. This book shows how progressive organizations, led by those concerned with and recognizing the current failures of the system, are already becoming more accountable and offering more transparency. It is hoped that this book gives you heart and may go towards restoring your faith in the free market capitalistic system that has served us so well in the past. The system has never been and will never be perfect. The problem facing us today is that a few bad performers have created political attention that has resulted in many stop gap measures to try and protect the public. These measures are not going to solve the long-term issues involved in building an effective framework in a new economy. As a reader of this book, you may be able to start putting the pieces together and contribute valuable thoughts and ideas about how we create a system that better serves us — society — in the future.

So read on and enjoy! While some of the material is detailed, the book identifies how we got to where we are today, how some are already responding to this challenge and how, if we think through what we want to do and where we want to go, we can enhance and modernize our governance structures so that once again we can have faith in the system from which most of us have benefited in the past.

PART 1

BACKGROUND

The first part of this book deals with setting the stage. At the beginning of the 21st century, both public and private sector organizations are under siege. The public seems to have lost trust in the ability of the legislative and accounting systems and their approaches to protect their interests. Continued scandals are appearing in the press that lead the public to conclude that both public and private sector organizations are both directed and managed, at the senior levels, by people who appear to have value systems in conflict with those that are "generally accepted" by the larger part of society.

The result has been political action to institute Acts, such as the *Sarbanes-Oxley Act of 2002* in the United States, which try to regulate and control organizations yet, in fact (many believe), add only greater complexity and fail to address the underlying issues. Contrary to popular belief as presented by the press, most directors and managers are reasonable people trying to do a tough job in a rapidly changing social and economic environment.

This first section looks at how we got here and why the issues that need to be addressed are greater and more complex than many perceive. In many cases the issues have already been addressed by new tools and techniques in place in many organizations at different levels. The problem is one of a patchwork without a clear "big picture" framework.

1

EFFECTIVE GOVERNANCE — MANAGING WITH INTEGRITY AND TRANSPARENCY

Signs of the times — in this chapter we identify the breadth and scope of governance by pointing to some key events that indicated the system was breaking down.

1. OVERVIEW

The concept of "governance" is not new. Since the time when managers were empowered to take resources, usually money, supplied by others and use it to deliver results, there has been a need for "oversight" on the part of the providers of resources to ensure that those using them were operating in some type of acceptable and controlled environment. This traditional model was true in the public sector, where the resources were provided by the taxpayers, through to the private sector where the resources were provided by investors.

To understand governance, we can start with the dictionary. The definition of "governance" comes from the root word "govern". Further exploration expands the definition to include the following:

- to make or administer public policy and the affairs of, to exercise sovereign authority;
- to control the speed or magnitude of;
- to control the actions or behaviour of;
- to keep under control, to restrain; and
- to exercise a deciding or determining influence on.

What is immediately obvious is that "governance" is an active role and not a passive one. How this responsibility is defined has evolved and developed over a long period of time.

In today's environment the rules have changed. Governance problems arise because the frameworks of the past are no longer effective. While still required, the traditional reliance on financial measures as being fully indicative of performance, and using third party auditors to assess these financial indicators against acceptable standards, is nowhere near enough to ensure sustainability of an enterprise, or to monitor the degree to which those entrusted with the key shareholders' interests are exercising due care and diligence.

Today's directors, leaders, and managers have inherited a model populated by dollars and cents, but also have a "sacred trust" of ensuring sustainability of their organization. This depends equally on how they protect the intangible assets of the organization, and how clearly they define their expectations in terms of not only *what* the organization is to do, but what is acceptable practice for *how* it does it.[1]

Good governance for the future will not come from making more rules and tightening up accounting standards. While these will remain important, what is now needed is the creation of a broader based governance structure that is consistently deployed from boardroom to the ultimate knowledge worker that deals with and embraces all of the aspects of organizational assets. Those empowered with accountability and responsibility for governance — whether oversight or implementation — must protect and deploy *all* the organization's assets, to improve credibility, insight, and success and to deliver the required level of performance results.

2. POINTERS FOR CHANGE

It has been apparent for many years that the current approaches to governing and managing organizations have begun to fail. While significant individual events may not seem to be connected, a further look will reveal a troubling continuum. Issues include the following:

- responses to corporate downsizing starting in the 1970s and continuing since have often resulted in the shareholders equity (value) being destroyed through depletion of intangible assets such as customer relationships and human capital;
- significant negative impacts to "brand image" that can be caused by conduct of some international organizations exploiting working conditions in lesser developed countries as they strive to meet price competition on a "lowest possible manufacturing cost" basis (*e.g.*, Nike). Also, brand damage done through corporate responses to product and service problems (Ford Pinto, and Ford/Firestone tire problems, both as compared to Johnson & Johnson's rapid response to the Tylenol problems);
- efforts to respond to competition through mergers and acquisitions have a poor record, resulting in failures on integration and again significant reductions in shareholder equity[2] (as well as severe societal impacts on

---

1 S.R. Lewis, Hay Group, "Leaders Must Weave Values into Fabric of Firms" *The Globe and Mail* (22 July 2002) Careers section.
2 Piller & Madell, "Merger Mania — the Financial Risks of Mergers and Acquisitions" *CMC Magazine* (April 2000).

other stakeholders). Examples cited include Quaker Oats/Snapple $1.6B loss 1994-1997; Boeing/McDonnell Douglas $4B write-off; AT&T/NCR $4B write-down on sale 1991-1995. Canadian examples include organizations such as Nortel write-off of approximately $12B in goodwill after the "dot-com" meltdown;

- the average tenure of the CEO within Fortune 500 companies had declined from approximately eight years in the early 1990s to less than five years at the turn of the century[3] as a similar trend has occurred in the CEOs of the top global 2,500 organizations over a similar period. Boards are forced to make changes as continuing problems arise. Problems can include poor results but also governance surprises such as unanticipated risks and exposure;

- efforts by the accounting profession globally to deal with the rapid growth in intangible assets making balance sheet values less meaningful, leaving valuation of public companies to be set by "the market" with no traditional bell weather book/price ratio as a guideline; goodwill remains the way to capitalize such costs based on a buy/sell transaction, but assessment of value remains questionable even using new accounting standards for reporting and impairment;

- fraud and other fiscal problems in the late 1980s such as BCCI, Vatican Bank, Savings and Loan, and Barings Bank, mostly laid at the door of the boardroom, due to a lack of corporate risk management, resulting in boards, directors, and shareholders not having visibility into issues until too late;

- further fraud and corruption in the late 1990s, that seemed to be as a result of both corporate greed (as well as management greed), and the inability of existing governance frameworks and reporting standards and rules to deal with newly emerging financial instruments such as SPC (Special Purpose Corporations), stock options, and emerging technology where fraudulent transactions become harder to detect through external audit.[4]

- declining willingness of individuals to serve on boards of both for profit and not-for-profit entities because of the increasing personal risk involved (possibly due to lack of transparency?) that leads to escalating liability insurance requirements;

- efforts by the public sector to improve transparency as a response to increasing levels of fraud and lack of accountability, as governments strive to balance demand for services with stabilizing or even declining revenues. Examples such as the Canadian federal government's "Re-

---

3 L. Dobbs, "Hail to the Chief" (September 2001) CNN news story.
4 KPMG *Survey on Corporate Fraud* 2003.

sults for Canadians"[5] program incorporating an overall renewal for public sector management called "Comptrollership Modernization" aimed at significant improvements in accountability.

It is clear that the growing focus on legislated changes is required, but is it enough? Is it addressing the root causes of governance failures or is it merely an effort to "reorganize the deck chairs on the Titanic"? Is the problem more deep-seated than it appears? Are there other converging issues that together are moving to create a sea change in the ways in which effective governance is practised? This book lays out an argument that the problem will not be addressed until a thorough rethinking of governance takes place. Such a review, while based on history and what exists today, must look to the future and to a system of effective governance that addresses the challenges of a 21st century economy. While not all the solutions may yet be in place, there are enough directional pointers to start creating a new framework that can be populated and improved as society moves forward.

---

5 "Results for Canadians" was a cornerstone of the 1997 *Throne Speech* that defined the future look of government.

2

TRADITIONAL APPROACHES TO GOVERNANCE

This chapter identifies why the systems developed for governance over the last century worked well for the economic and social realities of the times. However, these times started to change towards the end of the 20th century and problems in areas such as risk management became early indicators of growing issues. The chapter discusses initial reactions to these concerns — such as Sarbanes-Oxley and points out that legislative changes based on the traditional ideas of governance will not fix the problems.

1. WHY IT HAS WORKED IN THE PAST

Governance has been working — quietly in the background — often with most people not knowing it was in place. Board meetings were held, plans were established for management to execute, and annual reports were generated and audited for presentation to the shareholders at their annual meeting. The Directors appointed to the Board were protecting shareholders' interests. In the public sector, government plans and priorities were established and passed down to deputy ministers and under secretaries for deployment. Policies and procedures were established governing organizational conduct and audits by the Auditor General or GAO. As far as the public was concerned, the process was working; it was assumed to be working because there were no major or significant issues that had occurred that caught public attention or gave rise to investigations or charges based on either abuse of the system or of power. It was working because as the economy and society had evolved over time, the process of governance had evolved along with it. Generally the "fit" between the two was effective. Change, when it came, was often slow to evolve, allowing time for governance approaches also to be modified.

Up until recent times, even the word "governance" was not in common use. When discussed it was often not clearly defined or understood by the average individual. Limited visibility existed, depicting governance as something that only related to boards of directors. Most people lived in a world with an attitude of "we don't know what we don't know". Governance "worked" because we assumed it worked and those living within the system itself were often not motivated to change anything.

In the 1980s, things started to change. Organizations were faced with increased competition on both a local and international basis; to respond to this they moved high intensity labour activities to less developed countries; they outsourced and downsized; they flattened the organization and empowered managers to make decisions and respond to risks and opportunities. Advances in computer and communications technology allowed organizations to move information at previously unheard of rates. Paper transactions were replaced with real time transactions on a global basis.

The accounting profession, especially auditing firms, were faced with responding to the drive of organizations for cost reduction. They, too, became larger and multinational in scope. As audit became a commodity service, these firms repositioned themselves strategically to offer a broader range of "value-added" services to their clients. This often included technical specialized support, in areas such as taxation, and treasury advice, but also a wider scope of consulting services, through which they became more closely involved with their clients' day-to-day activities.

In the late 1980s it all started to fall apart. As is discussed later, all the components were in place for a major problem in corporate governance.

2. HOW AND WHEN THINGS STARTED TO FALL APART

Financial institutions started to see problems in the late 1980s and early 1990s. Initially, it was thought that the problems were caused by lapses in structures for effective risk management. Governments and institutions moved to create commissions to study the problem and make recommendations. Best known of these are the Cadbury Commission in the United Kingdom that reported in 1992; CoCo (the CICA Criteria for Control Committee) in Canada that reported in 1995, and COSO (Committee of Sponsoring Organizations of the Treadway Commission) in the United States, which reported in 1992. The main focus of all of these was improvements in governance required to better identify risks and ensure the adequacy of internal controls.

Parallel to this, securities regulators and the financial markets were also beginning to show concern over poor press related to the perception that Boards of Directors were "asleep at the wheel" potentially affecting the capital markets. In 1994 in Canada, the Toronto Stock Exchange developed guidelines for "Best Practices" of good governance for Boards of listed companies. These 14 points included the responsibility of Boards to ensure that there was an adequate framework for risk management in place. They also included, in a very practical and straightforward way, a list of best practices on what Boards should do to govern themselves effectively as well as how to ensure visibility in the day-to-day business of their organizations that had been delegated to management. Some of these points appeared prophetic when viewed in the light of events occurring later in the decade.

Various problems continued to appear through the early to mid-1990s that included a variety of scandals in both financial institutions as well as others: Barings Bank (1995), Sumitomo (1996), Bre-X (1997), Livent (1998). The next major upheaval came with the dot-com crash in March of 2000. The world was mesmerized by the economic well-being of the late 1990s, especially in the field of high technology. Knowledge and intellectual capital were being recognized as "king". Organizations needed little revenue, customer base, or tangible assets, yet investors scooped up IPOs lending millions of dollars to these organizations. Stock prices were "bid up" by 10, 15, or 20 times the issue price on the first day of trading. The merger and acquisition world became a frenzy of organizations trying to acquire these small upstart companies so as not to be left behind in potential technological advances. Billions were paid for goodwill based on future expectations of earnings. Not to be left out, stock analysts and promoters were realizing that it could be in their interests to select certain stocks so that market watchers would react to their advice, prices would climb, and they and their organizations could cash in on significant profits. The bubble burst. In many cases, like "the Emperor's new clothes", there really wasn't a commercial product or service behind the hype and eventually organizations had to face the facts and write off the goodwill on their balance sheets. Single major adjustments would turn normal operating earnings into billion dollar losses at the stroke of a pen.

The problems continued. The early years of the 21st century saw corporate scandals on a grander scale than before — Enron, WorldCom, Parmalat, to name a few. In addition, in 2004 the empire of Conrad Black appeared to be starting to fall apart amid allegations of excessive personal gain and control. Woven through all of this was the reporting of the media, not only on the scandal but identifying those involved and asking why it occurred. Just to add a little seasoning to the mix, the corporate scandals were also plagued by questions of monster pay raises, bonus payment, and profits from stock options — in many cases occurring in conjunction with the scandals.

Clearly, public opinion stated, governance is no longer working. Public and private sector organizations are out of control. Something needs to be done. Historians may research with interest the parallel reporting during these times with that at the time of the Wall Street crash.

As always happens, when public opinion shifts, the politicians take notice.

3. HOW MAJOR NATIONS ARE TRYING TO FIX THE PROBLEMS

Politicians are a savvy bunch of people; they watch public opinion and react to changing societal pressures. Entrusted to provide leadership, they can be limited to a great degree in their ability to "rock the boat" while still expecting re-election. Likewise, those who are already part of the governance picture in a very broad sense may be pressured to limit any changes to legislative frameworks that they may be contemplating. This is a fundamental challenge of politics in the 21st century; one can argue that democracy is no longer truly representative of the general public but of those who have vested interests and can influence the creation and passing of legislation.[1]

However, the governments of most countries have responded to the challenge through changes to legislation affecting both corporate law, regulations, and securities infrastructures. In the United States, the *Sarbanes-Oxley Act* generated significant additional rules and requirements for Boards and their organizations. In addition, it empowered and required the SEC to develop more stringent regulations on filings and reporting, supported by heavier fines and penalties. It also enabled the creation of the Public Company Accounting Oversight Board.

In Canada, progress has been slower but changes are taking place. Bill 198 enacted in 2002 applied many parallels to *Sarbanes-Oxley*. In addition, the OSC (Ontario Securities Commission) took over the TSX guidelines for Boards and further revised these requirements. As well, the Canadian Securities Administrators, the Office of the Superintendent of Financial Institutions, and the Chartered Accountants came together to create a Canadian Public Accountability Board to provide greater transparency and integration of financial standards and regulations.

Things are happening. Rules are being tightened up and new ones created. Ethics are being talked about as well as being included as a part of compliance reporting. Penalties for "breaking the rules" are becoming more onerous. The question remains: will this "fix the problem"?

4. WHY THESE CHANGES WILL NOT DEAL WITH THE NEW REALITY

Taking all of the events of the last 25 years or so in the broad context, it could be concluded that the changes being made by legislators are reactive; they come in response to public demand for action. They have been initiated because politicians could not wait for self-regulating bodies like the ac-

---

1   K. Phillips, *Arrogant Capital* (Little, Brown & Company, 1994).

counting profession to develop and implement adequate changes and standards to address the issues in a timely basis. However, while many of the changes will doubtless advance compliance and provide for a greater level of public trust and scrutiny, there are two problems. First, most managers are honest and have a desire to run and manage their organizations in an effective and transparent manner. In this case, added legislation has the potential to make an already overburdened corporate sector even more mired in analysis and reporting for pure compliance purposes. Second, these changes are only focusing on the traditional approach to governance — the one that is built on the major corporate asset being fiscal. The one that assumes that sustainability is based on the validation of financial results as presented according to financial reporting requirements. This is not the case as organizations move into the 21st century. The world has changed. Tangible assets represented on a balance sheet ignore significant aspect of corporate wealth — the intangibles. Nor is behaviour addressed, other than top-level compliance, with an ethics statement in the new rules.

The fact is that organizations must become much more transparent in areas that, traditionally, have not been addressed. A new approach and a new framework is required. Accountability to move forward with this will be less of a legislative agenda than one driven by the efforts of progressive shareholders, directors, and managers who realize that long-term sustainability and market credibility in a knowledge-based economy will not come from existing governance approaches. This subject is the focus of the remainder of this book.

5. A REFRESHER ON GOVERNANCE

Few books have defined governance. Before we proceed to establish the need for and framework of a new system, we need to create a context. First, governance is a very broad subject; it deals with the accountability for the overall direction and management of an organization's affairs. Organizations may be real persons (*i.e.*, individuals and partnerships with no legal attributes) or legal persons in either the public or private sectors. *All* categories require an approach and framework for governance. A good definition can be taken from the OECD:[2]

> *Corporate* governance is the system by which *business* corporations are controlled and directed. The *corporate* governance structure specifies the distribution of rights and responsibilities among different participants in the *corporation* such as the board, managers, shareholders and other stakeholders and spells out the rules and procedures for making decisions on corporate affairs. By doing this it also provides a structure through which *company* objectives

---

2 OECD — Organization for Economic Cooperation and Development, Paris, April 1999.

are set, and the means of attaining those objectives and monitoring performance.

Although this definition focuses on "corporate" and the "corporation", the word "entity" could just as easily be substituted and the framework definition would apply to privately owned organizations as well as public sector organizations. This is the "mandate" for governance: research can look in numerous places for specific accountabilities and responsibilities but, in many cases, these are both defined by enabling legislation as well as being custom-developed by the by-laws of an organization and by policies for internal self-government that may have been created.

For our purposes, we want to try and simplify the framework while at the same time make it holistic and integrated. Governance is a shared responsibility between those who represent the shareholders and those who have the delegated responsibility to manage the day-to-day affairs of the organization. The Board can be considered outward looking in that they represent the shareholders as well as all other stakeholders who have an impact on, or are impacted by what their organization does. In this way their role is complex, and involves the continual balancing of expectations in a way that ensures both short-term results as well as long-term sustainability. Thus, the Board can be considered as having the prime role for setting standards, expectations, and direction as well as clearly defining mandates, missions, and other criteria.

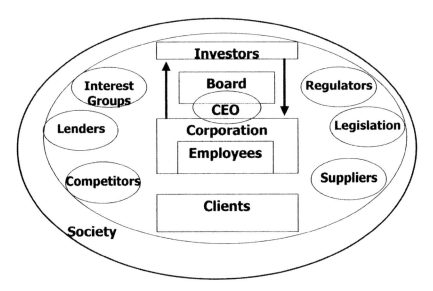

The Board must also — as part of its mandate — ensure that there are adequate policies and processes in place to ensure the effective "self-governance" of the Board.

The Board then interacts with those responsible for the day-to-day activities of the business; the first connection here being the Chief Executive or equivalent who is appointed to act on behalf of the Board to convert organization "intent" into operational reality. This person has the key role in ensuring consistency between all of the aspects of Board direction with the operational activity of the business entity.

This requires that there is clear direction between the CEO and the Board on *all* aspects of organizational activity. Traditionally, areas such as financial objectives and business performance exist and are, in fact, part of the best practice guidelines as developed by the TSE in 1994. However, purely focusing on this area alone leads to many of the governance problems of the 21st century. Boards and management must have a clear and shared view of not only *what* is to be accomplished but *how* it is to be done. This is where behavioural aspects become key to moving an organization ahead.

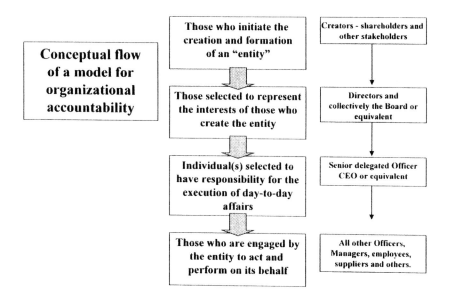

Conceptual flow of a model for organizational accountability

Those who initiate the creation and formation of an "entity"	Creators - shareholders and other stakeholders
Those selected to represent the interests of those who create the entity	Directors and collectively the Board or equivalent
Individual(s) selected to have responsibility for the execution of day-to-day affairs	Senior delegated Officer CEO or equivalent
Those who are engaged by the entity to act and perform on its behalf	All other Officers, Managers, employees, suppliers and others.

Organizational accountability for governance is therefore a continuum between shareholders, Boards and Directors, the CEO, and other key officers, and every employee within the organization. Every expectation must be clearly passed down. In addition, any reporting framework must be able to transfer back up the chain, the actual results being achieved.

3

THE NEED FOR CHANGE IN A NEW ECONOMY

This chapter discusses how frameworks for governance reflect societal progress and how they evolve as society changes. Such a time for change exists as we enter the 21st century; drivers such as global trade, technology, the growth of knowledge as a key organizational asset, and the growing concern in society for greater accountability are all bringing the need for a new approach into focus. In summary, the chapter discusses how the need for improved governance is closely interwoven with the need for an enterprise based risk management system — explaining to some degree why the CoCo framework is integrated with Sarbanes-Oxley requirements as a basis for ensuring effective internal controls.

1. GOVERNANCE PROBLEMS NOT A NEW ISSUE — THE LAST 20 YEARS

Humans often have short memories. The events of the day capture our attention and we often fail to take a step back and place whatever is occurring within the context of overall trends and changes. So it is with corporate governance. There is an inherent challenge in any society to balance responsibility for leadership and change with public accountability and transparency. Problems occur with governance under any political system. There is clear evidence that abuse of power takes place in dictatorships as well as within centrally planned socialist economies. However, governance approaches have been slow to recognize that the potential to abuse power exists in any system and when the potential personal gains inherent in a capitalist system are added to the mix, the temptation often becomes too great.

In addition, it is no longer enough to assume that individuals in postions of power and control, especially those heading large organizations will act in the best interests of both the shareholders as well as key stakeholders; indeed, in many cases, organizations have completely ignored certain stakeholders and exploited them for corporate benefit. The rise of the union movement (and the need for it to continue in some modified form as a balance of power) is an example of how abuse of labour had to be curtailed in cases where owners and managers truly were abusing the rights of individuals. What is important is that in all cases of effective governance, the majority of individuals will act in a responsible manner. What needs to be in place is an effective assurance system, that is as unobtrusive as possible so that those accountable for governance actually know whether their expectations are being met.

So the governance challenge facing us as we move into the 21st century should be no surprise. It reflects the need to change the way we govern in line with changes in the overall environment within which organizations operate; this covers individual, community, and international aspects.

2. AN HISTORICAL PERSPECTIVE

Change is permanent — it is taking place all the time — sometimes fast, sometimes slower. Often change is initiated by watershed events that occur in society. Governance is always required — it is the framework by which we hold our institutions and ourselves accountable for what they do. Whether a taxpayer, investor, or entrepreneur, all are expected to conduct themselves around a set of "norms". Sometimes these are "codified" into legislation, and sometimes they may be culturally or personally driven.

The end of the 20th century marks such a watershed, as the advanced economies move from the latter part of the industrial age, characterized by a shift to a service-based economy, into the knowledge-based economy. None of these phases is absolute; none occur simultaneously everywhere — however, they illustrate driving trends. As society changes, so do the frameworks by which society manages and holds itself and its institutions accountable. Little wonder that in the early days of the 21st century, the existing models for governance are in need of update and modification.

An important aspect here is to consider that the maturity of governance systems and approaches and the economic maturity of a society need to be in accord. Thus standards developed for application in Canada and the United States (*i.e.*, nations considered to be economically advanced and industrialized) may be too far advanced to be of practical reality in some less developed nations.

The drive for improvements in governance is seen everywhere. Governments at all levels are looking for increased transparency in what they do and how they report to their citizens. Non-profit organizations are seeking ways to be more open and accountable to those they serve. The private sector, besieged by problems in reporting, accountability, ethics, and various other issues is striving to re-establish a level of trust and confidence. Everywhere the challenge is underway to improve governance on a broad scale.

What has developed is a crisis of trust; a crisis where, increasingly, the public at large demands clear accountability from its institutions, where constant revelations about failures not only of these institutions to deliver on their own accountability, but where those traditionally relied upon to ensure that these institutions "play by the rules" and disclose their true operations have themselves failed to deliver. Left un-addressed, such lapses in confidence of major institutions can and are having a negative impact on the public's willingness to participate in the market system to make it work. In the large picture, the growing lack of participation in many nations in the voting process indicates loss of belief in the system and offers further insight into problems ahead.

So-called "lapses" in corporate governance have been increasing and cover a broad range of issues, e.g., lack of financial control in situations such as Barings Bank, boards of directors not being aware of key financial decisions in cases such as WorldCom, a lack of legislative governance strength in situations such as BCCI, a lack of effective application and interpretation of accounting standards in cases such as Enron, ineffective management of strategic risk taking in some of the dot-com meltdowns such as Global Crossing, lack of administrative attention in Canadian federal government situations such as HRDC and PWGSC. The challenge that we face is to identify the root causes and deal with these rather than reacting to the situation and looking for "bad CEOs and putting them in jail" or blaming the auditors and looking for new accounting standards.

3. SOCIAL CHANGE AND THE DEMAND FOR ACCOUNTABILITY AND TRANSPARENCY

Why is it that the public appears to be more "active" and outspoken in responding to some of these governance failures? Two key reasons — first, the good news: in many cases the problems are being revealed albeit with significant digging and analysis by reporters, auditors, forensic accountants, regulators, and others but, nevertheless, the public is finding out about things. Thus, there is some degree of transparency — however it is transparency by exception. The second is that there is a growing feeling of inherent "unfairness" in the system.

Classic capitalists of the traditional school will argue that the whole system is built to be unfair; however, it is a matter of degree. In addition, there has been and continues to be a subtle shift in the balance of power from those owning capital to those owning knowledge. Although outside the scope of this book, issues such as copyright laws and privacy, in the age of the Internet, are caused by the same drivers that parallel the problems of governance. Public perceptions are changing depending upon where you sit in society. Failure to see and respond to these changing perceptions is a significant barrier in moving ahead with effective governance changes.

Studies have shown that a key problem to organizational compliance with intended direction is poor communications. Some years ago, a number of assessments were carried out in organizations where certain priorities of the business were identified. The goal was to see what level of consistency of purpose existed within the organization between those setting the direction and policies (senior management), those responsible for deploying them (the middle managers), and those "in the trenches" that were responsible for carrying out the work. Seven priorities were established as being key to the organization's success. Individuals were asked to rank these seven items based on three sets of criteria. First — what do you think are senior management priorities? Second, what do you think your immediate supervisor's priorities are? And lastly, what do you believe is important to the long-term success and growth of the organization?

Business issues	Senior management	Your supervisor	Your personal view
Revenue and/or expense management			
Product or service quality			
Sales quota			
Employee morale			
Productivity			
Customer satisfaction			
Work schedules			

It should be added that most were considered well-run organizations. Interestingly, what emerged was often a complete mirror image between the message that senior management was trying to deliver and the message that employees heard on a day-to-day basis. The responses were as follows:

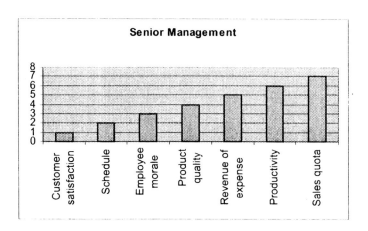

Senior management, those closest to the Board, believed that sales quota, productivity, and revenue and expense control were most important.

However, when employees looked at their immediate manager or supervisor, the priorities appeared to change. Although sales quota was again the highest, customer satisfaction and employee morale appeared to be what they were most interested in.

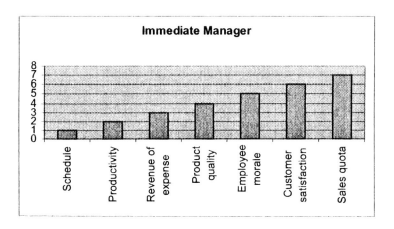

Finally, the employees had a clear personal picture of what the organization needed to succeed. First was employee morale, followed closely by product quality and customer satisfaction. The message here is clear.

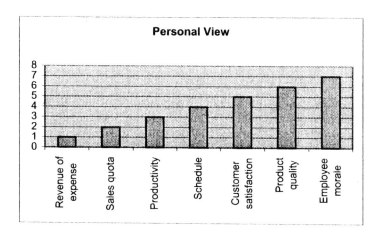

The organization had failed to demonstrate a consistent set of priorities down through the ranks. What was worse, it appeared that employees felt that management's priorities were wrong in terms of ensuring the long-term success of the organization.

What lessons does this have for governance? Primarily the following:

- If you are not assessing the opinions of people internally and externally, you cannot build an effective framework as their opinions change over time.
- If you fail to have a consistent message delivered, don't be surprised that what actually happens differs from what was expected.

The learning here is that those setting frameworks for effective governance are often out of touch with public opinion. In his book *The Naked Corporation*,[1] Don Tapscott starts out with a critical statement:

> An old force with new power is rising in business, one that has far reaching implications for almost everyone. Nascent for half a century this force has quietly gained momentum through the last decade; it is now triggering profound changes across the corporate world. Firms that embrace this force and harness its power will thrive. Those which ignore or oppose it will suffer. This force is transparency.

Social change is driving the need for transparency, and the need for greater transparency is driving the need for changing approaches to corporate governance. Shareholders and boards, together with senior managers, must take the leadership role in building these frameworks. However, they cannot do this without understanding individual and public attitudes. Many of these attitudes have, in fact, been created by the behaviour of the same people who need to reinvent the process, so change may be difficult. In commenting on the ongoing financial woes of Nortel in April of 2004, Robert Ferchat stated,

> I think the company became a very immodest company. It's always a danger culturally and personally when you start to believe your own press clippings. The problem is that Nortel had, as a culture, become drunk with ego, with an over inflated idea of its own infallibility.[2]

Strong words, though this statement is indicative of the "isolation" that creeps into dealing with reality when organizations and regulators fall out of touch with their constituency. Change will be tough:

> There is nothing more difficult to execute, more dubious of success, nor more dangerous to administer than to introduce a new system of things; for he who introduces it has all those who profit from the old system as his enemies, and he has only lukewarm allies in those who might profit from the new system.
> — Machiavelli "The Prince" 1513.

---

1 D. Tapscott & D. Ticoll, *The Naked Corporation* (Viking Canada, 2003).
2 G. Pitts, article following the firing of the CEO David Dunn and other senior executives over continuing financial reporting problems, *The Globe and Mail* (29 April 2004).

4. INDICATORS OF CHANGE — THE QUALITY AND ENVIRONMENTAL MOVEMENTS

Society around the world has been paying an increasing level of attention to "environmental management". This is a social change where the general public and interest groups, supported by scientific evidence, have convinced regulators that society must change the way it deals with both renewable and non-renewable resources. In Europe, statutory reporting against environmental goals and objectives is now a mandatory part of annual reports (accounting organizations such as the ACCA even sponsor best practice awards for these elements of annual reports). International Management Standards have also been developed by the International Standards Organization in Geneva and adopted as national standards by many countries through which best practice organizations can implement systems for managing environmental aspects and impacts on their business and receive certification after completing on-site assessment audits.

Quality Management has also progressed down the same route. International standards were developed and initially issued in 1987, which were also adopted by many countries as national standards. Again, these were developed based on management best practices for which organizations could obtain certification and recognition.

In both cases, these systems involve the development of a standard that defined general requirements, and is then used as a base against which an organization will develop its own responses, and ensure compliance through regular internal and external audits.

Progressive organizations are already adopting these changes. In a number of cases, Boards are now making reporting against environmental criteria a key part of their governance framework through management reporting and feedback. However, quality reporting has not reached the same degree of Board visibility, probably since there are less onerous legal liability impacts associated with non-compliance (although the financial risks are probably just as great if not more strategically important on the longer term). So again — change here is already underway. As we shall see later, some of the emerging frameworks for effective governance are already incorporating some of these aspects.

5. DRIVERS FOR CHANGE

Placing governance frameworks and approaches in a societal and historical context provides an opportunity to then study ongoing societal changes and predict what future frameworks and approaches to governance may reflect.[3]

---

3 B.A. Pasternack & A.J. Viscio, *The Centreless Corporation* (Fireside Books, 1998) pro-

Middle Ages	Up to 1880	1880 - 1945		1945 - 1985	1985 - 2030	Post 2030
Hunting	Agricultural	Industrial			Knowledge	Leisure/ cosmic?
		Manufacturing	Services			

Frameworks for societal governance (including institutions)

Governance frameworks evolve over time and reflect the current and historical reality of the society within which corporate entities and individuals operate. Frameworks that existed in the agricultural era were no longer effective as society evolved into the industrial age. Likewise, as services became a predominant sector within the industrial society, changes were again needed.

Change is often triggered by a "significant event". In terms of our current frameworks of governance, this occurred in the 1930s as society recovered from the Wall Street crash. Activists of the time were lobbying extensively for firmer controls on capitalists to protect investors' financial interests as well as to protect the rights and social conditions of the individual.

Even though "modern day governance" can be linked back to the emergence of the "industrial age", other links can be identified. In many ways, modern day governance both in terms of shareholders and their Boards, as well as the supporting management systems, have all been built around "command and control" type structures. Many of these grew as capital became the key ingredient of commercial expansion and, because of this, organizations grew in size and complexity. While we think of globalization as the era of mega corporations, we can trace the roots of these back to the turn of the century.

Early corporate governance frameworks came as the first "big business" developed. In 1891,[4] the Pennsylvania Railroad employed 110,000 workers; its size began to rival government whose budget that year was $387.5 million as opposed to $100 million of Pennsylvania Railroad. The logistics through which the owners ensured that their investment was effectively deployed, protected, and managed in an organization of this size would have been

---

vides a good insight into how an entity may be governed (*i.e.*, directed and managed) based on several evolving trends.

4   J. Rifkin, *The Hydrogen Economy* (Jeremy Tarcher/Penguin Books, 2002) at 81 *et seq.*

considerable. Likewise managers, trying to "manage" the day-to-day affairs of the business of this size, needed significant structures, systems, and controls in place. In fact, it was this complexity that created the start of the "modern management" framework.

The growth of "big oil" between the turn of the century, right through to the 1980s further increased these developments, and was at the source of industrialization. However, as organizations faced the changing economic environment of the 1980s, they started to flatten traditional hierarchical structures and eliminate bureaucracy that had built up over the previous 60 to 80 years in order to manage command and control. Layers of management together with key elements of internal controls were swept away in an era of downsizing and right sizing. There is little surprise then that as these changes started to occur at the macro level, gaps in governance started to become apparent.

Not until the late 1980s and into the 1990s did the problems of corporate governance start to make headlines and stir the consciousness of the average person. While not fully comprehending the issue, it was still apparent that the system that people thought was working "in the background" was, in fact, failing.

Based on the stirrings of discontent, we can step back and identify at least four key drivers that are all contributing to significant changes within our society. Already, each of these are being reacted to in some ways, but each form a part of the new knowledge-based economy, which is what future governance frameworks will be required to support.

As a final note before we move forward, it is worth considering how the current focus on protecting shareholders' interests was developed. Traditionally, the majority of shareholder capital was financial — represented by tangible assets. The majority of reporting, internal controls, standards, and audits developed with this in mind. This can be seen in the examples of the late 1800s and into the early 1900s when the predominant ingredient required to move industrialization forward was capital — money. While leadership was important, the command and control structures required the human ingredient to be there to follow direction, set by high-level leadership, and to be kept in control — hence the emergence of scientific management and Taylorism that strove to break human effort down into the lowest component parts and ensure that there was no waste and that people followed engineered instructions handed down from "specialists" above.

This driver of protecting shareholder capital became the framework of an agreed basis for reporting and accountability, supported by third party verification that has been in place for over 50 years. However, in all industries the importance of intangible assets has been growing as the knowledge-based economy is emerging. This is especially true in areas such as software and other businesses where applied intellectual capital is the predominant economic ingredient. Not that knowledge was not involved in the past;

however, it was a) employed by few as part of their requirement as human capital; and b) did not form the predominant role of organized labour. "Manual work" was the key component, as people were required to build and operate the capital equipment and move materials, in an age before high levels of automation. The governance system's inability to support the effective valuation and verification of the worth of these assets is behind much of the dot-com bubble in the late 1990s.

What will emerge in the future is a governance system, including standards, bases for comparability, and verification that reflect these changes. The development of the current system occurred through evolution, starting with the post-Depression period. So it will be for the future.

(a) Global Commerce and Competitiveness

The complexity of what governance, in its broadest sense, needs to address has increased substantially over the last 20 to 30 years. At first, shareholders, boards and management continued to use the old approaches assuming that they were adequate.

Today's reality of global operations, with decentralized decision making, a high need to be responsive and agile, and with products and services flowing across national boundaries, makes governance a challenge. Demonstrations that take place during G7 as well as World Bank, IMF (International Monetary Fund) and WTO (World Trade Organization) meetings show us that there are also significant social impacts to these changes. Managing far-flung enterprises, employing individuals with different cultures and backgrounds, and operating in different economic and political situations provides great complexity.

In addition, as international commerce has grown, many traditional "value added labour" jobs have been exported to lower cost countries, in order to meet global pricing and competitiveness pressures. This not only builds the complexity of managing the enterprise, but also encourages actions that can be taken by managers to come up with creative situations to cut costs to meet earnings forecasts. These pressures, especially when the locations are remote, bring the need for effective policies, principles, and verification procedures to the forefront. Added to this, the need to minimize corporate bureaucracy to allow managers to react and respond to competition puts a strain on effective governance including the due diligence of Boards to protect their key stakeholders' interests.

In the public sector, the implementation of ASD (Alternative Service Delivery) where the public sector establishes policy and the private sector delivers the service has also increased complexity. In addition, efforts to provide more "local" management flexibility in the public sector through the creation of special purpose entities such as Agencies (*e.g.*, Canada

Revenue Agency, Border Services Agency) have also added complexity to governance.

(b) Toward a Knowledge-Based Society/Economy

The increased importance of intangible assets was discussed earlier. The knowledge-based society, where intellectual capital and the use, development, and care of information are critical to maintaining a shareholder's worth is also driving the need for changes to systems of governance.

The challenge that exists is that historical frameworks for governance have primarily been based on the assumption that a) the major stakeholder is the shareholder; and b) that this stakeholder is primarily interested in financial capital in terms of accumulated equity. Both assumptions are incorrect as the new economy emerges.

Governance in the future needs to be capable of managing and monitoring stakeholders' assets in the areas such as brands, reputations, relations with client, relationships with suppliers, human resources, processes, patents, trademarks, copyrights, and technical know-how including application expertise. Although there are some areas where these intangibles can be added as a balance sheet asset for monitoring and reporting, overall current systems and frameworks are incapable of addressing this. Financially, this type of asset contributes an increasing amount to a stakeholder's value and the ability to generate earnings; however, the only place that it appears in the financials is goodwill (if a buy/sell transaction has occurred) or buried within the overall financial results as a "hidden return premium" in earnings.

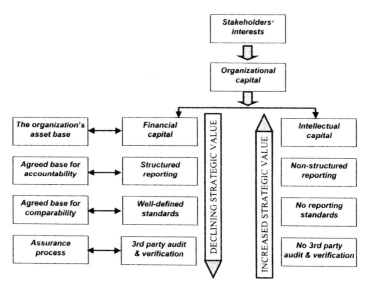

25

This is not to say that in today's accounting standards against which organizational balance sheet values are assessed cannot include some degree of intangible assets. They can and, in some cases do, however, the challenge comes in that they are usually hard to value and accounting, being the "exact science" that it is, excludes as assets in the balance sheet "things" that cannot have accurate cost and value attributed to them.

As the above schematic shows, financial capital, supported by a mature governance and reporting framework, needs to be updated because, in many situations, it is being replaced by intellectual capital where there is little or no existing framework for governance. This challenge is not unique to corporate enterprises or indeed to just "legal persons". Individual and national reputations and credibility, as well as even religious institutions, can be impacted significantly by scandal and wrongdoing.

(c) Management's Inability to Manage

While this may appear an overstatement, it is a key driver of "bottom up" governance change. Best practice managers have known for over 20 years that managing and reporting the performance of their enterprise cannot be done effectively through a focus on only the traditional review of financials. In their preface to the book *The Centreless Corporation*[5] Pasternack and Viscio write:

> This book has been born out of upheaval. It is rooted in our experiences working with top executives at large corporations around the world trying to grapple with the turmoil in their business environments. In our interactions we noticed a decided change in what executives wanted. While still mightily concerned with cost structure, business process reengineering, and maximizing operational effectiveness, they had shifted their focus to issues of how to be more effective global organizations, how to build capabilities for faster growth, how to attract and retain the very best people, how to become a true learning organization and how to develop leaders at all levels in the company.

In their search for best practice methods to help them through these challenges, executives and managers have tried many initiatives. These would include such approaches as:

- centralization/decentralization;
- TQM (Total Quality Management);
- customer service and customer-focused initiatives;
- benchmarking and best practice comparisons;
- activity-based management and activity-based costing;
- process-based management and process re-engineering;
- zero-based budgeting;

---

5 Above, note 3.

- balanced scorecards,[6] dashboards, and integrated performance measurement systems;
- models, frameworks, and award schemes for organizational excellence;[7]
- comprehensive and operational audits.

Through this search, many management teams have come to realize that there is no one answer — the issue is a *renewal of the approach to managing an enterprise*. This is what is coined as "Supermarket Management" — leaders who try solutions that are flavour of the day and, while intentionally probably quite valid, end up often distracting employees and failing because they do not become part of the woven fabric of how the organization is governed. We have seen the era of layer upon layer of new ideas and fads.

Progressive leaders and their management teams have already implemented operational changes that allow them a far greater level of visibility into the health of their enterprise so that they can manage more effectively. These lessons can provide significant direction in where the future of comprehensive governance approaches needs to develop.

These changes span both public and private sector. Organizations such as CCAF[8] have done considerable work in driving management reporting as well as "transparency" and disclosure changes in the Canadian federal government as well as other institutions.

(d) Emergence of Social Accountability for Corporate Performance

The fourth driver for change starts to move in a totally different direction. There has been much focus on the changed social attitudes to the "corporate world" and linkage of this with the changes in governance expectations. What needs to be considered is "what is cause and what is effect"? Organizations with inadequate frameworks to govern have been unable to execute their responsibilities effectively and so have, in many cases, acted irrationally and in a way — especially in hindsight — that is counter-productive. Examples of how corporate principles, or the lack thereof, can drive business decisions can be discussed using Johnson &

---

6 As an example, R.S. Kaplan & D.P. Norton, *The Balanced Scorecard: Translating Strategy Into Action* (Boston: Harvard Business School Press, 1996).

7 One can see that there is a developing level of "content consistency" emerging between the various International Models for Excellence when one compares the frameworks with the seven key aspects of management activity starting with Leadership. See chart, p. 18.

8 Originally the Canadian Comprehensive Audit Foundation, CCAF has done much work to expand public sector reporting see http://www.ccaf-fcvi.com/entrance.html

Johnson's positive and fast reaction to the Tylenol scandal and Ford's reaction to product problems such as the Pinto and the Explorer "rollovers".

Behaviour of organizations is no different than that of individuals. Act in bad faith and you develop a bad reputation; act openly and honestly and it tends to build the reputation and "put money in the reputation account" for when those occasional problem situations occur.

The public's declining trust and faith in its institutions is driven to a great degree by examples of institutions taking actions that are considered by the public as being unfair, unreasonable, or even illegal. Perception creates the reality that these organizations live with, so that the building of a renewed framework for governance becomes imperative to restoring trust and credibility with the public. These "publics" form the key stakeholders whether as shareholders, client, suppliers, employees, or just members of the society within which the organization operates.

These concerns of transparency have broad application to the public. Traditionally, organizations in the private sector have resisted suggestions that they have a societal corporate responsibility, arguing that their primary responsibility is to their shareholders and that their key interest is a return on investment. However, society (as well as investors) is now putting pressure on organizations to recognize that a key part of shareholders' expectations is that their investment is sustainable in the longer term. This requires that governance be broadened to address aspects traditionally seen as peripheral to governance.

Finally, the conduct of some corporate executives has further eroded public trust; examples of using corporate resources for personal gain as well as generating significant personal financial benefits through enhanced pay plans, including stock options and profit sharing, have raised some eyebrows (what Alan Greenspan has referred to as "greed"). While Boards may have condoned such activities, in many cases the results have appeared inconsistent with the affairs of the business itself. The example of executives enjoying pay increases and bonuses while at the same time freezing or reducing salaries of other employees and "laying off" staff, does not appear to fall in the "fair and reasonable behaviour" category. This issue becomes a key aspect that drives the focus on organizational leadership as a core component of effective governance.

6. RISK MANAGEMENT AS THE GUARDIAN OF ACCOUNTABILITY

Previously in this book was discussed the emergence of accountability for risk management as one of the early indicators of governance problems. Risk management is inherently tied to governance frameworks; risk exists in everything that an organization does. It is broad and pervasive and includes risk associated with including or excluding certain stakeholders; taking or not taking action to ensure compliance to statutory requirements of all kinds; risk associated with business planning; risk associated with effective internal controls and process management; risk to the brand when making market place based changes; risks to continuity when remaining in a key business area or venturing into a new one. No Board or management can deal with governance without addressing risk. The approach should be straightforward:

- identify all organizational risks;
- determine impacts of risks to the organization (probability of occurrence and impact in financial and other terms, *e.g.*, reputation, community, loss of staff, *etc.*);
- decide upon an approach to risk management (set a policy);
- deploy resources to underpin effective governance through tracking and monitoring of key risk areas.

Risk is an enterprise issue. In their 1999 book,[9] about carrying out control self-assessments for risk management, Wade and Wynne make a strong case that this is an approach that is here to stay. Control self-assessments developed as a tool in order that organizations could respond to the problems that arose in risk management during the past 20 years or so; however, as the book indicates, risk management is not new. The key here is that while a traditional aspect of business management, it must now move into the mainstream and be looked at as an enterprise issue. This is especially important in that responses to risk that have been identified often take resources.

Both Boards and management must always ensure that scarce resources are applied to the most critical area. In developing an organization wide approach, visibility is critical. In addition, effective identification of where risks are and what actions are being taken to address them will ensure that Boards have visibility in setting policies, developing business plans, and ensuring consistent feedback reporting.

> Like it or not CSA (Control Self Assessment) — in one form or another — is here to stay. No matter how much you may be irritated by the hype, envious of CSA consultants' earnings, or despairing of the unthinking acceptance of claims that this is something original and life saving, the momentum is strong, its broad acceptance so widespread, and the reasons for its adoption in some cases so compelling that no internal auditor, line manager, senior executive, audit committee member, or company director can afford to ignore its merits and impact.[10]

---

9 K. Wade & A. Wynne, *Control Self Assessment: For Risk Management and Other Practical Applications* (John Wiley & Sons, 1999).

10 Above, note 9.

7. WHY TRADITIONAL GOVERNANCE MODELS ARE NOT TELLING THE WHOLE STORY

Traditional models worked well in the past or at least we believe that they did. They were never perfect, continually being modified to deal with changing situations such as the protection of minority shareholders' rights and other concerns; however, today enough change has either already taken place, or is about to, that will require new approaches. We have discussed the key gaps and this is where we can move forward:

- legislation alone cannot address all the problems, especially those related to organizational behaviour and ethics;
- focusing on improving governance through increased control and legislation may in fact create added barriers to competitiveness, rather than address the root causes of governance problems that exist today;
- financial reports fail to tell the whole story, missing certain assets that are key to shareholder value;
- there is an inadequate framework for planning and reporting non-financial aspects of an organization's activities;
- there are aspects of non-financial governance already taking place in organizations such as addressing environmental and quality management (part of intellectual capital);
- trust in institutions has declined and, to remedy this, greater visibility and transparency is required;
- boards have not been aware of what has been going on in the day-to-day business of the organization; management has not been adequately directed and controlled;
- systems and procedures for identifying and managing risk have not been dealt with on an enterprise basis thus not allowing management to establish priorities and assign resources effectively;
- both financial accounting, auditing, and management accounting are impacted by changing requirements but have been slow to develop tools and approaches to handle this;
- governance concerns are impacting trust in both public and private sectors and many aspects of what needs to be improved are consistent in both sectors;
- management has been struggling for the last 20 years to identify and apply new management approaches to help them run the day-to-day business more effectively.

Overall there is a lot of momentum to call for an improved approach to corporate governance. Some way needs to be found to bring together the best of what is in place and combine it with new approaches. Through this, a framework for governance for the emerging economy of the 21st century will begin to be applied.

PART 2

FOCUSING ON SURVIVAL

Why is it that some organizations seem to weather storms of change and survive while others flounder or resort to questionable tactics as they try to steer through the storm? What is the difference in their thinking? Why does this matter and what does it have to do with the future of corporate governance? The answer lies in "sustainability" — the ability to think in the long-term and strategically so that the day-to-day challenges of running the organization are always made in the light of ensuring continuity of the enterprise.

Accounting has taken a lead role in the past in providing an assurance framework for accountability — mainly because the model of governance was based on financial capital. However, the profession is now failing to meet the challenge of providing adequate information for shareholders, directors, management, and others through which they can be accountable for sustainable performance. Sustainability today is about more than financial capital — it is about the economic value of the enterprise. While financial capital is one element, there are a number of critical elements of value that the system of accounting fails to address. No balance sheet shows the value of people, relationships, processes, or the inherent ability of the organization to be a leading edge innovator.

Even proponents of "intellectual capital" have not yet been able to develop meaningful measures that address these economic values. One might argue that purists in the "sustainable development" area are also missing the boat, as there seems to be disagreement on whether this means "doing things right" or "doing the right things". The fact is that *both* are critical to an organization's success; current and past writings on organizational effectiveness have continued to focus on *both* the importance of correct strategy as well as "flawless execution". It is not a case of "either/or".

This next section of the book starts to explore activities that are already underway and which provide some direction and building blocks for a future effective governance framework.

4

BUILDING FOR SUSTAINABILITY

Much work is being conducted internationally to address the concepts of sustainable development. In a 21st century knowledge-based organization, sustainability is much more than dealing with social changes that reflect concern for the social and natural environments. It goes right to the heart of the ability of an organization, whose main assets are intangible, to continue to exist. Unless sustainability is addressed, a growing number of organizations will lose their competitive advantage, and will either fail, be taken over or, if in the public sector, cost increasingly more to run yet deliver sub-standard outcomes. This is the theme of economic sustainability. This chapter identifies the place for this activity and how it creates a parallel and critical framework for future governance. This activity needs to become one of the mainstream drivers for change in governance and accountability as the concepts embodied deal with the current lack of transparency that many investors, directors, and even managers have in responding to social expectations.

1. TOWARDS A SUSTAINABLE FUTURE

The journey towards renewal has begun. Legal changes are being made that mandate increased compliance in areas of oversight and reporting. They also mandate increased accountability for boards, directors and managers for the work they perform within the enterprise. Interest in corporate and organizational ethics is also growing to provide an underpinning for decision-making.

There is also a convergence of thinking taking place that brings together many of the individual initiatives that are underway. These approaches, of which three are discussed here, attempt to bring "integrated accountability" to the broad aspects of organizational accountability.

A key aspect of legal persons is that they should last a long time — transcending the careers of individuals that may over time be shareholders, directors, officers, managers, and other employees. To do this, the foundations need to be deep and strong. A tree that grows quickly but does not put down a strong root system will fail when change starts to challenge its ability to survive. So it is with legal entities.

What is emerging is an approach that is holistic, integrating the expectations, needs, and desires of all the stakeholders into a strong framework that is then established and monitored by the Board and deployed throughout the organization. Key aspects of such a framework include:

- setting key policies for governance including both compliance and discretionary items;
- integrating these policies with a management model that is inclusive of the core components that make up the stakeholders' interests (*i.e.*, *all* of the aspects that contribute to value);
- ensuring that business plans as well as the framework for monitoring and measurement are aligned with the comprehensive management model;
- ensuring that there is clear accountability as plans are deployed throughout the organization to ensure effective use of resources;
- an effective rewards system that links internal and external interest; and
- a feedback and reporting system both internally and externally that is comprehensive, aligned, and transparent.

While any such approach will continue to ensure management's key responsibility to "Plan, Organize, Staff, Control, and Direct", these considerations need to take place within the context of an expanded management model. Components of this could come from "learnings" that management has developed as it has struggled over the last 20 years to find the right elements — components and levers — to allow it to manage effectively.

Risk exists everywhere within and around an organization with respect to how it acts, where it acts, and what it does. It follows, then, that an effective framework for governance will include a fully integrated approach to expanding the organization's handling of risk management to one that is integrated and comprehensive, embracing all aspects of an enterprise activity.

2. ROLE OF ETHICS IN SUSTAINABILITY

Ethics form a foundational element of any approach to sustainable reporting as well as the ability for any organization to survive — but what are ethics? Many organizations today are hiring ethics officers to oversee their performance in this area. Ethical behaviour means doing what you believe in, with the assumption that this generally aligns with the values of the society within which you operate. The challenge is to understand what these values really are. Values are generally defined along the following principles:

> A system of moral principles, rules or standards that govern the conduct of members of a group. Ethical codes of conduct approach human behaviour from a philosophical standpoint by stressing objectively defined, but essentially idealistic, standards (or laws) of right and wrong, good/evil, and virtue/vice such as those applicable to many of the professions.

Ethics are the key differentiating feature of any body of professionals. They form the basis of a Code of Ethics (or Conduct) that clearly defines what they stand for and then are supported by a set of interpretive guidelines so that individuals can "go behind the words" and understand them in a way that applies to their everyday work. Examples can be found in many places — one would be the Code of Conduct of the Canadian Association of Management Consultants.[1]

Sustainability as a belief system is then founded on an organization acting in a manner consistent with what its stated beliefs are. Therefore, ethics as a practice must be founded on a clear understanding of the principles behind how any organization, and those connected with it as suppliers, employees, directors, and others, actually behaves.

Step one in establishing a framework for sustainable development is to ensure there is a stated code of ethics; a framework to ensure people associated with the organization know it and are committed to it and a framework to report on how well it operates and deals with situations that deviate from the core beliefs. How many organizations have this framework running through their structure from the shareholders, to the Board and senior management, to the most junior person in the organization?

3. CONCEPTS OF SUSTAINABILITY

(a) The Challenge of Organizational Self-interest

Sustainability is built upon beliefs about what aspects of an organization's activity are critical to long-term survival. One key challenge is that organizations tend to act in their own self-interest and, if survival means a trade-off between pure economic aspects such as the cost of doing business and remaining competitive, and acting in a way that society would prefer or expect an organization to act — which may not be purely in its self-interest — then a problem arises. This aspect of corporate behaviour and the challenges that it creates in expecting private sector organizations to become committed to really balancing long and short-term interest is discussed in a book written by Joel Bakan,[2] an eminent law professor and legal theorist. Bakan argues that whenever situations arise where an organization has to choose, it must act in the benefit of its shareholders rather than the whole of society. CEOs doing otherwise will be subject to removal by their Boards for not acting in the shareholders' best interest.

However, Bakan also argues that as corporations are in fact creations of society in the first place, then society can require that these creations

---

1 http://www.camc.com

2 J. Bakan, "The Corporation – The Pathological Pursuit of Profit and Power" (Simon & Schuster, 2004).

amend the ways that they act or have their charters revoked! This argues that shareholders and their Boards *must* be the prime drivers for setting expectations of broad-based sustainable performance *or* legislation will be brought in to mandate such criteria. This might go some way towards changing the situation — as has been the case in Europe as it relates to environmental aspects that are enshrined in both corporate law and reporting — but this will never be a long-term solution. The drive to entrenched sustainability, and the frameworks to create such a way forward, must come from organizational leadership at the highest levels.

(b) The Triple Bottom Line Concept

Sustainable performance is often "framed" as being a "Triple Bottom Line" approach to corporate governance, behaviour, and reporting. (This term appears to have been originally developed by AccountAbility[3] — a leading organization in developing solutions for the future approach to governance such as the AA1000 sustainability self-assessment and reporting framework).

A number of approaches to sustainability deal with the "Triple Bottom Line". Initially embodied in the work of the World Business Council on Sustainable Development, this concept has become a common "umbrella" for sustainability. The three factors are:

* economic;
* social; and
* environmental.

Traditionally, elements of society have tended to limit their agenda to focus on one area: the private sector. Whether perception or reality, it is seen as focusing on economic aspects. However, because this focus has been based heavily on accounting aspects of measurement, the growing importance of intangible assets that accounting fails to recognize as an organization creates them, is becoming meaningless. The public sector, driven more by political and social interests has attempted to deal more with the social and environmental aspects. The reality is that all three components are related — economic viability in the long term can only be assured by reflecting environmental and social concerns and by addressing the much broader aspects of economic sustainability that are not yet well understood or captured by traditional reporting.

---

3 See website http://www.accountability.org.uk

(c) Social Sustainability

The free enterprise capitalist system, including both the public and private sectors of all types, builds heavily on a perception of trust and reasonableness. The public expects those who risk their own wealth by taking risks to reap the rewards of doing so; however, in recent years this public trust has been lost because so often it is *not* the owners of capital that are reaping the rewards, it is the "paid help" — senior managers who lead organizations. Examples are many:

- stock options that provide major capital gains to senior managers;
- excessive pay and salary levels;
- excessive short-term profit sharing and pension benefits;
- misappropriation of funds for personal benefit — entertaining at a lavish scale as well as purchasing items that are clearly not business related;
- excessive personal financial protection built into merger and acquisition agreements;
- cutting back on contributions to community while maintaining excessive salary levels.

The list can go on. Each of these situations builds a level of distrust between the general public and organizations. These are the contents of good media coverage and the general public begins to see the corporate world as one of self-serving greed. However, there are organizations that seek balance in understanding the needs of the communities within which they operate and try to address these while remaining competitive. Examples include:

- purchasing and sourcing decisions that encourage local participation and job creation;
- support for local institutions such as schools and colleges;
- support for local charities including organizations such as United Way as well as special appeals for specific projects (arenas, sports facilities, and others);
- allowing employees time off to contribute to the community such as building houses for the homeless;
- maintaining "connectedness" with the community through supporting social and community functions for both employees and their families;
- serving on local boards such as Chambers of Commerce, hospitals, associations, and others;
- serving on local trade and professional associations.

The list goes on yet the organization that ignores the community within which it operates will, ultimately, face disconnection and eventual alienation.

Organizations of the future need to remain connected with their communities and this means understanding the aspects of being located within a community and the impacts of being a part of the fabric of that community. The challenge for managers here is to assess and determine what level of investment activity should occur and what the payback, in traditional financial terms, is from such actions.

(d) Environmental Sustainability

The second key element of sustainability are the aspects and impacts that an organization has on the natural environment within which it operates. Clear examples of where this is critical would be the approach that resource organizations take towards the natural resources that they rely upon to generate revenues and profits. If forests are depleted and not replaced as part of an ongoing effort to ensure a long-term supply of materials, then the forestry industry will fail in the longer term. Environmental activists have succeeded to some degree in getting their agenda on the public radar and, through this, organizations are both regulated as well as closely watched in how they interact with the environment.

However, there are broader impacts of the use of resources that are not measured by traditional reporting upon which governance is based; not just the sustainability of the resources that are consumed but also the aspects of outcomes that are generated from the use of these resources. An example is the generation of large amounts of waste and pollution that future generations of society might be required to make good on.

Effective environmental sustainability means addressing both the aspects of the work that is done — *i.e.*, what processes are used, what inputs are consumed in the process such as energy and supplies, and the impacts of these aspects on the environment within which the organization operates. In this area, effective sustainability comes from "minimizing the footprint" that the organization leaves on society, from an environmental perspective through the work that it does and how it performs it. The three key areas to be addressed to ensure sustainability are:

- minimizing or eliminating the usage of materials and supplies that are non-renewable;
- minimization or elimination of any levels of waste generated in the process; and
- minimization or elimination of any negative impacts on society from the production and sale of the products or services provided.

Thus in this sector we have all of the "green initiatives" such as waste management programs, green purchasing initiatives, renewal of natural resources, recycling programs (the 3Rs — reduce, reuse and/or recycle).

40

Again the challenge of sustainability in this area is in determining where the financial rewards come from to justify the investment initiatives. However, several case studies have been developed over time that show savings in areas such as reduced raw materials costs, reduced waste disposal costs, reduced legal costs, and others. While payback may, on some level, take an extended period of time, some measure of return on investment can be determined.

(e) Economic Sustainability

In short, economic sustainability means managing an organization in a way that allows you to stay in business over time. In traditional triple bottom line terms, this closely relates to the ability of an organization not to exploit its factors of production in a way that they are exhausted and the organization thus fails. Both social and environmental aspects link strongly with economic aspects.

However, in this book we argue that the model for sustainability must incorporate both the social environmental agenda but that there are much greater aspects to economic sustainability than those typically addressed. As an example, traditional models for sustainability deal with areas such as employee health and safety but, while these are important, the environment that an organization creates for its human resources overall has a probably much greater impact — even in the short term — than some of the other factors. In addition, the linkage made in the book between models for governance and frameworks for enterprise-based risk management need to incorporate the economic impact of financial risk associated with social and environmental as well as all other areas of organizational capital that is required for long-term viability.

An interesting linkage here would be that of quality management. Effective quality management systems should, if deployed in the correct manner, address waste and eliminate it. This approach goes beyond compliance to create a fundamental culture of continual improvement. Poor processes create not only waste which very often impacts an environment with wasted raw materials, wasted energy, or excessive scrap to dispose of, but they also waste significant other resources such as human capital. Yet in many organizations today, accounting fails to identify waste to any real extent. Even in situations where standard costing is used and "variances" are identified, these often fail to reveal the real waste problems because the standards themselves have been created to meet generally accepted accounting principles, meaning that the "normal" level of waste is built into the standards against which performance is measured. Quality management systems are responses to assessed levels of risk — processes are re-engineered and controls put in place to minimize risk to an acceptable level — yet again today many organizations fail to integrate effective process mapping, analysis, and design with their risk management systems. (An example of a worksheet that can be used to do this is included in the appendices to the book).

Economic sustainability must include *all* tangible and intangible factors of production that need to be in place. Financial viability needs to be maintained and data to support this comes typically from the existing financial reporting; however, the intangible aspects of sustainability through failing to address intangible assets as well as the impact of the organization on the long-term sustainability of society, both from a human and community perspective as well as a natural resources perspective, are all critical.

This becomes the societal aspect of sustainability — the overall impact that institutions have upon wider groups of stakeholders, beyond taxpayers and investors within a national economy, as well as the impact that they have globally in the ways that they act and the impact on future generations of today's approach to consumption. None of this has been effectively addressed to date by models for governance and accountability.

Some might ask whether the institutions currently in existence are capable of making this transition. The accounting profession in particular faces some challenges in adapting to the new realities — although part of these deals with the incapacity of this profession to address the issues based on its traditional mandate of what falls within its area of accountability for reporting. What might evolve are whole new areas of professional activity capable of operating in a new paradigm. One only needs to look at history to see situations where giants of the past disappeared as new realities came forward — examples being the demise of many companies when the transistor was invented and then again the demise of many main frame computer companies when the PC was introduced. One either adapts to a new reality, or others will move in and occupy the space.

4. THE ISSUE WITH TRADITION AND VESTED INTERESTS

As new frameworks for governance evolve, they will have to be melded into a practical approach that balances risk through controls, and the ability for innovation and flexibility. However, as financial managers and others participate in this process, there will be exciting opportunities to develop new skills, to become more involved in overall governance of enterprises, and to bring existing knowledge of effective approaches to the table.

Financial managers, as specialists in the area of providing management with performance plans and results information, will be able to play a leading role in the enhancement and development of effective governance.

(a) The Need for Change

The drive for improvements in governance is seen everywhere. Governments at all levels are looking for increased transparency in what they do and how they report to their citizens. Non-profit organizations are seeking ways to be more open and accountable to those they serve. The private sector, besieged by problems in reporting, accountability, ethics, and other various issues, is striving to re-establish a level of trust and confidence. Everywhere the challenge is underway to improve governance on a broad scale.

What has developed is a crisis of trust. One where the public at large increasingly is demanding clear accountability from its institutions; one where constant revelations about failures not only of these institutions to deliver on their own accountability, but where those traditionally relied upon to ensure that these institutions "play by the rules" and disclose their true operations have themselves failed to deliver. Such lapses in confidence of major institutions, if left unaddressed, can and are having a negative impact on the public's willingness to participate in and make the market system work.

(b) Moving Beyond Classical Sustainability

Much of the existing work on sustainable reporting focuses on integrating social and environmental aspects of corporate performance; this book moves beyond this definition and aims to look at organizations' accountability in the broadest possible terms. This approach incorporates the work being done elsewhere but seeks to add recognition and accountability for the accumulated existing value of an organization's equity in terms of the capacity that has been developed to operate and execute in a manner that optimizes a shareholder's wealth. As has been mentioned earlier, organizations seeking sustainability must do the right things and do things right.

An organization that demonstrates social accountability and corporate social responsibility may in fact fail because it excludes sustainability of its existing capacities to innovate and execute. If this were the case, new frameworks for accountability would just add additional breadth of reporting without addressing the move of organizational value from tangible components to including significant intangible components.

Organizations such as the Association of Chartered Certified Accountants in the United Kingdom are already well established in their move to shift the profession to considering the broader aspects of accountability and performance reporting. The Canadian Association of Chartered Accountants also sponsors annual awards in this area. While recognition is growing, responses and frameworks remain *ad hoc* — yet concepts are gaining ground including frameworks for assessment such as AA1000 available through "Accountability" and the emergence of new models over the last ten years such as GRI and the newer UK-based SIGMA framework.

While models such as the GRI provide a good basis for developing broad measures, they fail to integrate the measurable and accountable impact of intangibles in terms of a shareholder's equity built up over time. The approach used here of "economic sustainability" embraces both societal and environmental aspects but also seeks to move beyond the accounting aspects of investor resource management to include intangible resources that in many organizations are the real components of past wealth creation and future wealth capacity.

5

RESEARCHING A NEW MODEL FOR ACCOUNTABILITY

This chapter deals in some depth with the needs for a new model of governance and continues to explore many of the existing initiatives that can be brought into a new model for governance and accountability. While the basic need for accountability has not changed, the components of what needs to be addressed have, as the economic and social realities within which organizations operate have become affected by new challenges and issues. The Board, supported by a renewed accounting profession, can reach out to develop new governance approaches as well as models for excellence and emerging management standards to establish new operating frameworks.

1. IDENTIFYING AND PROTECTING SHAREHOLDERS' AND STAKEHOLDERS' INTERESTS

(a) Defining Governance Expectations

Governance is viewed by some to be a new and evolving subject yet in fundamental terms it has not changed. What is required is a definition that moves beyond either corporate governance (typically used for the private sector) to one that embraces the good governance aspects of all entities.

> Governance is the framework through which the affairs of enterprises are directed and controlled. Good governance ensures that the rights and responsibilities of all stakeholders are identified, recognized, and protected; that there is clear agreement of organizational principles and values, and that a process exists through which the enterprise's goals and objectives are executed, performance is monitored, and results delivered.

Using various sources[1] and the above definition as a reference point, we can create a starting point. Approaches to improve organizational governance must address a number of key issues. These include:

- the way in which accountability for good governance is established, either legislatively and/or through other means;

---

[1] Mathiesen 2002, Shieifer and Vishny 1997, OECD April 1999, Cadbury Report 1992, Financial Times 1997 et al. See Encyclopaedia of Good Governance, www.encycogov. com

- the ways in which all stakeholders are identified and decisions are made about the degree to which their needs will be considered and incorporated;
- the way in which the rights of stakeholders are to be protected, through legislation, standards, and other approaches;
- the way in which accountability for good governance is split between various parties;
- the way in which the principles and values of the organization are developed and deployed to ensure ethics and behaviour are considered in concert with financial performance;
- the way in which goals and objectives for the enterprise are created and communicated; and
- the process through which those responsible for execution plan, perform, and report on their accountability to deliver the desired results.

It is too easy to blame Boards of Directors, CEOs, auditors, managers, and every other potential culprit for the symptoms of poor governance. The question that needs to be asked is *whether the right tools are in place to ensure effective governance*. These range from the clarity of shareholders' expectations and requirements, the selection of directors, the creation of well-defined high level governance frameworks, the use and application of effective third party assessment approaches (such as audits), and any other standards that are to be used. These tools all need to be supported by an adequate framework for translating and managing the deployment of strategy and for ensuring that a) all facets of direction are identified and communicated, and b) there is an adequate ability for feedback on compliance and performance results in all relevant areas.

In many cases, some fundamental issues exist at the Board level such as disagreements over terminology and assumptions about what directors *really know and understand*. (As an assistance for readers, please refer to the glossary of terms in the appendixes. This may be the best starting point for improvement).

What must be recognized, though, is that we are currently seeing the impact of the post-industrial revolution. The old economic order, which was heavily based on tangible assets, large national organizations, a clear line between public and private sector, and the gradual adoption of new technology, has been replaced. Every one of these aspects is now altered. Today, many organizations have a greater reliance on intangible rather than tangible assets and, in many cases, there are no accounting standards to provide assurance of effective governance in these areas. Organizations are moving fast, adopting new technology, and changing rapidly to deal with local, national, and international issues. They are operating globally and are of such a size that any sort of effective, central control is almost impossible. The line is also blurred between the public and private sectors. Every one of these issues creates a reality within which traditional approaches to governance need to be not only strengthened but also re-invented.

(b) The Basic Need Has Not Changed . . .

Our earlier definition of governance retains many of the traditional views: it remains about ensuring that the key stakeholders' needs are understood and managed; it is also about establishing the "play box" within which management is authorized to operate and, within this, creating and approving high level strategy and plans to move the organization forward, *i.e.*, the expectations. Finally, it is about "closing the loop" — ensuring that what has been committed to and planned is in fact occurring and that results are in line with expectations (ensuring management capacity).

The role of review and audit, whether it be through third party statutory audits in the private sector or by the OAG, Treasury Board, or GAO at a federal government level, assures transparency of the conversion of governance to execution. In most organizations, this interlocking circle is where the critical role of the Chief Executive or Deputy Minister sits, through which the expectations are translated to actions and results delivered.

Therefore, we can establish a *high-level governance framework* within which these actions take place. Note that we have shown risk management as a key aspect of the capacity to execute and, as will be discussed later, this is why integrated risk management is a critical issue in today's environment.

Governance - direction

Risk Management

Governance expectation
(Shareholders, Boards and Directors)

Senior Officer (CEO)
(Review/audit)

Management capacity
(Officers, Managers, employees clients, suppliers, and others)

Transparency

A high level view of governance is about a) defining clearly what is expected in *all* aspects of performance, b) ensuring that the designated officer(s) who link expectations to execution are fully conversant with expectations and capable of providing the leadership and communication skills to ensure consistency of deployment, and c) a framework for management process and accountability that provides assurance to both the officers and the Board that management has the capacity to execute as well as the ability to continually report against the expectations that were initially established. Overall, we have an integrated and closed loop system.

(c) . . . but the Components Have Changed

In positioning for effective governance in the future, the concept model remains but the reality within which it operates needs to be re-assessed. A diversion exists today between governance and management that has been created out of the different worlds in which the two operate. This is well defined by Leighton and Thain who show an example of a frustrated CEO who "... wants to be left alone to get the job done that he was hired for ... ."[2]

A number of factors are critical for effective future deployment of this high level model.

1. In setting expectations, the Board and Directors supported by shareholders must be fully apprised of organizational risk.
2. Tolerance and approach to risk management must be part of policy.
3. The individual identified as the officer responsible for aligning Board and management plays one of the most critical roles in ensuring alignment.
4. There must be a clear process through which direction is passed down not only to the key management officer (CEO) but also from that position throughout the organization.
5. There must be a management system and structure in place that has the capacity to convert plans into actions.
6. There must be a clear and well-defined system of reporting the results of plans and actions back to the Board in a clear and consistent way that covers all elements of Board expectations and policy.
7. There must be, within both the upper circle (Board conduct) and lower circle (management capacity), an effective subset of monitoring and reporting systems that allow for full control and continual self-assessment of effectiveness and value added.

---

2   D. Leighton & D. Thain, *Making Boards Work* (McGraw-Hill Ryerson, 1997), at 6.

(d) Leadership Starts with the Board

Changes throughout the 1990s across the world have worked to strengthen the Board's traditional governance accountability and, more specifically, to define what Boards should and should not be doing. For example, see the guidelines that the Toronto Stock Exchange adopted, as a result of the Dey report, that are used as a basis for recommended changes and updates in the recently published final report on the Joint Committee on Corporate Governance.[3] A great deal of this work is extremely beneficial in starting to clearly define expectations of what questions Boards should be asking and what level of involvement they should seek. However, it is disturbing that in a parallel report published in 1999, many of the suggested improvements from the Dey report in 1995 have yet to be implemented in many organizations[4] (a symptom, perhaps, of traditional Boards of Directors believing that "the Emperor indeed does have clothes" when all around seem to disagree). Now events are beginning to shake the status quo.

Boards have to be concerned with meeting both legislated and mandatory requirements for governance but also ensuring that there is a broad framework for clear transparency on the management of the business. This role, although delegated cannot be abrogated. No Board can protect itself from criticism of the way in which an organization operates, even though it may be legally compliant by responding, "we didn't know". Therefore, Boards have to step back and ask themselves whether the affairs of the organization for which they are responsible have changed and, if so, in what way. The outcome of such discussions should drive the evolution of discretionary Board expectations that will be incorporated in policy setting, planning, measurement, and reporting.

Boards must evolve to recognize that their upward role in reporting to shareholders (as well as their downward role of providing supervision, guidance, and direction to management activity) has become more complex. As a simple example, traditional simplicity had a well-defined set of shareholders as investors with either passive or similar expectations (i.e., financial returns at or above industry average). The Board knew this and represented this need in the way management was directed and monitored.

Fast forward. Investors are no longer homogeneous. Some are concerned about the environment, and some hold the investment because it is strategic to their own business. Some hold it as a long-term capital gain, some may hold it expecting regular and growing earnings. Even the vehicles for investment have changed with key investors now being other "operating"

---

3 Joint Committee on Corporate Governance, "Beyond Compliance — Building a Governance Culture" (November 2001), at 34 *et seq.* www.jointcomgov.com
4 Institute of Corporate Directors and TSE, "Report on Corporate Governance — 5 years to the Dey" (1999).

corporations as well as investment organizations such as unit trust and mutual funds. Representing the shareholders is much more complex and given that some shareholders have a belief that their investments should practise certain principles that involve representation of other types of stakeholders, then again the Board has to expand its scope of representation.

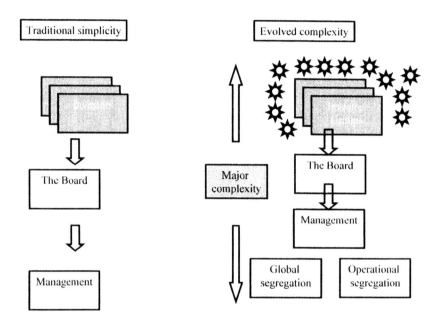

Looking downward, life is more complex. Instead of centralized homogeneous organizations with clear command and control structures, many organizations today are far flung, decentralized in decision making, bound by different legislation and standards of reporting and conduct and, in many cases, engaged in a wide range of differing activities. Operations are segregated and decentralized, as is the global arena of activity.

In moving forward, we will define the upper part of the governance model (the expectations that we discussed earlier) as the "intent" aspects of governance. Intent being defined as what must be done for legislative compliance as well as what shareholders, the Board, and the Directors collectively establish as the discretionary policies of how the organization will operate.

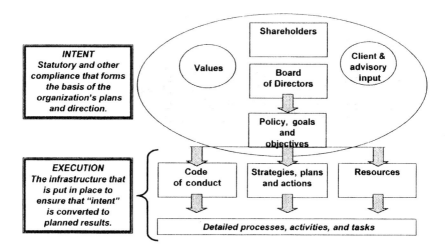

The lower half of the model that will be discussed in more detail is about "Execution" — making it happen. This is where intent is converted into action and results.

2. DILEMMA OF THE GUARDIANS: THE ACCOUNTING PROFESSION

Boards, as well as shareholders and the general public, have traditionally believed that the auditors from professional accounting firms played the key role of guardians of their interests. The development of the accounting profession is by definition intrinsically interwoven with the development of corporate governance.

Historically, the main role of accountants was compliance management. Professional accounting firms developed and grew in order to support the emerging commercial entities' needs for compliance audits required by legislation. This was further supported by increased complexity in government legislation requiring specialists in areas such as taxation. Increased global trade, with its myriad of international currencies and taxation frameworks, also required specialized support.

Parallel to this, management accounting was also developing. While its roots can be traced back to the 1700s and 1800s, it was in the 1900s that it began to grow. Organizations such as General Motors under its President Alfred Sloan developed sophisticated models to track and monitor performance variances against planned results. This activity was linked back to the work of Taylor who, as an industrial engineer, provided budding cost accountants with the physical time standards upon which detailed manufacturing costing could be based. Direct labour, as a key component of manufacturing cost, was closely monitored and tracked with all time being fully accounted for.

Both areas of the accounting profession developed parallel to the needs and requirements of economic activities. Financial accounting has generally been focusing more on standards and compliance issues while management accountants focus more on the internal analytical activities of assisting management in making the optimum use of resources.

The governance turmoil has focused on the role of the public accountant, in many cases, but the profession is in trouble on a broad front. In the financial accounting area, professionals and their organizations (including their professional bodies at the national and international level) are struggling to develop new standards and compliance frameworks that meet updated statutory requirements, and meet a defined set of generally accepted accounting principles. The problem in this arena is significant. Business and commerce are international yet there remains a proliferation of national standards. While international standards are growing in acceptance, especially in Europe, there is a long way to go in achieving global consistency. In addition, a crucial struggle remains between those who build standards as "rules-based" (such as the United States) and those that use a "principles-based" approach. This difference is fundamental especially when one considers the role of accounting standards as a core component of governance. One rests on behaviour and one rests on following (or getting around) defined rules.

Additionally, in an effort to ensure clear independence of third party auditors, new rules are being developed within legislation, guidelines to good governance, and securities legislation which have a significant strategic impact on the professional firms. These have grown as "full service" organizations (consistent with principles of excellence — getting to know the customer and their business) and are now being asked to disengage from all "non audit" functions.

What is being lost in the whole governance discussion is the role and contribution that management accountants, as a significant part of the profession, play in advancing effective governance. This part of the profession supports both shareholders, through ensuring effective internal controls in partnership with internal financial accountants, as well as supporting managers, through effective advice in the areas of planning, analysis, and reporting. This portion of the profession is significant; as an example the Institute of Management Accountants (IMA) in the United States boasts about 70,000 members; the Certified Management Accountants in Canada 45,000 members and students; and the Institute of Chartered Management Accountants in the United Kingdom 62,000 members and 80,0000 students in 155 countries.

The problem that this area of the profession has is that the tools developed during the industrial age for analysis and cost management are becoming outdated. Tools such as standard costing, especially as it applied to the large resource known as "direct labour", worked well when a large portion of the work force was accounting for its time through time clocks and time sheets that could be allocated to specific tasks, products, and services. Some industries still use this tool but, in many cases, especially the service industry, this analysis is not undertaken. While management is moving towards a process-based approach to management, accountants in this area are slow to develop and adopt new tools such as Activity Based Costing (ABC) and Resource Cost Accounting (RCA). Thus, even internally, the profession is slipping in value in its ability to provide meaningful advice to management. One can link this problem to the unplanned side-effects that occurred during downsizing when management focused cost reductions on the basis of departmental cost accounting (*i.e.*, who spends the most money) rather than process-based accounting (*i.e.*, what processes consume the greatest resources and need to be re-engineered to eliminate resource consumption).

The accounting profession, while important as part of an overall assessment process, cannot play the major quality assurance role through reliance on an audit function. Even if legislation currently being put in place creates more independence as well as a higher level of Board review through a strengthened Board audit committee (as required by both American and Canadian changes), the scope of a fiscal audit cannot address key aspects of organizational activity. The profession itself will need to embrace significantly improved standards related to intangible assets and will need to seek new and improved approaches to performance assessment.

3. LEARNING FROM GLOBAL MODELS OF BEST PRACTICE

(a) Models for Improvements in Board Accountability

Legislated changes are already underway; examples include the changes to the U.S. securities laws, enacted as a result of *Sarbanes-Oxley* together with the many new rulings that the SEC has developed to "enable" these requirements.

In Canada, while evolution of the overall approach to securities regulations continues to be discussed, there is evidence, such as Bill 198 in Ontario, of changes in the securities laws that, in many ways, mirror many of the changes brought about in the United States by *Sarbanes-Oxley*. In addition, changes are already underway — albeit as guidance for Boards, to enhance disclosure and "good practice" for those organizations listed on the TSE (now the TSX). These started as a result of the Dey report in 1994 followed up by an "implementation" review in 1999 (that indicated that in spite of the importance of good governance, adoption varied quite widely).

The major groupings from both the draft (1999) paper from the OECD[5] on Corporate Governance Guidelines, as well as the 2004 update, identify the following key principles on corporate governance:

I.   The rights of shareholders. II.   The equitable treatment of shareholders. III.   The role of shareholders in corporate governance. IV.   Disclosure and transparency. V.   The responsibilities of the Board.

Within each category there are several specific guidelines as to how the particular area should be addressed. In all there are 23 subsections within these five areas that outline more specific guidelines. As an example, there are four points in the "Disclosure and Transparency" section that deal with areas for disclosure: preparation of materials using high quality standards of accounting, financial and non-financial disclosure and audit, the overall audit process, and the need for dissemination of the information. This section starts by stating the following:

Disclosure should include, but not be limited to, material information on: I.   The financial and operating results of the company. II.   Company objectives. III.   Major share ownership and voting right. IV.   Members of the Board and key executives and their remuneration. V.   Material foreseeable risk factors. VI.   Material issues regarding employees and other stakeholders. VII. Governance structures and policies.

The guidelines adopted initially in 1994 by the TSX, and later taken over and incorporated by the OSC, are available from the OSC website: www.osc.gov.on.ca.

(b) Models for Management Excellence

For over 20 years, management organizations around the world have been seeking solutions to manage their enterprises more effectively. If

---

5 Organization for Economic Cooperation and Development, Paris.

management is seeking new solutions, would these not also provide some insight into what different types of information might be required at the Board level to also assess management performance? If accountability for dealing with these emerging issues stops at the Chief Officer (CEO or other) level, there is immediate governance disconnect.

We have carried out studies that review the results of many of these models. One challenge is that many began life as models for excellence in quality management, and have therefore already been discounted by potential users who may see them as just another quality program dreamed up by consultants. However, most have already dropped the word "quality" from their nomenclature and today focus on *organizational excellence*. The following chart shows a summary of some of this work. Note that the chart is not exhaustive nor have all of the details incorporated within any one of the seven headings been shown. The important aspect is to illustrate the degree to which a) the models are consistent, and b) given this consistency, the degree to which factors affecting management excellence may be helpful in creating a "governance excellence" approach.

Five "models" have been selected for illustrative purposes only. The abbreviations shown on the top of the chart refer to the following:

- NQI — National Quality Institute (Canada) who administers the Canadian Awards for Excellence.
- Baldrige, the U.S. National Quality Award for Performance Excellence. (Note that almost every State within the United States also has an equivalent award. Analysis shows that components are very similar.)
- EFQM originally referred to the European Foundation for Quality Management; however, this organization is now called just EFQM and its Model is the EFQM Excellence Model (hence EFEM — European Foundations Excellence Model).
- OPS — the Model for the Ontario Public Service developed as the "Cornerstones" model in the mid 1990s. While a hybrid, this model was based on extensive research on global best practice, and created with a focus on the public sector.
- ISO 9000-2000 — although not a best practice excellence model *per se*, it is illustrative. The ISO 9001 standard together with the ISO 9004 Guidelines on Continuous Improvement[6] focus on the eight principles that management need to follow to create a "quality organization".

---

6 See Appendix F of the eight principles of quality management.

Factor	NQI	Baldrige	EFEM	OPS	ISO 9000 (2000)
Leadership	Yes	Yes	Yes	Yes	Some
Customer/Citizen focus	Yes	Yes	Yes	Yes	Yes
People Focus	Yes	Yes	Yes	Yes	Some
Planning	Yes	Yes	Yes	Yes	Yes
Process Mgmt.	Yes	Yes	Yes	Yes	Yes
Partners/Suppliers	Yes	Yes	Yes	Yes	Yes
Results	Yes	Yes	Yes	Yes	Yes

What is clear from these models, and from the complementary global models elsewhere, is that there is a high level of consistency and agreement with what makes an organization "excellent". These models have been refined over some 20 plus years and seem to present best thinking on the subject. Key principles that appear in almost all models and have content that is in excess of 85 per cent to 90 per cent the same, include:

1. **Leadership** is the first key ingredient of excellence. In terms of our governance approach, leadership provides the consistency of purpose in what is done and how it is to be achieved. Leadership is also what is required to convert "intent" into action.

2. Having a **customer/client focus** (or citizen in the public sector) is key to ensuring that the organization is driven by those to whom it is providing services. Again, from a governance perspective, what we see is the importance of a key stakeholder.

3. Next is a **people focus.** Organizations have talked about "people being their greatest asset" for many years, and here they are as a key component of excellence; the linkage with effective governance is again a) another key stakeholder, and b) the importance of the human dimension *especially when we consider the emergence of the knowledge-based economy.*

4. **Planning** is next. Effective planning of what needs to be done and then ensuring the plans are deployed is a key part of management excellence. In addition, this issue is at the heart of good governance. The ability to translate plans of all types of expectations into action and results is at the core of effective governance.

5. **Process approach.** In most cases, work is carried out and results

achieved through effective process management. For governance perspectives, effective processes are a core part of intellectual capital. No one could argue that the processes developed and honed by organizations such as FedEx form an inherent part of their worth; yet they are nowhere on the balance sheet — a key asset under-reported and not recognized as part of assessment, evaluation, audit, and disclosure.

6. **Partners/Suppliers** are core to success in most organizations as they form part of the supply chain through which inputs, activities, and outputs are linked together in one continuum. In the case of governance, again the existence of key partners is critical. Organizations that have developed strong distribution networks to get the product to market have a core asset in place; in addition, many organizations create a key asset when they work closely with key suppliers. For governance purposes, these are both key assets and key stakeholders.

7. **Results.** Finally, it all comes down to results which, in the case of these models, means the ability to track, monitor, and deliver results in all the previous key aspects of the framework *i.e.*, above and beyond just financial results, but incorporating information on clients, suppliers, and employees as a minimum. In addition, an effective model links this with "learning" — the ability of the results to drive continual improvement back into the planning process.

These seven points demonstrate that a major learning can be acquired by understanding that management, in its search for effectiveness in the management process, has already arrived at which components should be included; this is a key learning for building future governance models.

(c) Models for Reporting and Accountability

In addition to the *Models for Management Excellence* and *Guidelines for Board Conduct*, there is also a growing initiative to develop organizational reporting frameworks that are comprehensive in nature. Many of these fall under the umbrella of sustainable development. It is not unusual for people to think of sustainable development as being related to environmental issues, but this is far from the truth.

Sustainability is a concern, in its broadest sense, to those accountable for organizations. In this context, sustainability deals with the long-term economic value created by the interaction of tangible and intangible components. These components of sustainability can include areas such as maintaining good brand recognition and reputation; maintaining the "stock" of human capital both as it related to retention as well as to succession planning; ensuring the sustainability of core business processes through which work gets done; ensuring sustainability through providing investors with a competitive return on investment, both in terms of capital appreciation as well as cash flow; and sustainability in terms of sources of supply of core materials — many of which will have aspects or impacts that affect the natural environment and many other factors.

In recent years, a number of these approaches and models have developed outside the mainstream of corporate reporting yet bring together many of the aspects of a broad-based approach to effective governance. Such models are slowly emerging led by the efforts of progressive Boards and managers who have already recognized the significant *value of going beyond the minimums required in legislation*, and acting in a way that gets the message out that they are a "good corporate citizen" and are already addressing the broader issues of behaviour and conduct in the market place to ensure sustainability of the enterprise.

The CICA's (Canadian Institute of Chartered Accountants) overall award for corporate reporting in 2003 went to the Royal Bank of Canada, who can be used as an example. The Bank provides both financial reporting to meet statutory requirements as well as a supplement called "Corporate Responsibility Report and Public Accountability Statement". In addition to the CICA award, the Royal Bank was also named the most respected corporation in Canada by a KPMG/Ipsos Reid Poll. A summary of the award release is shown below.

January, 2004 — For the second year in a row, RBC was named the "Most Respected Corporation in Canada" in the annual KPMG/Ipsos Reid poll, appearing in *The Globe and Mail*.

RBC achieved this ranking by placing first in six of nine categories, including "Most Admired & Respected," "Corporate Governance," "Human Resources Management," "Financial Performance," "Corporate Social Responsibility" and "Long Term Investment." RBC was the only financial institution in the Top 10 in "High Quality Services/Product," reinforcing our commitment to providing a superior client experience.

For the eighth consecutive year, RBC was named the top corporation in the category of "Corporate Social Responsibility." This not only recognizes our charitable giving, sponsorships, environmental and community activities, but also celebrates employee volunteerism in communities across the country where we live and work.

For a second consecutive year, RBC placed first in the category of "Human Resources Management." This reflects our commitment to building strong relationships with employees and our Total Rewards philosophy which recognizes the importance of

---

> not only competitive compensation and benefits, but also sup-
> ports all aspects of work environment as well as providing strong
> learning and career development opportunities.

The breadth of the Royal Bank report is considerable and includes a framework called "Leadership in Corporate Responsibility" whose components include:

- Governance and ethical behaviour;
- Respect for diversity;
- Respect for the environment;
- Respect for employees;
- Products and services;
- Sponsorships;
- Gifts-in-kind;
- Sharing business and financial knowledge;
- Employee volunteer contributions;
- Donations.

The report goes on to identify in a good level of detail the degree to which the Bank has initiatives, takes action, and delivers results in these areas.

Many of the emerging models have as a key component "corporate social responsibility". While, traditionally, this has a perceived bias as an environmental based initiative, CSR is, in fact, closer to integrated governance and thus provides some effective insight into the required components.

The World Business Council on Sustainable Development[7] (WBCSD) is a coalition of 170 international companies united by a shared commitment to sustainable development via the three pillars of economic growth, ecological balance, and social progress. Their model provides a clear framework on which organizations can structure their future broad-based good governance reporting. The three pillars are:

1. *Eco-efficiency.* The WBCSD defines eco-efficiency as being achieved by the delivery of competitively priced goods and services that satisfy human needs and bring quality of life, while progressively reducing ecological impacts and resource intensity throughout the life cycle, to a level at least in line with the Earth's estimated carrying capacity. The Council has identified four aspects of eco-efficiency that make it an

---

7 See their website at http://www.wbcsd.ch that provides a background to the organization and its activities.

indispensable strategic element in today's knowledge-based economy. These are:

- de-materialization — developing ways of substituting knowledge flows for material flows;
- closing production loops — the biological designs of nature provide a role model for sustainability;
- service extension — the movement from a supply-driven economy to a demand-driven economy;
- functional extension — the manufacture of smarter products with new and enhanced functionality and selling services to enhance the products' functional value.

2. *Innovation* — which is at the core of creating a more sustainable world. Society will not succeed in achieving sustainability by focusing merely on doing things more efficiently tomorrow.
3. *Corporate social responsibility.* WBCSD's work is based on the fundamental belief that a coherent CSR strategy, based on sound ethics and core values, offers clear business benefits. In other words, that acting in a socially responsible manner is more than just an ethical duty for a company, but is something that actually has a bottom line pay-off. The WBCSD's basic message has always been very simple: business is not divorced from the rest of society. The two are interdependent and it must be ensured, through mutual understanding and responsible behaviour, that business's role in building a better future is recognized and encouraged by society.

The WBCSD started in 1992 and has grown and developed since that time. It started life as a group of 50 CEOs as the Business Council for Sustainable Development. In 1995, the Council merged with the World Industry Council for the Environment (WICE) in Paris — a brainchild of the International Chamber of Commerce (ICC). As part of this evolution, the organization has maintained its three core areas of focus identified above but has developed a concept of integration through the focus on cross-cutting themes that also include risk management, ecosystems and sustainability, and markets.

WBCSD members are drawn from more than 35 countries and 20 major industrial sectors. The Council also benefits from a global network of 45 national and regional business councils and partner organizations located in 40 countries, involving some 1,000-business leaders globally. The WBCSD's activities reflect the belief that the pursuit of sustainable development is good for business and business is good for sustainable development.

A second, and newer organization is GRI — the Global Reporting Initiative. Started in 1997, GRI became independent in 2002, and is an official collaborating centre of the United Nations Environment Programme (UNEP) and works in cooperation with UN Secretary-General Kofi Annan's Global Compact. The GRI[8] (Global Reporting Initiative) framework is similar — basing its framework on economic, environmental, and social criteria. Underpinning these are four principles of reporting that include transparency, suitability, and inclusiveness (*i.e.*, the ability to address broad-based stakeholder requirements).

GRI's rapid evolution in just a few years from a bold vision to a new permanent global institution reflects the imperative and the value that various constituencies assign to such a disclosure framework. The GRI process, rooted in inclusiveness, transparency, neutrality, and continual enhancement, has enabled GRI to give concrete expression to accountability. Support for creating a new, generally accepted disclosure framework for sustainability reporting continues to grow among business, civil society, government, and labour stakeholders.

The third example is the latest model called SIGMA[9] and was developed in the United Kingdom (including the participation of the Association of Chartered Certified Accountants — ACCA). The SIGMA Project — "Sustainability–Integrated Guidelines for Management" — was launched in 1999 with the support of the UK Department of Trade and Industry. It is a partnership between the British Standards Institution (a leading standards organization), Forum for the Future (a leading sustainability charity and think-tank), and AccountAbility (the international professional body for accountability). SIGMA brings together many existing initiatives in a way that some of the other models do not clearly achieve. SIGMA also embeds the role and importance of "capital" reporting but increases the breadth of this to include financial, social, human, and manufactured (reflecting many of the aspects of intangible assets addressed earlier).

SIGMA partnership with AccountAbility[10] also provides linkage to an assessment and evaluation tool know as AA1000. To quote from the AccountAbility website:

> Launched in 1999, the AA1000 framework is designed to improve accountability and performance by *learning through stakeholder engagement.*

> It was developed to address the need for organizations to *integrate their stakeholder engagement processes into daily activities.* It has been used worldwide by leading businesses, non-profit organizations and public bodies.

---

8 See their website at http://www.globalreporting.org
9 See their website at http://projectsigma.com
10 AccountAbility website can be found at http://www.accountability.org.uk/aa1000/default.asp

The Framework helps users to establish a systematic stakeholder engagement process that generates the *indicators, targets, and reporting systems* needed to ensure its effectiveness in overall organizational performance.

The principle underpinning AA1000 is inclusivity. The building blocks of the process framework are planning, accounting and auditing and reporting. It does not prescribe what should be reported on but rather the 'how'. In this way it is designed to complement the *GRI Reporting Guidelines*.

(d) The Role of International Management Standards

One area that is starting to grow, but has limited visibility, is the gradual emergence of standards which apply to areas other than financial management. Many of these have been initially developed in Europe but are making their way around the globe. Organizations that wish to improve their overall governance now have another opportunity to obtain feedback from either internal audit sources or even through the work of third party Registrars, to assess the organizations' state of operational effectiveness.

This will develop as a key area of attention especially as it relates to process management — a proven approach to support the requirements of paragraph 404 of the SEC/*Sarbanes-Oxley* requirements pertaining to management's ability to assess their process of internal controls. Current standards include areas such as:

- risk management;
- privacy;
- design of products and services, and project management;
- quality management;
- e-commerce;
- customer complaints management;
- social accountability;
- environmental management.

Each of these standards can provide support for elements of the good governance model and encourage organizations to create a basis upon which to assess their level of achievement against best practice as determined within a generic global standard. Although there remains some high degree of scepticism about the need for either national or international standards in many of these areas (Oscar Wilde once said that consistency is the refuge for those with a lack of imagination!), they will have an increasing role to play in assessing organizational performance in the future. One of the main advantages over some of the other historical approaches is that organizations seeking certification to such standards have to pass both an initial audit by a third party as well as maintenance audits and, in addition, must show an internal capacity to maintain these systems through structured internal audits conducted on a regular basis.

4. SETTING ROLES, RESPONSIBILITIES, AND ACCOUNTABILITIES

Effective governance requires a clear framework for accountability and responsibility. In building a new model for the future this must be included. Earlier definitions of governance that were discussed, such as the "English language" definition and the OECD definition, both indicate a comprehensive framework within which governance includes those setting and providing direction as well as those implementing and holding accountability for work execution.

In moving forward with a new framework, the earlier split defined by the two interlocking circles shown below will be used and this will be the basis for developing the structure for accountability.

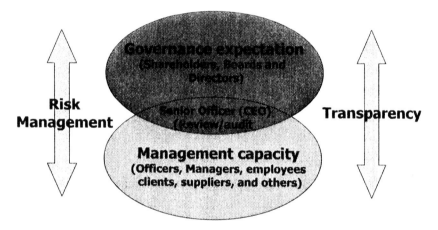

Primary accountability, in most cases defined within enabling legislation, must rest with those holding organizational accountability on behalf of the major stakeholders — either shareholders or the public for government institutions and non-profits. It is clear from the problems of the last twenty years that Boards and directors *must* be providing clear direction and must know, through an effective accountability reporting framework, the degree to which management actions comply with intended direction. This requires that Boards, as part of their own development, provide internal operating processes that clearly define their own accountability as well as a framework for how they will relate to management.

Management, although holding delegated powers as either officers or as designated managers, also hold a key component of accountability. In this case, it is accountability for the lower part of the interlocking circles. The first component of this is the accountability of the CEO for clear direction and leadership in converting Board direction into a management framework that has a capacity to execute within a clearly delineated structure of delegated responsibility and no further. Boards must define clearly and hold accountable the Chief Executive for such action.

During an investigation into problems identified with the "sponsorship" programs in the Canadian federal government in 2004, a senior cabinet Minister responsible for PWGSC, the department administering the funds in question, indicated under oath that

> . . . while he was responsible for the Public Works Department, *he did not manage it*, and took the proper action when he knew there were problems.[11] [emphasis added.]
>
> . . .
>
> 3. (1) There is hereby established a department of the Government of Canada called the Department of Public Works and Government Services over which the Minister of Public Works and Government Services appointed by commission under the Great Seal shall preside.
> (2) The Minister holds office during pleasure and has the management and direction of the Department.[12]

Abrogation of accountability cannot be achieved when things go wrong; a Chief Executive holds a clearly defined area of accountability and responsibility that should be defined and continually reviewed by the Board. The final part of clear accountability is the creation of an internal (*i.e.*, for management purposes) framework of accountability and responsibility. This is often referred to as the "delegation of authority or DOA". This document takes the delegated powers from the Board to the CEO and further breaks these into a framework, consistent with the organizational structure and management model. This framework then creates the basis for all further work on internal controls and process management activity. It also provides a structure against which audit and assessment can take place.

5. SHAREHOLDERS EXERCISING THEIR MANDATE

While accountability starts with the Board, shareholders must in fact "set the stage". In the past, shareholders have been somewhat passive in the evaluation and assessment of organizations in which they hold investments. Traditional focus has been on "what" is delivered rather than the "how". Recent situations have changed this. Shareholders have been surprised and embarrassed by situations created by management, or even Boards, that were inconsistent with expectations.

Shareholder activism and representation has grown significantly in recent years. In the United Kingdom, organizations such as Hermes, whose

---

11 *The Canadian Press*, March 18, 2004, Ottawa.
12 *Department of Public Works and Government Services Act*, S.C. 1996, c. 16, s. 3.

website introduction is shown below, have taken a leading international role in governance improvement.

> Hermes' corporate governance programme is founded on a fundamental belief that companies with interested and involved shareholders are more likely to achieve superior long-term financial performance than those without.
>
> Hermes places great emphasis on exercising its ownership rights in all the companies in which it invests. The objective is to add value to Hermes' clients' 3,000 public company investments worldwide. As a significant portion of our clients' investments are in index-tracking portfolios, they are necessarily shareowners in under-performing companies. By always voting at company meetings, Hermes aims to ensure that companies are run by managers and directors in the best long-term interests of their long-term investors. A pioneer in corporate governance and shareholder engagement, Hermes is a leader of the debate in the UK and abroad.
>
> Furthermore, Hermes has taken its corporate governance programme to the next level by being the first major investment institution in the world to establish shareholder engagement funds. The Focus Funds invest in underperforming companies which are fundamentally sound but are undervalued due to a variety of strategic, financial or governance issues.
>
> Hermes believes that good stewardship contributes to superior corporate performance. Its vigilance and involvement as long-term shareholder thus enhances returns on its clients' assets.[13]

In the United States, organizations such as CalPERS[14] (California Public Employees Retirement System) have been leaders in demanding a higher level of accountability from institutions in which they invest. What is important in the work of both organizations is that they represent a movement of proactive involvement by shareholders in the affairs of the organization. This interest continues to focus on financial returns but is also increasingly focusing on "how" these returns are generated both in terms of corporate conduct and accountability but also within the wider sphere of sustainability.

These organizations are expanding shareholder activism beyond the earlier aspects of "green investors" or "ethical investors" and are striving to restore balance to the conduct of private sector public organizations. Such activities not only include broader involvement of key stakeholders but are demanding a more balanced and reasonable approach to areas such as senior executive compensation and rewards.

6. EFFECTIVE BOARDS AND DIRECTORS

Boards and their equivalents today are managing enterprises using tools, techniques, and approaches that, in many cases, did not exist ten years ago.

---

13 For the Hermes website see http://www.hermes.co.uk/about/introduction.htm
14 For the CalPERS website see http://www.calpers-governance.org/forumhome.asp

It is therefore critical that those engaged in governance at the senior level are at least connected with and understand the issues that the enterprises face and those which management deal with on a regular basis. (The author has attended at Board meetings where key directors, in some cases chairing key committees of the Board, have indicated that they do not understand such issues as technology and e-commerce and the issues of business partnering — a real problem in today's environment). Therefore the composition, experience, education, and training of the Board including the length of term and other issues must reflect current needs — moving away from the "old boys' network" of which many Boards have been accused. If Board members have not managed an operating enterprise in more than 10 years, they should probably not be serving.

Director accountability must be clearly defined. While statutory requirements provide a starting point (see extract from the *Canadian Business Corporations Act*, below), effective Boards today are going far beyond this in developing expectations.

> 122. (1) Every director and officer of a corporation in exercising their powers and discharging their duties shall
> > (*a*) act honestly and in good faith with a view to the best interests of the corporation; and
> > (*b*) exercise the care, diligence and skill that a reasonably prudent person would exercise in comparable circumstances.[15]

Sources of direction for improved Board level governance can come from areas such as the original TSX guidelines, that have since been improved and modified and are currently being considered as a wider set of guidelines for both Ontario[16] and national purposes, as well as "best practices" in sources such as John Carver's[17] *Boards That Make a Difference* and Leighton and Thain's[18] *Making Boards Work*.

Examples of transparency in moving in this direction can be found in the 2003 Annual Report of the TD Bank Financial Group (TDBFG[19]) which includes statements of governance practices and also includes examples of the actual responsibilities of key Board positions (such as Chairman of the Board), roles and accountabilities of Board Committees, and key qualities for directors at TDBFG.

---

15 *Canada Business Corporations Act*, R.S.C. 1985, c. C-44, s. 122.
16 For Ontario Securities Commission see http://www.osc.gov.on.ca
17 J. Carver, *Boards That Make a Difference*, 2nd ed. (Jossey-Bass, 1997).
18 Above, note 2.
19 For TD Bank Financial Group Governance website see http://www.td.com/governance/index.jsp

(a) It's No Longer Just About Accounting Controls and Standards

So the issue of updating and improving governance needs to be seen on a broad scale. For those at the level of overall governance such as the Board of Directors, ministers, and deputies, the need is not only for enhanced financial reporting and transparency but for a broader approach that encompasses the realities within which the organization operates. Governance approaches must be brought into line with the changes taking place in the social and economic environment as well as the practices that are being used in managing enterprises. This drive for increased transparency has been further enhanced by the publication of *The Naked Corporation*[20] by Tapscott and Ticoll.

Thus, we have the basis for not only improving the competence of the Board, but for updating the tools, techniques, standards, and approaches through which a Board ensures that its governance scope is aligned with what management is *actually doing*. If the Board cannot ask the right questions and the third party audits and reviews fail to cover all the key aspects of the business, effective governance will surely fail.

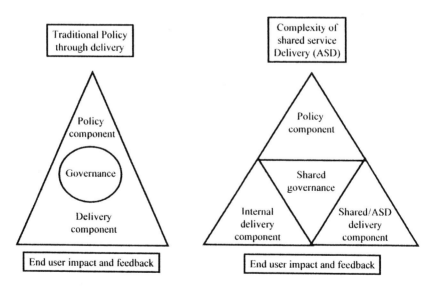

As discussed earlier, the challenge is ensuring that governance frameworks move ahead as society moves ahead. The example above illustrates this issue. In the public sector, policy and delivery of services within gov-

---

20 D. Tapscott & D. Ticoll, *The Naked Corporation* (Viking Canada, 2003).

ernment used to be one — an integrated approach, managed and governed internally. However, recent changes in the practice of government through outsourcing of delivery of services and, using techniques such as ASD (Alternate Service Delivery) models, have significantly changed the risk profile and, therefore, the governance issues being dealt with by *both* partners in the process. New systems for planning, evaluation, control, and reporting are all needed if those accountable for the execution of policy are to be able to manage the process and ensure "intent" has indeed been converted into "execution".

It has been said, as part of the dialogue on the Enron situation, that the success of free enterprise is all about finding ways to get around the rules to gain a competitive advantage. After all, the Americans broke the original rules of warfare when they beat the English — doing things like acting independently, not all advancing together, and not wearing uniforms. If these rules include and principally rely upon accounting standards, then we should not be surprised that no matter how well we write the standards, efforts will be made to find ways around them. Maybe a key issue is more values and principles than adherence to standards?

7. CREATING BOARDS THAT WORK

Significant change has already taken place in developing and improving Board performance. These changes have resulted from a combination of new legislation, tightened securities, guidelines, and regulations and pressure from investor activists. Board renewal and improved accountability requires that a number of actions be taken. These include:

- creating clear definition of roles, accountabilities, and responsibilities for Board members;
- recruitment of Board members based on competencies and value brought to the governance function (this includes ensuring that the Board complement includes the required competencies to deal with the issues facing the business as well as placing a high value on "knowing the business" itself);
- providing Board members with effective orientation on their accountabilities and the organization itself (only focusing on what is required to ensure competence and value added with a reasonable level of time commitment);
- defining a clear process for Board to regularly assess their own performance and to take action where value is not being added;
- ensuring that Board representation adequately reflects both executive Board members as well as non-executive (external members) to add objectivity;
- structuring Board Committees as well as resources to ensure that Boards

can deliver effective oversight (*e.g.*, audit, governance, compensation) *including* having resources available (funding) to allow them to carry this work out, external to Management. *(Note:* this would also suggest moving budgets for audit fees out of the operating expenses and into a separate Board budget category.)

Much of this work is already in progress — however, the failing will be that improved Board structures and accountabilities will not necessarily broaden the perspective of Board oversight to the level required to meet effective sustainability and economic viability for the future unless the information that the Board demands and addresses also reflects the breadth of issues in a 21st century economy. Boards will remain "in the dark" unless their oversight extends to reflect the broad base of stakeholder interests at the planning level as well as a framework for planning and reporting that includes the metrics required to evaluate performance from a broad perspective of strategy formulation and implementation.

8. SETTING DIRECTION: VISION, MISSION, VALUES, GOALS, AND OBJECTIVES

Before any work can be done to create a sustainable and comprehensive governance framework that starts to complement and support the new economy, someone needs to set some direction. This *must* be the initial primary role of the Board together with the shareholders (and other stakeholders).

Boards — and through them owners — define the scope and breadth of an organization — in effect defining the "play box" within which approval is given to operate. This is critical, as management needs to have a clearly defined sphere of operations. If management strays outside the defined mandate, then Boards are no longer able to ensure that their governance expectations can be maintained. Rules for governance are established based on the type of business an organization is engaged in and, therefore, straying outside of this can invalidate such rules. This forms the starting point of effective governance — responding to the question "what are we trying to do here?" Determining a clear answer to this is core to protection of shareholders, and other stakeholder's interests. This defines the beginning of the previously discussed "upper circle" of the governance model that deals with "intent".

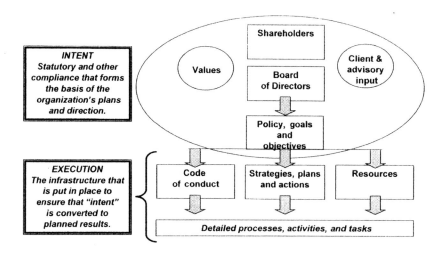

In addition to defining the upper circle of the governance model, this approach serves as the starting point for the model discussed earlier that creates an aligned framework at the top of the governance deployment pyramid (see exhibit below). The top portion of the model includes setting clear direction from which plans to execute can be derived. Without clear direction, plans will continually change, becoming confusing for those required to plan execution.

Connecting Approved Strategy to Successful Action

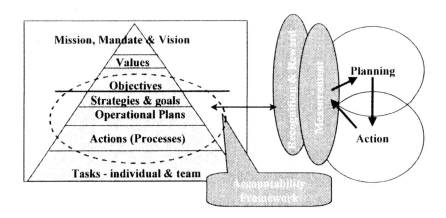

To a great degree, mission and mandate will link with the defined purpose in the organization legislation — either through the articles of incorporation or through the enabling legislation for public sector organizations.

Mission/Mandate	Defines the framework within which the organization is authorized either through legislation or decision of the shareholders to operate. Words like "limited to" or "operating within", "focusing on" or "engaged in" might be appropriate.
Vision	Defines the long-term high level view of how the organization will be perceived as it continues its journey of development. Words such as "leaders in" or "solutions to" or "seen as" might be appropriate.
Values	Defines the ways in which the organization will be seen to behave as it engages in the works defined by the mission and vision.
Goals	Defines the medium- to long-term expectations set by owners, boards, or others who are accountable for the achievements of the organization.
Objectives	Defines the medium- to short-term measurable performance that the owners, boards, or others expect (indeed set) as criteria for management to achieve.

As an organization moves through the five criteria above, a clear pattern should develop that results in a set of objectives being defined in such a way that management is left in no doubt about what performance is expected in terms of results as well as the behavioural criteria expected as the work is performed. It sets scope, behaviour, and outcomes in both objective and subjective criteria.

As an organization sets its objectives, it therefore becomes critical that consistency exists between what is expected and what is actually happening. Management and measurement models and approaches need to be aligned that verify for the Board that:

- the scope of operations is being maintained within those defined in the mission and mandate;
- the strategies being employed are consistent with the vision that has been established;

- the behaviour is being managed in a way that is consistent with the values that have been defined;
- the goals are being worked towards as business plans are being developed; and
- the objectives are being achieved in terms of short-term milestones on the journey that the enterprise is engaged in.

Without this linkage and aligned approach, Boards will be unable to assess performance within a defined framework and management will not be able to ensure that plans being developed and executed are, in fact, aligned with the board's expectations. In this type of situation, it is impossible to define accountability.

This approach has some interesting linkages to other aspects of management performance. Effective product quality depends upon clear specifications of the product or service being provided. These have to be created with client (user) input while being developed in a way that planning for creation as well as assessment of compliance are clear. Specifications typically have clear metrics in areas such as time, quality, cost, and availability (volume). Specifications for services will usually include both objective (tangible) as well as subjective (intangible) measures, which could include satisfaction — a clear part of which is the behaviour of those delivering the service, and a clear part of the organizational specifications.

We have already discussed that, in the past, TQM (Total Quality Management) was one of the approaches that management applied to try and improve the effectiveness of management. The problem is — and here we see the governance linkage — that if the specifications for management performance are not clear (i.e., as set by the Board) then the execution will be flawed.

One of the key aspects of poor quality is excess costs[21] which is a shareholder issue rather than a customer one; yet quality managers have continually found it difficult to focus on what this opportunity is and to attract senior management's attention to the opportunities involved.[22] If the negative impact of poor quality was part of management reporting metrics, and the Board used this to assess the integrity of the intangible assets (process performance), then more attention would be given to quality. The problem is that existing financial metrics and the accounting profession do not see themselves as part of the quality management approach and therefore no such reporting ever becomes part of the accountability for management.[23] The result is that management is failing to meet an "unwritten" board

---

21 J. Campanella, ed., *Principles of Quality Costs*, 3d ed. (ASQ Quality Press, 1999).
22 C.G. Cobb, *From Quality to Business Excellence: A Systems Approach to Management* (ASQ Quality Press, 2003).
23 G.D. Beecroft, G.L. Duffy & J. W. Moran, *The Executive Guide to Improvement and Change* (ASQ Quality Press, 2003).

expectation (specification) of "*no waste of shareholders' resources*" yet are completely unable to see what such waste is costing as they review performance measures.[24]

9. MANAGEMENT'S CHALLENGE: PLANNING FOR ACCOUNTABILITY AND CONTROL

Having dealt with the challenges of the Board and owners in having a framework through which clear direction is established, we need to address "alignment". This deals with the ability to ensure that management's framework for accountability reflects and complements the intent of the Board.

In order for this to happen, the lower circle of our high level framework needs to be linked to the upper circle in all aspects of converting intent to execution. However, management's focus must be to ensure that an effective framework is in place, starting with the planning stage from which objectives are translated into executable strategies, plans, and actions.

The traditional problem has fallen into at least two main categories. First, both planning and reporting have been focused on financial aspects of performance, which fails to deal with both intangibles as well as behaviour. Second, in many organizations there are no direct linkages between

---

24 H. Atkinson, J. Hamburg & C. Ittner, *Linking Quality to Profits* (ASQ Quality Press, 1994).

board level policies in many areas and strategies for executable deployment within the day-to-day activities of the organizations. Results of this include:

- creation of policies and plans that appear inconsistent with organization values leading to morale problems;
- behaviours in many areas, that are inconsistent with values (such as management/staff, organization/suppliers, organization/clients, and others;
- activities being undertaken by management outside the scope of oper-ations anticipated by the Board;
- miscommunications of the performance intent with the behaviour (*e.g.*, improved performance through costs cutting that leads to values prob-lems);
- short-term performance decisions that may be contradictory to longer term goals and expectations;
- depletion of organization's intangible values through focus on financial performance (loss of staff, reduced innovation, customer defections).

In all cases, the failure is usually not just poor management but a poor infrastructure that fails to ensure alignment between intent and execution. The key aspects that need to be in place to ensure such accountability are covered in the lower circle of the governance model. These ensure that linkage exists and that each intent criteria is mirrored by an execution capacity.

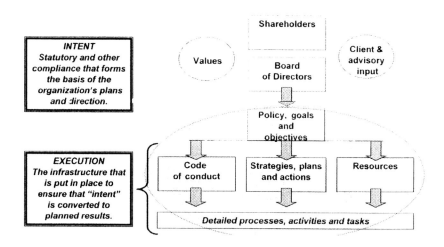

In creating such a model for linkage, we can consider where the con-nections might be and what needs to be in place and why.

Aspect	Examples of Management Model linkages
Mission/Mandate and Vision/Goals	• Effective leadership skills — deploying communications up and down the organization on where we are going versus where we are now; • Planning — developing realistic plans that link current, short-term, long-term and benchmark performance criteria; • People development — education and training through both orientation and regular "where we are" updates; • Measures and learning systems — feedback systems that allow learning of employees as plans proceed to ensure direction is maintained.
Values	• Planning — ensuring that plans include both objective (outputs and outcomes) as well as subjective (outcomes) measures; • Planning — ensuring that planning process as well as aspects include key stakeholders; • Process management — ensuring that process design includes both the methods as well as behaviour anticipated; • People development — ensuring orientation, training, and feedback deals with what is done as well as how it is done; • Measurements systems — ensuring measures from key partners include values based aspects (*e.g.*, surveys).

Aspect	Examples of Management Model linkages
Objectives	• Planning system — defined performance expectations in all aspects of organizational activity (financial and others). • Planning — developing alignment in the planning, doing (execution), checking (measures), and acting processes to develop continual improvement in all areas of execution; • Leadership — linking high level organizational plans with expectations at the individual level (clarity); • Measures/feedback — ensuring that consistency exists between breadth of objectives reflecting board expectations and breadth of metrics to assess actual performance.

It is important for readers to stop and consider the last several years of governance problems and ask how many are, in fact, related to fraud and legally defined issues versus ones that can be laid at the door of bad management or board performance? We cannot blame individuals (directors and/or managers) if we do not have the tools in place to do the job. Today's governance frameworks do not provide such tools. The danger is to over-react on the legislative side and just create additional constraints rather than focusing on greater flexibility and the capability to deal with the broad range of possible control deviations.

10. FUNDAMENTALS OF A NEW MODEL FOR ACCOUNTABILITY

(a) Introduction

When we look at our high level governance model, we see that many other changes are indeed either taking place or are in the process of evolving, to reflect the changed realities of managing enterprises in the post-industrial age. However, there are also considerable changes taking place within management.

In particular, we see various international models for management excellence that focus on a broad range of what needs to be managed to deliver results, as well as the movement towards a more broad-based measurement system for results and outcomes — often based on the Balanced Scorecard[25] (BSC). However, when we look at the linkage between the Board level governance issues, the review and assessment linkage area, and the management circle, we begin to see a major area of disconnection.

Traditionally, there has been heavy reliance on financial performance reporting as well as controls through third party audits as the vehicles for assurance that the "assets" of the organization — most particularly the investments made by shareholders — are indeed protected and managed effectively. This is the area of accounting standards that auditors follow to ensure consistency and compliance. However, these audits, based heavily on financial aspects of the organization's activity, only deliver one aspect of the requirement. Kaplan and Norton give the example of Skandia, a Swedish insurance and financial services firm that has moved to using a BSC type format called the Skandia Navigator[26] format to report to its Board.[27] There remains much to be done, and one of the key organizations working in this area is the World Business Council on Sustainable Development[28] that has been discussed earlier.

In building a model for the future and creating a way ahead, we will break the discussion into the following points:

- designing the framework for good governance;
- populating and deploying the framework;
- verification of the effectiveness of good governance.

Each of these distinct phases requires a thought process of what needs to be done as well as how it will be executed. By following these steps, an organization can develop the framework that is right for its reality, while building in both existing and developing "best practices".

---

25 R.S. Kaplan & D.P. Norton, *The Balanced Scorecard: Translating Strategy Into Action* (Boston: Harvard Business School Press, 1996).

26 To learn more about Skandia and contact them see www.skandia.com

27 Readers should note that Skandia is also used as a leading example of an organization that has moved almost all of its governance practices, including management, away from traditional areas. While the company delivers leading edge performance on a continuing basis, it has moved away from budgeting as being an inhibitor to growth and accountability and has also fully embraced the concepts of identifying, valuing, measuring and managing intellectual capital — often referred to as knowledge management. This company provides a good example of an integrated approach where the whole framework has been shifted in recognition of a post-industrial society based enterprise.

28 For more information see www.wbcsd.org

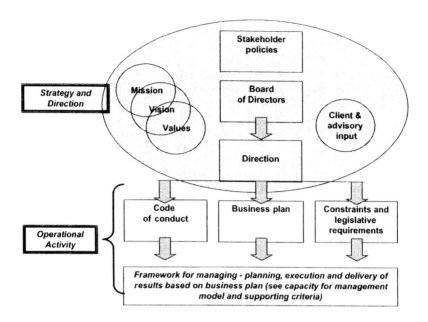

(b) Phase # 1 — Direction

In this first phase, an organization must define what its philosophy of operations will be. The initial directors or equivalent will have been selected and will be in place based on legislation or ongoing elections through annual meetings. Their principle task must be to ensure that a clear governance framework is in place for the enterprise. The aspects that need to be covered in this stage are as follows:

- What are the organization's mandate, mission, and vision? Where do we want to steer this ship? What is the enabling legislation that empowers us? What are the boundaries and accountabilities?
- Who are the stakeholders that require representation? For example, traditionally, the representation has been financial but an increasing number of Boards exhibit selection criteria that include individuals who meet the broad criteria of:

  - representing key investors;
  - bringing specific sector experience and representation;
  - bringing specific functional and/or technical expertise; and
  - bringing specific geographic expertise.

- What are the sources of external input that we require to establish direction for the organization? Is there legislation that we must comply

with? Are there trade and professional associations that we participate in/take a lead role in?
- What should we be considering in order to position our enterprise to be on a sustainable basis for the future?[29]
- What are the roles, responsibilities, and accountabilities of the Board, *inter alia*, the CEO as the key representative of management through which the direction of the Board is communicated?
- What approaches, methods, and processes are there in place to establish direction for the entity and to communicate such direction to management? What are the processes and feedback mechanisms that ensure the Board has visibility to the organization's activities, and can monitor actual performance, results, and other key issues?

In addition to the mechanics of what needs to be done at this "direction" stage, the Board of Governance also needs a process for managing its own activities. This is where much of the work has been done to increase Board effectiveness. Resources for Boards to assess their performance in these areas include checklists[30] as well as self-assessment against good governance standards such as the TSE requirements.[31] In addition, self-assessments of Board effectiveness can be made through considering "key success factors for an effective Board"[32] and "characteristics of good governance."[33]

(c) Phase # 2 — Execution

Traditional approaches to governance rely, to a major degree, on two pivotal connections:

- the Chief Executive Officer/Deputy Minister as the main conduit through which direction is communicated and feedback is received;
- the independent third party of audit and/or assessment that provides validation of the organization's compliance with pre-determined standards.

With the rate of change in the operational environment, the complexity encountered, and the scope of activities, this linkage becomes critical.

---

29 For example, using the checklist from the World Business Council on Sustainable Development that covers corporate values and issues, communication, and others as one source: www.wbcsd.org

30 As an example for non-profit organizations, the "Quick Check" list by the Institute on Governance available through www.iog.ca

31 For guidelines currently in place see www.tse.com and look at "Resources" section, Company Manual, Sec. 474 (1- 14).

32 Above, note 2, at p. 143 — six factors of leadership, legitimacy and power, job definition, competence, board culture and board management.

33 See www.unescap.org/huset/gg/governance.htm from the United Nations.

While the ability of the CEO to satisfy financial requirements remains key — protecting the assets and generating a return on investment at or above the levels expected, this no longer tells the full story. In fact, traditional financial reporting no longer tells this story with many organizations now moving towards the use of EVA[34] (Economic Value Added). However, effective deployment of today's organizational "value" includes many intangibles that also need to be assessed, managed, and protected in order to ensure sustainable development. These include areas such as relationships with key clients and customers, attraction, motivation, and retention of key employees, the effective functioning of key processes including information about the effective quality delivered by such processes, and the level of innovation and development that is taking place.

One approach to these issues is to allow the Chief Executive Officer to be assessed on results delivered, using the assumption that "all must be well if the results are there". One classic example of this (although now eclipsed by more recent issues) was the departure of Paul Stern from Nortel, at a time when financial cost cutting was taking place to "make the numbers". The impact of this was revealed later as being critical, based on the negative impact it was having on both innovation agenda as well as client relationships. Although in the early years of the 21st century, Nortel's governance problems appeared to continue in a wide range of other areas — again a reflection not just on the manager but on the ability of an organization to have the governance capacity and tools to do the job. Nortel has exhibited most of the symptoms caused by poor frameworks.

Another alternative is to rely upon the third party auditors' opinions of the ability of the organization to operate as a "continuing business" — however, the problem here is that auditors rely upon management's opinion of this and we therefore come full circle. There is a codicil to the audit approach and that is the deployment of a broader based operational audit. However, without the statutory requirements for compliance with such a vehicle, the weight of this is limited. (Although one should note the success of this in the public sector, where the quality of management as well as compliance is now frequently reported upon).

The recommended option is to create linkage between the evolving tools that management needs to manage the enterprise and Board reporting, and to recognize these as being the same tools and information vehicles that are required for good governance. There are three aspects to this that we suggest.

The first is the expansion of the interpretation of an organization's "market capital" (*i.e.*, its worth) from one that includes just financial capital (*i.e.*, that which is represented by the traditional financial statements), to

---

34 See www.sternstewart.com as the copyright holders for this approach.

one that includes intellectual capital. The following model [35] shows the three prime components as being the people (human capital), the structural capital (the process and other organizational knowledge and infrastructure), and the customer capital (the relationships and worth of items such as brand image, distribution networks, and others). This approach mirrors that of the Skandia Business Navigator [36] outlined earlier, that includes financial focus, customer focus, human focus, process focus, and renewal and development focus.

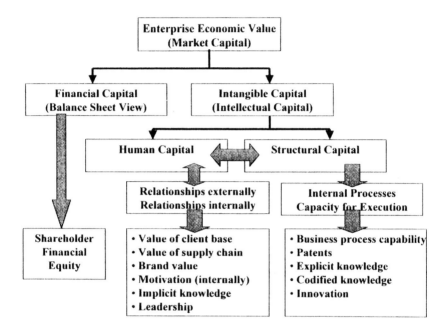

The second aspect is to embrace the reporting that many management organizations are moving towards in terms of the balanced scorecard. Through this approach, an organization tracks and maintains a multi-dimensional basis of planning, managing, and reporting its activities. In this approach (adapted from the Kaplan/Norton, Balanced Scorecard Model (BSC)), we maintain the central linkage to the governance vision, strategic direction, and core capability (*i.e.*, mission/mandate), then define this as the financial perspective (the traditional financial model of reporting), and then add the aspects of customer relationships, internal processes, and learning and growth. In this model, the human dimension is assumed as subsumed into the ability to achieve innovation and growth. In addition, in this example

---

35 From Danish Ministry of Industry, based on Skandia.
36 See details in note 25, above, at pp. 211-217 for complete linkages.

we have added into the BSC the areas where the previous "intellectual capital" aspects would fit.

The Balanced Scorecard

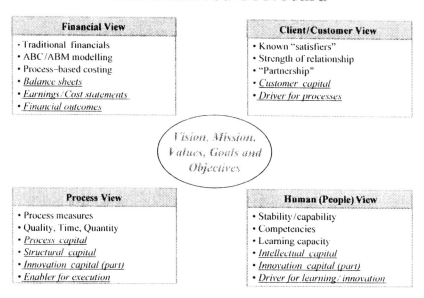

Financial View	Client/Customer View
• Traditional financials	• Known "satisfiers"
• ABC/ABM modelling	• Strength of relationship
• Process-based costing	• "Partnership"
• *Balance sheets*	• *Customer capital*
• *Earnings/Cost statements*	• *Driver for processes*
• *Financial outcomes*	

Vision, Mission, Values, Goals and Objectives

Process View	Human (People) View
• Process measures	• Stability/capability
• Quality, Time, Quantity	• Competencies
• *Process capital*	• Learning capacity
• *Structural capital*	• *Intellectual capital*
• *Innovation capital (part)*	• *Innovation capital (part)*
• *Enabler for execution*	• *Driver for learning/innovation*

The third aspect, and the one that most closely fits in with leading edge practice in management execution as depicted by many international models for excellence, is a framework both for governance direction as well as management execution and reporting that fully reflects all the aspects of performance management.

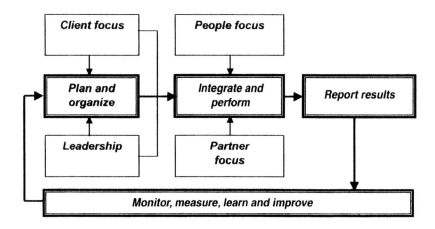

In this approach, the traditional hand-off from governance direction to execution is through the *planning and organizing function*. While there will be interaction between the Board or equivalent governance relationships to agree upon what is to be done, management must then take the plan and organize to execute it. Next, management "runs" the operation — performs what has to be done to deliver results — and this is the traditional final step to feed back the results to those holding the primary governance responsibility. Traditionally, the feedback from results to planning would be through monitoring and measurement of the financial aspects, as these were the primary values that required governance.

However, today's organizations operate in a broader framework that is of value to both those governing as well as those executing strategy. Considering the functions, we start with *leadership*. The role of leadership becomes critical in ensuring that the mission, vision, and values of the organization are translated from a governance requirement into operational reality. This would include, for example, the ability of the organization to act in a way that it committed to do in meeting sustainable development. Without the leadership linkage, there is no assurance that the values and principles established by the Board as a framework for operations are even being considered as part of execution.

Second, we have a *client focus*. All of our prior discussion about the intangible worth of this asset, as well as its importance as a key stakeholder, indicates a need for some level of monitoring and reporting from an external aspects viewpoint of the organization. This again serves to validate the words that the Board has created as part of the organization's position in terms of its relationships with key external stakeholders.

Next we have the *people focus*. Again, this has been discussed as part of the intangible capital of the organization and is also one of its key stakeholders. The organization's ability to manage its human resources is a critical component of sustaining its activities into the future. The guidelines for good governance established by the TSE and others include the need for effective recruitment and succession planning for the CEO; but good governance requires that issues such as this are fully deployed across the organization.

Next we have "partners" as a key category. Most organizations today recognize that there are sets of stakeholders that are partners in the enterprise's activities. These may be suppliers, third party service deliverers, or others, but in all cases the ability of the organization to execute against its strategy means that these relationships must be created, nurtured, and grown in order to be fully effective. This again can be considered an area of intellectual capital in many organizations — especially those where sole sourcing has been put in place, or in the case of government where ASD (Alternative Service Delivery) has been implemented resulting in a critical degree of dependence on a party external to the traditional governance framework.

Finally, we have the ability of the organization to not only *measure* all of the key aspects of what it is doing but to learn from what takes place so that it can use these learnings to grow and improve. In many organizations, there is a large gap between stated governance intent (to be a learning, continually improving organization) and the actual practices in place through which this is supposed to happen.

What we therefore have with this third aspect, is an ability to create a consistent linkage between what management knows that it needs to manage to be effective (excellent) on a continuing basis and those aspects of what management is engaged in doing that the board of governance needs to know about, to plan, and to monitor. This provides a solid model for conversion of an organization's intended governance into actual practice.

In the remainder of this book, we will address each of the aspects of this model and explain possible frameworks and metrics that can be developed to populate such a model.

11. INTEGRATING RISK MANAGEMENT WITHIN THE MODEL

Prior to the most recent current governance issues, a great deal of work was underway to improve the capacity of organizations to identify and manage risk. However, risk management is, in fact, a subset of the good governance framework that needs to be created for the future.

Using the interlocking circles concept model, there are three key areas where risk management needs to be addressed, which should be incorporated. These are:

- risk related to organizational/structural governance — *i.e.*, those risks resting with the decision making of the "governing" body prior to execution;
- risk related to the translation and deployment of the governing strategy to the performing organization; and
- risk related to the independent assessment process in fact providing adequate information upon which evaluation of performance as well as oversight and course correction can be based.

Effective approaches to addressing these three areas can be addressed through creating and implementing ERM (Enterprise Risk Management) approaches that were discussed earlier. However, this should not be yet another separate initiative within an organization. If risk exists within the areas identified within the new approaches, then an effective governance model will, in fact, create the framework for a risk assessment as well as for a management framework. Thus the need to take an integrated approach to risk management, which seems to be the most effective and preferred route, becomes part of the approach to addressing each of the areas of organization performance. Risk assessments, therefore, need to a) start with Board level risks and b) align and deploy through operational risks. In terms of operational risks, these will exist within each of the aspects of what is being planned, managed, and measured. As an example, risks will exist with aspects of people management. Therefore, the risk assessment program needs to address this. This same approach can work for all aspects of the governance "deployment/execution" framework.

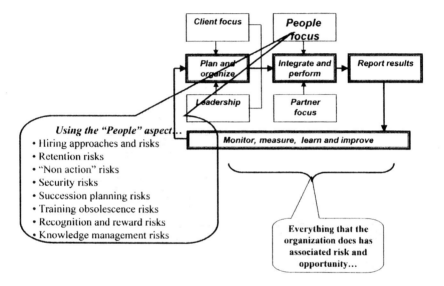

Using the framework that we have created we can now consider risk under all of the main categories; these would include risk related to:

- external stakeholder relationships, including societal issues and concerns and the risks related to compliance with organizational values and principles;
- risks related to the effective governance of the Board and its assigned roles and responsibilities (including competence, succession, and others);
- risks related to the process of translating opportunity into action from Board through to CEO decision making;
- risks related to the capacity to perform in *all* areas of the model — planning, process, results, leadership, client, partners, people, measurement, learning, and improvement.

Using this approach, as will be discussed later, a complete capacity assessment can be created that will fully integrate the identification and planning for risk within each of the key elements of the capacity model.

12. CHECKLIST FOR A GOOD GOVERNANCE FRAMEWORK

Earlier we discussed what would be required as a framework for creating good governance; this can now be reviewed against the model that we have created to ensure that all areas have been addressed.

Area to be addressed	Method of approach
The way in which the accountability for good governance is established either legislatively or through other means.	Governing Board accountability in effective creation of mission, vision and of representative body to ensure legislative needs are met.
The ways in which all stakeholders are identified.	Governing Board review of all stakeholders and ensure that all have been identified, relative policies set to determine rights and priorities.
The way in which the rights of stakeholders are protected, through legislation, standards and other approaches.	
The way in which accountability for good governance is split between various parties.	Board initially through defining its role and responsibilities including job descriptions and through the CEO the creation of an accountability framework.
The way in which the principles and values of the organization are developed and deployed.	Governing Board creates high-level values for the organization for which CEO is then accountable through leadership to create code of conduct and ensure alignment of stated views through all areas of planning and execution.
The way in which goals and objectives for the enterprise are created and communicated.	Governing Board and CEO and then CEO through the creation of the planning portion of the capacity model.

Area to be addressed	Method of approach
The process through which those responsible for execution plan, perform, and report on their accountability to deliver the desired results.	CEO through the management framework that ensures that goals and objectives are deployed throughout the organization, and that the measurement systems align with and support governing Board intent.

In the next section, we will review how such a framework is supported by either existing standards or other areas that are emerging to support the transition to new approaches to governance.

13. MOVING FORWARD

At this stage, we have discussed the existing problems with governance frameworks; identified alternatives that are emerging in various areas including legislative changes and, in addition, we have identified that these other frameworks deal with a broader range of performance and conduct criteria. We have also identified an operational approach that deals with each of these criteria and allows them to become part of the management model through which Board intent is translated into plans and action.

1. Boards create the direction and define mandate, values, goals, and objectives.
2. These are linked to management execution capacity through an integrated model that starts with the Board governance aspects and also includes a defined management model, business planning, and a measurement and feedback system.

We have also identified that this type of approach, being holistic and aligned, will also form the basis for integration of risk management throughout the organization.

In the next sections of the book, we will review each of the key aspects of performance reporting, starting with the traditional financial area, and will review how the aspects of each area are included in policy at the Board level, integrated into business planning, and then executed through effective management. In addition, the metrics required as part of an effective performance measures system will be discussed as will the aspects of risk management for each. This will allow for the creation of a blueprint from which an organization can move forward and build a governance approach for the 21st century. Such direction should place organizations following their own development on a parallel and complementary course to the emerging models for sustainable development.

PART 3

BUILDING BLOCKS OF A NEW APPROACH

Reflecting on history, thinking about the reality of our current capacity to ensure organizational accountability, and learning from current trends, we can start to create a new model for the future; a model that has the depth and breadth to rebuild confidence in the public, complement existing approaches that work, and gradually shift reporting and accountability into a framework that more effectively reflects the societal expectations of the 21st century.

In the previous section of the book, we looked at areas that are either already in place or starting to be implemented — models for excellence, international standards, guidelines for reporting on a broad basis, and others. In our final section, we will distill these components into specific elements that must form a part of future accountability. Only through addressing each of these areas will shareholders and other stakeholders, directors, managers, and others become knowledgeable as well as accountable for the accumulated economic value of the enterprise which they seek to guide and manage.

This breadth of accountability will lead us to realize that effective governance cannot be achieved through a focus on legislation and financial reporting. What is required is a renewed framework which deals with economic sustainability — the ability of an enterprise to deal with its tangible as well as intangible assets — and to ensure that the "wealth" that has been accumulated over the years in knowledge and capability is being sustained and grown for the benefit of shareholders and recognizing its place in society and addressing the changing expectations of all stakeholders.

The approach proposed here builds on such a concept and identifies what is required in terms of the aspects of enterprise performance to be reported.

6

ACCOUNTABILITY FOR FISCAL PERFORMANCE

Financial performance will remain a key element of accountability, as investors pay out cash to create a share in the wealth of the entity. Likewise in the public sector accountability for the use of the financial resources collected and expended remains a key factor. However, the accounting profession's ability to manage intangibles must be re-engineered if economic valuation of the organization as a system of both tangible and intangible assets is to be made transparent.

1. THE ROLE OF STANDARDS — ONGOING ACCOUNTING DEVELOPMENTS

The role of the external auditor and the compliance with external accounting standards will continue to be an important part of ensuring an effective governance framework; however, an expectation of solving the good governance crisis by focusing of tightening up standards is, at best, misleading. There will always be an element of situational interpretation required in some instances and in *all* of these cases the *values* of the organization should be a solid enough driver to ensure a correct and reasonable interpretation.

In the case of Enron, one might observe that the major driver could have been the desire to maintain the stock prices so as to benefit option holders (and, in many cases, this is a valid concern if a large number of employees have their savings invested in company shares). However, the key was that there was inadequate disclosure of factors that would have had a material impact on peoples' judgements. An interesting study that begins to address this in terms of shareholder versus management driven values was recently summarized in *Report on Business* magazine.[1]

The obvious gaps in accounting standards need to be addressed and these events should encourage the profession to move faster to develop and position standards in a way that responds to a number of issues. First is the speed with which new tools of management are developed, thus dealing with issues such as handling the impact of stock options expense. Second, to deal with the need for international harmonization, and third, to start to address the growing gap between the book value of enterprises as depicted

---

1 S. Foerster, "Does Management Look After Itself First?" *Report on Business* (June 2002). Also see study on www.sternstewart.com website – report created by Hackett Group.

by accounting records and the valuations that develop where there is a high proportion of intangible assets to tangibles and investors have no real way of assessing the organization's underlying worth and strength to generate a future earnings stream.

2. FINANCIAL MEASURES AS THE ULTIMATE VALUE

Financial performance measurement has long been used as the best common denominator of an organization's overall performance. It synthesizes every aspect of activity into a single set of measures through which performance can be benchmarked.

Essentially, shareholders and owners want to know whether their investment in the organization is increasing or decreasing in value-based managements and their Board's effectiveness in using their money. Investors focus on two key aspects of financial performance: their equity value based on their year-to-year balance sheet value, and the "worth" of their investment based on the current share price and/or the value of their portion of the investment should they sell it.

History and the evolution of financial reporting have brought these measures into a stage where:

- accounting approaches (GAAP) are integrated with legal requirements for incorporated entities;
- standards have been developed to deal with approaches to the many types of financial transactions that occur;
- financial benchmarks have been developed that allow organizations to compare their financial performance with others to identify "best practice";
- reporting frameworks have been developed that ensure consistent presentation of information through earnings statements, balance sheets, source, and application of funds as well as required supporting information such as management discussion and analysis (MD&A), notes to the accounts, segmented information, and others;
- the market place has been able to create a base value for organizations using the balance sheet values, plus or minus adjustments for other values not included on the standard financial reporting;
- criteria have been developed that allow the development of sectoral financial ratios to be developed that identify typical relationships between "book values" and share values (PB — Price to Book) as well as "normal values" for price to earnings and others;
- a whole profession has been created to provide compliance assurance that financial reporting does follow the rules.

All of these developments have created a mature framework for those outside the organization to have a level of transparency (knowledge and visibility) as to what is occurring internally. The goal obviously has been to provide for both accountability between owners, boards, and managers as well as to provide for informed decisions by interested parties such as investors and others. Verifying that an organization complies with these rules has been a core aspect of exercising due diligence in investments.

The challenges facing financial reporting today in the private sector are that, for many organizations, balance sheets no longer truly reflect the value of the organization. The alternative is to use "market value" but this is a poor indicator reflecting both overall market expectations as well as the hype that a particular stock might have depending upon the most recent write-up of an investment analyst. Investors want greater visibility and transparency into the real potential and worth of their investment and, as we have discussed, traditional accounting is becoming less relevant as the principle indicator.

3. PUBLIC SECTOR FINANCIAL REPORTING

Standards have also developed that allow public sector organizations to report their performance in a consistent way. However, in the public sector the investors as such (the taxpayers) have traditionally not been overly concerned with detailed financial reporting and few have read public financial statements with the same degree of interest that they would if they had "shares" in the organization that increased or decreased in value depending on what level of performance management was delivering. The focus has been on the "big numbers" — levels of taxation coming out of the individual's pocket and the level of either surplus or deficit positions.

In addition, because there is no basic financial equity in a non-profit or public organization, the accounting has focused mainly on sources and application of funds; sources in terms of the revenues collected in the year and application in terms of the expenditures made to fund programs. While expenditures of governments have traditionally included what the private sector would deem "capital" investments, where benefit accrues over time and this "expense" is charged against operations based on depreciation, governments have basically paid for these out of "current" incomes and appropriations and, in many cases, from an increase in the public debt. This approach has negative implications in that significant expenses for infrastructure might be avoided as governments seek to balance budgets.

It could be argued that this problem is at the heart of the decline in Canada's federal, provincial, and municipal infrastructures in terms of roads, bridges, schools, mass transit, military installations, and equipments and many other traditional "capital" purchases.

If there is no balance sheet then financial decisions related to the treatment of expenditures between capital and operating are not needed but neither is there a need to worry to a great degree about the timing of expenditures. However, this again creates problems in terms of both current expenditures for future benefits, the current consumption of "capital resources" already paid for out of past revenues (understating the real cost of operating), and the problems with funding longer term programs as well as creating "accruals" for future commitments.

Public sector financial management challenges are further complicated by both the inadequacy of the time periods involved where very significant strategic directional decisions can change 180° every four of five years, as well as the timing of the budgeting processes in terms of providing an effective framework for linking financial plans to action plans. Situations occur today in governments where operating managers only receive their financial budget six to eight months into the operating year making any sort of financial planning, management, or reporting a dysfunctional element of effective governance.

Finally, the public sector is starting to address some of the capital versus current expenditure issues through the adoption of accrual based accounting; government "assets" will now be identified, "capitalized", and then "expensed" over time to more effectively present ongoing program costs versus those expenditures dealing with infrastructure, which has a longer life and supports the overall development of the national economy.

4. PROTECTION OF STAKEHOLDERS' EQUITY

Market capital and the value of an organization stems from a combination of financial and non-financial aspects. While the reporting and transparency problems of traditional public sector accounting are starting to be driven by changes in standards for the public sector as well as by the move towards "accrual accounting" (which will begin to put public and private sectors on a somewhat similar presentation basis), the challenges in the private sector are not yet being addressed in any meaningful way. While some changes are being made to standards that pertain to issues such as stock options and to deal with "special purpose entity" (SPE) accounting (one of the Enron problems), there remain significant issues that either cannot be addressed by accounting changes or that need to be made to have accounting viewed as a clear developer of increased transparency.

To begin, we must go back to the discussion on shareholders' equity not represented by valuation on organizations' financial statements. There are two distinct issues in this situation that financial reporting must address if this element of accountability is to contribute to effective governance.

5. INTANGIBLES

Intangibles are those items such as patents, trademarks, brands, relationships with clients that establish market share, distribution channels that are in place with supply and client partners, market intelligence not shared by others, and reputation, as well as the entrenched knowledge of employees and the value of internal processes through which an organization's products and services are created.

The accounting profession does have rules for intangibles, *e.g.*, a past event, that has a measurable effect and a future benefit,[2] but these are generally guided by the overall principle of "conservatism" that guides the creation of any financial statements. It is because of this problem that the profession is having such a hard time of addressing the increasing economic value of such assets. This challenge was clearly identified by the International Accounting Standards Committee (now Board — IASB) in dealing with the issue, even taking into account the creation of IAS 38 — the current standard for intangibles.

Thus, the profession may not be able to address the issue while maintaining the conservative integrity of traditional financial reporting. However, some standards have been developed and are in place but these deal with a smaller proportion of the intangibles that typically create a significant difference between book and economic value. These include trademarks, patents, and other items where the cost of acquisition can be more effectively determined.

> . . . the conservative approach of the IASC and other national standard setting authorities is not very surprising. The standard setting bodies are not expected to take the lead in the issue of accounting for intangibles; in complex matters they are supposed to take the position of codifying best practise.[3]

The problem, however, is significant. It has been estimated that

> in 2000 US private firms invested over $1 trillion, a level that matches investment in tangible assets, and further that capital stock of US intangibles has an equilibrium market value that exceeds $5 trillion, approximately 50% of the total market value of all US corporations.[4]

So — something needs to be done; a growing proportion of investors' assets are not represented by financial reporting as and when they are created and, because their value is at best "uncertain", it is likely that the accounting

---

2 FASB presentation, Nakamura 4th Annual Intangible Assets Conference, Ross Institute, New York University, May 2001.

3 Extract from paper presented at workshop on intangibles in Brussels, February 1999.

4 B. Lev & J. Hand, eds., *Intangible Assets: Values, Measures, and Risk* (Oxford University Press, 2003), chapter 1, "A trillion dollars a year in intangible investment and the new economy", by L. Nakamura.

profession will be the solution to the problem. However, the profession does have one answer, albeit flawed — goodwill.

6. GOODWILL

Readers may be tempted to believe that goodwill on an organization's balance sheet is, in fact, the value of the intangibles. Goodwill is created when an organization buys another for a value that exceeds the value of the tangible assets as depicted by the balance sheet. This can be demonstrated as follows:

Assets transferred	*Dollars in millions*
Book value of business — assets	$15
Liabilities	$5
Net book value	**$10**
Purchase price	$100
Goodwill paid (for intangible values)	**$90**

In this situation, the selling organization was reporting performance against a financial book value of $10 million; however, the buyer was willing to pay $100 million for the business, thus deciding that there was "other" value greater than the $10M on the balance sheet. As the accountants have to now deal with where the $90 million went in the books of the buyer (*i.e.*, if the transaction was for cash where did my $90M cash go?), then the purchasing business will create on its financial books a transaction that puts the assets in the books at $15 million and liabilities at $5 million, and then creates an entry called "goodwill" valued at $90 million. An interesting approach!

Overnight our balance sheet value has increased 10 fold. What happens now? This becomes a greater challenge. Accounting now has to ensure (based on the rules of prudence and the ability to demonstrate that values shown in the accounts provide a "true and fair view" of the value of the organization) that this $90 million has not been "impaired" — *i.e.*, it is still worth the same amount. If it is determined to be worth less, we have to write it down to a lower value or write it off but, if it goes up in value, it is still worth $90 million. If it is not acceptable to initially create the goodwill when it existed in the seller's books, then how can it be acceptable, once created, to determine a fair value? As a director, I would certainly want to know whether management is increasing or decreasing the value of intangibles in the business for which I am accountable.

7. MAKING GOODWILL MEAN SOMETHING

There are two aspects of solving this problem; either the creation of goodwill initially has to be accepted at some level of value (which is doubtful given the earlier statements and the risk impact of attributing a value to an intangible) or, when created, the impairment test has to at least be linked with some type of objective assessment. While valuation of the intangibles will be dealt with later as we discuss each category, the approach can be demonstrated by the following (using our last example).

First, we determine exactly how the goodwill is attributed. This would require an analysis of the purchase price on a buy/sell agreement to intangible assets. This might be one or more of the following:

- brand name/reputation in the marketplace;
- channels of distribution/client relationships;
- knowledge of people, including value of the "team";
- value of processes in place to deliver products and services;
- "learnings" and knowledge, including R&D value of work in process;
- value of undeveloped technology *e.g.*, "idle patents";
- access to raw materials through exclusive agreements or advantageous pricing/supply.

Once these attributes have been determined, then the task must be to develop valuation criteria that attempt to at least establish a point in time value that makes up the economic consideration of $90 million. If approximations can be made, then the same model can be used to re-evaluate the future worth. However, a key problem with the accounting concepts, as currently constructed, is that in many mergers and acquisitions the identity of the assets acquired are lost as the operations are integrated. Examples would be goodwill paid for services organizations that are then followed by the integration of branches, staff, and system as well as by client base. At this point, identification of worth or impairment becomes extremely difficult to undertake and produce a credible result.

8. THE WAY AHEAD FOR FINANCIAL REPORTING

Many changes being proposed to strengthen the roles of audit committees as well as to improve accounting standards are important and will contribute to improved integrity of financial reporting. However, the main challenge for the profession is going to come from two issues:

- challenges of accounting for intellectual capital, currently handled through goodwill; and
- broadening reporting so that organizations are accountable in both financial and non-financial measures.

Current research indicates that the profession is going to have a challenge in responding. Models have been proposed to financially quantify intellectual capital but the problems with these are that they are, by definition, dealing with degrees on uncertainty. Approaches[5] include market-to-book valuations, application of Tobin's Q, creating a calculated value of intellectual capital by assessing premium earnings, and re-stating financial reports by ignoring traditional rules in order to create a capitalized "knowledge bank". All are fraught with problems and all create variable answers that can provide misleading impressions if not well understood.

Rather than trying to create a new series of measures, organizations may be better advised to use the existing financial framework in cases where it works best — the tangible areas — and then develop a new supplemental framework for those areas that are excluded.

The best course is to focus on the true determined valuations of goodwill. As we proceed through this book, we will create financial and non-financial measures related to the various components of intellectual capital that go to support an organization's non-financial capital — in effect, the sources of the added value.

In doing this, an approach modelled on the concepts that underpin traditional financial reporting remains valid. Organizations may have intellectual assets (the balance sheet) but are they using them effectively (the earnings statement and creating an ROI)? One of the problems with financial and non-financial measures currently in development for intellectual capital is that the tendency is to focus on what exists in the way of assets rather than the effectiveness with which we deploy them. If pursued, the model would look as follows:

---

5 For further detailed reading see T.A. Stewart, *Intellectual Capital: The New Wealth of Organizations* (Bantam Doubleday Dell, 1997).

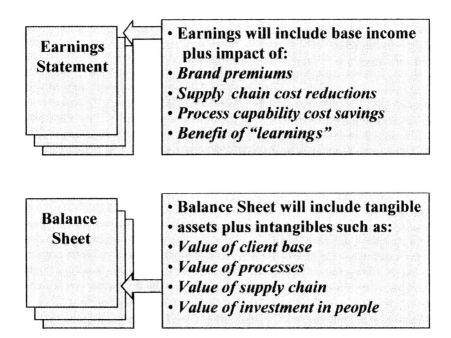

Such a system would recognize that "premium earnings" created by intellectual capital exist through lower costs and marginal revenues, and that intangible assets exist and are part of the balance sheet — some of which can be identified through existing accounting rules and some remain classified as intellectual capital. Developing measures that support such a scenario will be covered in the remaining chapters. In the final chapter, we will discuss how an Integrated Performance Measurement System[6] can be implemented to provide a comprehensive and aligned measures system.

9. MEASURES VERSUS INDICATORS

Before going further, here is a final point in moving away from reliance on financial reporting: financial reporting has been a good and valuable tool because it brings all things to a common denominator — monetary value. This has then been supported by a series of principles and standards (conservative in nature) that tend to stay away from creating measures that cannot be quantified with some specific level of accuracy. This works well when rules can be applied but, in cases where there are no rules or where accounting does not recognize such assets and performance criteria, *the current alternative is often no information at all.*

---

6 Also referred to as a "balanced scorecard" as per Kaplan & Norton, chapter 5, above.

What is being promoted in the new approach to effective governance is a combination of improvements to "monetarize" intangibles along with an effort to include new non-financial measures. Thus, future mechanisms for reporting information to support effective governance will include:

- definitive financial measurements where value can be determined through accounting standards and principles;
- financial quantifications of criteria that have a subjective factor to them (*i.e.*, they cannot meet the standard accounting criteria but an approximate value can be determined); and
- non-financial measures that supplement the financial information and provide added breadth, colour, and understanding to the state of affairs of the organization being "governed".

Purists may determine that measures are absolute, whereas indicators are just that — items that indicate direction. If a definition is required as the material moves forward, then only the absolute criteria of definitive items justified through standards can be determined to be measures, with all others being treated as indicators. Some indicators may be predictive (what may happen) and can be linked to possible future outcomes of both a financial, tangible, or intangible nature while others may be lagging and may tell us what has already taken place. Our goal is to have a broad portfolio of information that provides a combination of leading and lagging items so that planned action can be implemented rather than relying on reactive responses.

7

ACCOUNTABILITY FOR VALUES, ETHICS, MARKET REPUTATION, AND BRANDS

One of the greatest intangible values that an organization can create is its reputation. This impacts internally in terms of the principles through which the organization operates and behaves, and externally in terms of the impact created by its way of doing business — a positive or negative perception that adds to or reduces its value in the market place. Many of the problems that have exploded into the public perception about a lack of accountability can be traced back to the behaviour of an organization, including that of its employees and CEO. If public trust is to be rebuilt, there must be a framework for not only setting policy for values and ethics but also monitoring compliance in the deployment of this and the resulting value that is created.

1. THE VALUE OF A REPUTATION

From an economic perspective, reputation has value. At the individual level our reputation is one of the key "values" that we bring to our role in society; this is a key component of any professional organization — its "code of conduct" or ethical practice supported by a process of self-regulation. One individual using unethical practices reflects on the whole profession. There is no better example of this than the impact on Arthur Andersen as a result of the Enron situation or in fact any professional organization serving a corporate or individual client.[1]

The majority of people working for Arthur Andersen were, by all accounts, committed, diligent, and ethical professionals. The problems occur when organizations either change and lose their focus so that the ethical commitment becomes less clear or, for some other reasons, individuals caught up in specific situations make a decision that turns out to be incorrect, or are forced to choose between having a job and acting in a way that contravenes the organization's values as well as their own. (Of course there have been this and several other cases where destruction of the evidence has further worsened the situation and deemed it to an organizational rather

---

1   For those interested in the behind the scenes impacts see S.E. Squires *et al.*, *Inside Arthur Andersen: Shifting Values, Unexpected Consequences* (Financial Times/Prentice Hall Books, 2003).

than an individual problem). It is also interesting to note that the one person who eventually "blew the whistle" on Enron was Sherron Watkins — herself a CPA and thus a member of a professional body.

While the example demonstrates the issue of reputation at the individual level, so it is with corporate and organizational reputation. There is a value behind a reputation that requires investment in time and resources to create and sustain, and this value — real or perceived — creates behaviour in a market place that can have either a positive or negative value. Thus behaviour either adds to, or detracts from, a reputation and this in turn impacts the behaviour of other third parties as well as adding to or reducing the ultimate economic value of the enterprise.

2. ORGANIZATIONAL VALUES AND BEHAVIOUR

The core values of an organization as

the organization's essential and enduring tenets — a small set of general guiding principles; not to be confused with specific cultural or operating practices; not to be compromised for financial gain or short term expediency.[2]

Collins and Porras then go on to identify the combination of these values with the defining purpose of the organization as being at the heart of the organization's core ideology. This corresponds to our previously discussed framework where the organization's mandate and mission, leading to its vision, *must be a part of an integrated approach.*

The work of Stephen Covey also sheds significant light on the issue of values — although in his work the major focus is on "principles". However, the work is relevant as principles are derived at the individual level whereas the "legal person" *i.e.*, a corporate entity, cannot have principles *per se* as these are individual traits that are formed as part of an individual's genetic road map. Principles include such aspects as fairness, integrity, honesty, human dignity, quality, excellence, potential, patience, nurturing, and encouragement. While these can be easily linked to the behaviour of an individual, they only become corporate behaviours if, collectively, members of the organization share and demonstrate them. Thus, they become corporate values because they are adopted as "the way we do things here" and are reinforced and demonstrated by the consistency of individual behaviour within the organization. One individual alone can therefore create inconsistency in this behaviour.

This is a critical issue. Single events can have significant impact on the internal activities as well as on the external perception and, ultimately, economic value of an enterprise:

---

2   J.C. Collins & J.I. Porras, *Built to Last: Successful Habits of Visionary Companies* (Harper Collins, 1994).

- behaviour that supports, involves, and listens to clients will both attract and retain clients (all things being equal);
- negative behaviour (as defined by the client) depletes intellectual capital in terms of lost clients and eventually reduces revenues and drives up costs to replace the clients and the income derived from the relationship;
- behaviour that encourages and supports staff through coaching, mentoring, supporting, and developing creates added value and enables motivation; behaviour that does not achieve this depletes intellectual capital causing lower productivity and higher employee turnover;
- behaviour that encourages learning, results in developing intellectual capital through better application of human capital to all other aspects of organizational activity (improved client relations, better processes, innovative products and services, and faster cycle times — including take to market of new products).

Thus, the alignment of behavioural norms within an organization is critical to create the stage on which the intellectual assets will perform. As an example, human "assets" without motivation are wasted in the same way that an expensive piece of equipment is wasted with inadequate operations, care, and maintenance. The problem is that we can track and measure machine down time but totally lose sight of people down time when caused by a lack of motivation.

The importance and role of setting, communicating, integrating, and monitoring organizational values becomes a key component of effective governance. Without this, managers and directors are incapable of accountability for protecting existing capital, as well as effective development of future potential of intangible assets.

3. BRANDS

Brand image and reputation are prime examples of intangible corporate assets. Trends today include a degree of moving away from branded products and services in favour of generic items. However, there is a cause and effect at play here. Brands that are not sustainable do in fact die; their intangible value depletes until the market no longer places any value on the brand. An organization's behaviour, in the way that it interfaces with the market place and its clients and the way in which it focuses its resources on sustainability, has everything to do with either building or depleting a brand. Brand values can be a significant corporate asset; as an example, the top three valuations from the 2003 Global survey of brand[3] values were Coca-

---

3 For more information, see Top 100 global brand value listings produced by Interbrand at http://www.interbrand.com.

Cola at $70.45 billion, Microsoft as $65.17 billion, and IBM at $51.77 billion.

These would appear to be valuable corporate assets. If actions were taken that start to deplete such values, would this not be a governance concern? The top 100 global brand list equates to almost $1 trillion in 2003 — certainly a key part of accountability for protection of corporate value. What is also of interest is that the brand values of the top 10 organizations globally remained fairly stable over the 2001 to 2003 period, while the best 10 increased their values by almost $13 billion and the bottom ten lost over $25 billion in value in the same period.

Brand value is a key component of sustainability and should be included as a component of economic assessment for governance purposes. While this may not be a "year by year" item that warrants specific controls and actions, it is key to assessing the leadership of a CEO and the way in which an organization's values and behaviour are being translated into reality.

Later in the book we deal with customer relationship value as well as people aspects of intellectual capital. "Brand" is an underlying component that drives the customer component and, in terms of calculations of brand value, is intrinsically derived from actual performance numbers by Interbrand.

From a governance perspective, brand value is also an indicator over time of increased or decreased sustainability. As an example, we can take the case of Levi Strauss, a well-known and important brand name. According to Interbrand, Levi Strauss brand value performed as follows over the 2001 to 2003 time period.

Year	Value in $B	Cumulative Change
2001	3.75	
2002	3.45	-8.0%
2003	3.30	-12.0%

Compared to some other organizations, this is not a bad performance, but the question that should be asked is "why is the brand value declining?" In effect, $450 million has been depleted from the economic value of the organization. Is this a predictor of future decline in earnings or other tangible performance? Is it because current activity is depleting the perception of brand value in the market place? If so, then what are these actions and what changes should be made? Is it because the competitors are closing the competitive gap so that there is less product differentiation than before and, if not checked, will this continue to erode margins and market share? These are questions that Boards should be asking to assure themselves that management is creating sustainability of the brand value.

The prime linkage to behaviour and values here is that the values must also have linkage to sustainability. Being "close to the customer" or "customer driven" can be defined as values. This should result in an organization knowing where the market place is going and taking action that sustains the brand and reflects changing tastes. Could it be that Levi Strauss sees declining brand value because they lost sight of who their key customers were and/or that the market place changed and they failed to comprehend what the impact of these changes would be?[4] A powerful part of an organization's history and intangible investment over years and years of development is having values that are drivers of building a reputation and, through this, a brand. Slow to build but quick to lose, brand reputation is a key asset.

Organizations that pay excessive attention purely to financial performance reporting without complementary economic sustainability, can make decisions that quickly start to deplete brand value as well as contradict stated organizational values. In fact, these actions can often be traced back to reactive response to business performance problems. Improvement of the numbers has proven to be a short-term solution, yet in reacting this way, *billions of dollars of value are removed from the "intellectual capital bank" through lower brand value, decreased morale, employee and client turnover and many other outcomes.* These take years to re-build and, in some cases, cannot be re-built and lead to the demise of the organization. Effective managers and Boards need to ensure that, as part of establishing values and deploying them throughout the organization, they are included as policy, incorporated into planning, developed through effective leadership and reported on, to both management and the Board. Gertz and Baptista aptly identify this issue and the response required in the book[5] that they wrote at the height of the "downsizing" era. They identified the following aspects of effective governance (as should concern both management and the Board):

- customer franchise management;
- new product and service development;
- channel management; and
- foundations for growth that include an effective value proposition, economies in the overall supply chain, and flawless execution.

These four points have clear connections through both the creation of driving values and the related store of intellectual capital in areas such as relationships with employees, suppliers, and clients, and effective internal

---

4   For further reading on brand movement and, in particular, the chapter on Levi Strauss, see D. Dearlove & S. Crainer, *The Ultimate Book of Business Brands* (Capstone, 1999).

5   D.L. Gertz & J. Baptista, *Grow To Be Great: Breaking the Downsizing Cycle* (Simon & Schuster, 1995).

process management, none of which currently appear as part of corporate reporting and accountability at most Board levels.

4. CONVERTING VALUES TO PRACTICE

In order to convert theory to practice in the area of organizational values, managers and Boards need to ensure that the framework for accountability includes questions such as those set out in the following checklist, and that these are then traced back in terms of outcomes through effective organizational reporting metrics. In this way, setting governance policy for values and then deploying them is no different from setting any other type of policy and supporting it with an aligned deployment infrastructure.

#	Question	Yes	No	If No — action required?
1	Has a clear set of values been identified?			
2	Have the values been linked to organizational planning?			
3	Are values incorporated into management development, employee orientation, and assessment?			
4	Are the values incorporated in HR strategies — how?			
5	Are the values incorporated in client relationship strategies — how?			
6	Are the values incorporated into business process development and management — how?			
7	Has the expression of values been quantified or qualified in order to create metrics?			
8	Are there reporting metrics for management that demonstrate application of values?			
9	Is the Board tracking the consistent application through reporting metrics?			
10	Are values checked out on a regular basis against key stakeholder perceptions of the organization?			

Values "enable" organizational sustainability:

> Like money in the vault, values are the company's treasure. Values reflect what the leader holds worthy, what the organization assigns worth. They are ideals, principles, and philosophy at the centre of the enterprise. They are protected and revered. They reveal the company heart and soul. They energize the covenant.[6]

In the book from which this quote is taken, the author researches and develops key success criteria for service organizations (which make up over 65 per cent on average of most post-industrial economies — *i.e.*, this is the majority of enterprises that are being governed) to identify factors that must be focused on in order to increase the probability of success. In a similar (and earlier) study on managing service companies,[7] published in a book by the Economist Intelligence Unit, the same linkage was determined as a key success factor in the creation of culture; culture then being defined as a core component of surviving organizational change.

5. VALUES AS THE COMMON ENABLER

Before we move ahead, we can recap the discussion on organizational values. First, they clearly lie at the heart of organizational behaviour, through which the individuals within the organization interact with others and between themselves. Second, reputations, including the value of intangible assets such as brands, are driving the behaviour of third parties in relating to the organization and making decisions to do business with it.

Third, in order to operationalize values, there must be a clear linkage between intent (values as described) and execution (values as deployed). Fourth, if values are not operationalized, they mean little and, if not implemented, can (and have based on some of the quoted research) reduce intangible worth of the organization that may, over time, be converted in loss of tangible performance (lost sales, lost clients). Finally, if values are a key enabler, and the aspects of performance that are enabled can be directly linked to the overall worth of the organization, then systems for effective governance must incorporate a structured and traceable ability to convert intent to execution and to measure the outcome of such activity. Without this, accountability cannot be achieved. The model discussed earlier identified values as a core component of our upper circle of governance. In order to convert it into the lower circle, there must be linkage.

6   L.L. Berry, *Discovering the Soul of Service:The Nine Drivers of Sustainable Business Success* (Free Press/Simon and Schuster, 1999).
7   K. Irons, *Managing Service Companies* (Economist Intelligence Unit, 1994).

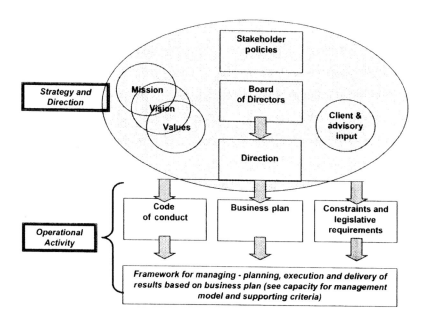

For this to happen, there needs to be some level of conversion between stated values and how these are deployed through operational activity. Statements such as being "customer focused" need to be supported by operational activity as well as by performance measurement that ensures a) customers see this commitment in the way that the organization deals with them and b) that there are specific activities in place that support this commitment such as running focus groups, involving clients in design and development activity and other initiatives. Values mean nothing unless they become demonstrated through the operation of the organization. Directors today receive very little feedback to assure them that the values that underpin organizational behaviour are, in fact, deployed, functional, and delivering results.

The checklist identifies some key opportunities to operationalize values. In addition, a basic tool used in effective organizations is the creation and use for training at all levels of a "code of conduct". Through such a checklist, real life situations dealing with all of the intangible components of organizational behaviour can be converted into examples or vignettes that reinforce within the specific organization (area, division, department, situation) aspects of how values are demonstrated in real life.

Checklist

Example of Values and Principles of Effectiveness Governance

Item	Assessment	Result			Action plan anticipated
		Yes	No	NI	
1	Has the Board established a stated set of behaviour principles for the organization?				
2	Has the Board identified the intangible value of organizational values and where this affects competitive advantage and intangible value?				
3	Have these principles been documented and converted to a code of conduct or equivalent?				
4	Have methods been established to train every participant in how these principles affect their work?				
5	Does the Board have feedback metrics to assess compliance with stated values?				
6	Has a risk assessment been completed that identifies potential areas of lapse in values and have these been addressed?				
7	Has a conversion been done between "intent" and "executions" so that application in all areas of management are identified?				
8	Have values been built into key business processes (design, delivery, service, *etc.*)?				
9	Have values been incorporated into the leadership training for all managers and supervisors?				
10	Have values been incorporated into organizational marketing and sales activity?				
11	Have values been incorporated into supplier/vendor relationships?				

Item	Assessment	Result			Action plan anticipated
		Yes	No	NI	
12	Does management have a process for reviewing managers and supervisors value of "performance" as part of the review process?				.
13	Do performance measurement metrics incorporate values issues?				
14	Have values been built into areas such as conflict resolution and complaints management approaches?				

List of Typical "Capacity" and "Performance" Metrics for Values and Principles

Capacity/Balance Sheet Metrics	Performance/Earnings Metrics
• Annual survey — recognition index/percentage of clients linking values to demonstrated relationships • Annual survey — recognition index/percentage of employees linking values to demonstrated relationships • Annual survey — recognition index/percentage of suppliers linking values to demonstrated relationships • Annual survey — recognition index/percentage of community linking values to demonstrated relationships • Annual survey — recognition index/percentage of investors/financiers linking values to demonstrated relationships • percentage of employees trained/tested in corporate values	• number of problems/complaints linked to deploying values and principles • number of process improvements (and other areas) linked to values deployment • number of positive press clippings/mentions • number of negative press clippings/mentions • client losses (percentage or number of) due to relationship problems • number of grievances related to problems with values deployments • number of unplanned terminations based on behavioural problems

8

ECONOMIC VALUE OF CLIENTS AND RELATED STAKEHOLDERS

While the foundation of an organization's values and ethics impacts its reputation and its ability to behave effectively, this, as well as its capacity to meet its commitments to clients, and the relationships that have been created through doing this, creates an economic value in its customer or client base. In the private sector this is an important intangible asset that must be nurtured and maintained as it has required resources to create and, while not shown as an asset, would in fact be treated as one if the organization were to be acquired. Likewise in the public sector, relationships with key client groups can have a significant impact in ascertaining policy direction but also in ensuring that actions taken minimize negative impacts that can generate undesired political repercussions. This chapter deals with the identification, assessment, and measurement of this corporate asset.

1. CLIENT RELATIONSHIPS AS A KEY COMPONENT

Having a client focus has been identified as one of the key elements of an effective management model; because clients represent an intangible economic asset that is crystallized into a value. When an organization is sold, it needs to be considered as an element of future governance frameworks, as constituting a key element of sustainability. The model shown below summarizes the framework that has been discussed earlier.

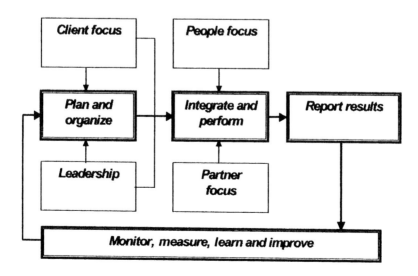

Planning and organizing have been discussed in depth as the critical transition phase between the Board and the CEO through to the management team. The tools and resources that management use to execute the intended strategy are incorporated in all of the remaining aspects of the framework. Thus as we go forward we can a) identify how each is an intangible asset, and b) whether either contributes to the execution of strategy, has an intangible economic value that Boards and management need to be accountable for, or provides part of a feedback infrastructure through which the governance performance reporting is achieved.

In this aspect of an organization's activity — whether public or private sector — clients are those to whom products or services are provided. In the previous chapter, we discussed values, reputation, brands, and behaviour; all of these impact each other because they deal with relationships. In the private sector (in most situations) the client is making a discretionary choice when they deal with the organization (as few suppliers have absolute monopolies). Their choice may be determined by the supplier organization, the brand, the location, or other factors. Lest free market capitalists be offended, price will also enter the decision making process. However, the way in which an individual or another organization makes a "buying choice" is important as it relates to competitive advantage, and relationships between buyer and seller have a value that either adds to or detracts from such competitive advantage.

Organizations spend considerable resources in building these intangible assets, however, in accounting terms they are considered as "expensed" items and (because it is very hard to determine future value) they are not considered to be a financial asset and are not allowed as an item on the balance sheet. If Boards consider all expenses to be "sunk money" — *i.e.*, anything spent in the current fiscal year that accountants do not allow to be treated as having a future value and can therefore be capitalized onto the balance sheet, then all is well. However, if Boards and management, in their deliberations, decide that certain expenses made today are made to generate future earnings (even if the accountants will not recognize them), nevertheless they have made an implicit decision to create something with future value albeit not reflected in the accounts. This is the heart of the issue of client relationships — being an important intangible asset that needs to be considered as part of an effective governance framework. After all, continued success (sustainability) comes from continuation of relationships with clients.

2. PRIVATE SECTOR RELATIONSHIPS

Client relationships in the private sector can have a multitude of characteristics. While we generally speak of "the client" as being the asset there are many relationships that are created through the expenditures of ongoing resources that contribute to value in this category. These may include the following:

Category	Characteristics
Reputation	This intangible asset is created over a long period of time and creates an overall character of the organization; ethical investors often choose organizations based on their reputation for behaving in a certain way. This is driven by the ability to have, implement, and sustain the "values" that have been discussed.
	It also has value because existing and prospective clients do business with organizations that have a reputation of acting in a consistent way. As an example, advertising a warranty and then not delivering on solutions to client's complaints quickly creates a bad reputation. (It's not what you say it's what you do).
Brand	This intangible, often closely linked and supported by reputation, is important as it has two key benefits. First, it drives buying decisions and therefore contributes to customer retention and attraction. Second, it should contribute towards savings in certain marketing cost areas. (A brand name that is being sustained outweighs the benefits of ongoing marketing programs to generate new buyers).
	An example of brand value is to compare the amount of money the "Big 3" automakers have had to spend to "recreate" the value of their brand in the market after years of competing with imports that established their brand by delivering on quality and value.

Category	Characteristics
Agents	In some organizations, a series of agents is created through which products are moved to the market. Because many buyers do business through established relationships, having these agents in place has an intangible value (it would be costly to recreate or replace such a series of relationships in terms of developing market, product knowledge, and new client relationships).
Affiliates/Franchisees	Many organizations "go to market" through intermediaries such as franchisees or affiliates. These usually take time to develop and are the "front line" relationship with the client. An effective and committed network of such organizations or individuals has an intangible value and again would be costly to re-develop or recreate. There is an added issue here that any organization that has such a "take to market" framework needs to maintain a high level positive relationship with its partners in these situations, as they are in fact "the clients". Many organizations have depleted their intangible asset bank by allowing poor relationships to develop with franchisees.
Distribution channels	Although this could be considered part of intangible process capability, distributors do become part of the "take to market" channel in the same way that agents and franchisees do. However, in many cases significant underlying client capital exists between the distributor and the ultimate client as well as value in areas such as product knowledge and application expertise between product distributors and their end customers. To recreate such networks

Category	Characteristics
.	would again cost a significant sum of money — so having one in place again has a value.
Locations	In many cases, access to locations through which products or services are sold can have a significant value. While this is often considered as part of a retailer's intangibles (in terms of potential market availability, *etc.*) location also plays a key role in other areas. For example, food vending locations close to sports stadiums; parts selling locations close to major industrial consumers; office equipment and supplies locations close to major conference centres; hotel locations close to vacation locations — especially being "first in" and the value associated with the operating losses incurred as market development took place.
Geographic representation	This is a key intangible and one that many North American organizations fail to grasp. While establishing and staying in certain North American communities can create an intangible asset in terms of loyalty from the client base, this issue becomes critically important when entering export markets. Nowhere is this more important than in Asia and certain other Eastern European countries where business is conducted much more on a relationship basis. Taking time to develop such a relationship is, in fact, investing in an intangible asset. Walking away and hoping to "come back" when the market improves will often end up in a constant cycle of failed expectations in terms of market share and penetration.

There are clearly a number of areas where an organization goes about its day-by day business and, through effective management driven by underlying beliefs and capabilities, develops client-based relationships. While these are typically not covered in the accounting area, they should be areas for accountability. The challenge is to establish a way of monitoring the "worth" of such relationships. At the high level it has been shown that there are positive correlations between brand value and share prices.[1] However, using such a measure alone will have risks. First, it is a volatile indicator that can be impacted in the short to medium term by other variables, some of which are not rational bases for establishing value (*e.g.*, overall stock market sentiment at any given point in time.) Second, this is a lagging indicator in the same way as reported revenues are an indicator of customer relationships. Those accountable for effective governance need more rapid representations of such relationships so that corrective action can be taken at the beginning of a shift to negative territory rather than waiting until the customers have already defected.

3. PUBLIC SECTOR CLIENT RELATIONSHIPS

The public sector has a unique situation; purchasing decisions may not be either by choice or discretionary in terms of the provider. Governments, in the main, provide monopoly services. However, no politician would argue the fact that the results of service delivery and taxpayer satisfaction have a specific impact on one of their key performance criteria which is the ability to get re-elected. In addition, poor client relationships cost extra money in terms of responses and so drive costs higher and increase the needs for appropriated funding.

However, client relationships and satisfaction should not be limited to the political aspect although this is important. Public sector managers also need to be aware, as part of the governance aspects of responsible steward-ship,[2] that delivery of services to a taxpayer can be more cost effective if positive relationships are maintained. Although these cannot at the current time really be classified as intangible assets *per se*, maintaining positive relationships will have significant benefits from both a political and cost of delivery perspective.

One example that could be pointed to, that has both taxpayers as well as bureaucrats scratching their heads (the traditionalists anyway), is the Canada Revenue Agency initiative of "fairness". Many taxpayers would question whether CRA can be client-focused, however, the organization has developed a set of values of which fairness is one, and is trying to embed

---

1 B. Lev & J. Hand, eds., *Intangible Assets: Values, Measures, and Risks* (Oxford University Press, 2003). See Chapter 6 "Brand Values and Capital Market Valuation".

2 For more information on developing aspects of responsible stewardship in the public sector, see Modern Comptrollership agenda *e.g.*, http://www.tbs-sct.gc.ca (for Treasury Board/Canadian federal government).

this value in both the human behaviour of its staff as well as its processes. Are they doing this because they like taxpayers? Well, maybe yes, but the more probable reason is that a value of fairness may well be a way to head off a potentially costly escalation of tax issues to both the appeal process within CRA and then, possibly, the courts. Fairness in this case is all about saving money — *totally consistent with responsible stewardship*. The question then becomes whether those responsible for directing and managing CRA (those accountable for its governance) have the ability to identify whether fairness as a value is being deployed or whether such deployment is improving or declining, and finally whether such deployment is creating the anticipated outcome. Not knowing the answers to these questions is an abrogation of governance accountability. This is why in creating the current Canadian federal government's accountability framework,[3] a structure for values underpins the intent.

Governance and strategic direction	Public Service Values			Results And Performance
	Policy and Programs	People	Client-focused services	
	Risk Management	Stewardship	Accountability	
	Learning, Innovation and Change Management			

One of the key aspects of providing products and services is for the organization to be able to "make it easy for the client to do business with us". In the case of the public sector, client satisfaction with the use of new tools in "doing business" is critical. As an example, counter delivery of taxpayer services on an assisted basis is an expensive way to operate "one-on-one". As a result, governments have taken a number of steps to reduce their costs by providing effective delivery methods:

• provincial and federal government economic development areas team up to make business registration a "one-stop shopping experience" by co-locating and sharing facilities;

---

3 Available at Treasury Board website (as of September 2004) at http://www.tbs-sct.gc.ca/maf-crg/mafb-crgb_e.asp

- provincial governments put kiosks in place where simple tasks such as renewing car ownerships or driving licences can be done "on line" by the consumer.

In both cases, the dual goals will be enhanced taxpayer satisfaction as well as lower costs. However, again from a responsible stewardship perspective, failure to deliver effective service at such locations will then result in complaints that have to be dealt with through other processes such as customer service "hot lines" or face-to-face interventions at a regional location (*i.e.*, one that is inconvenient for the taxpayer). This increases the cost of doing business in other areas as well as creating taxpayer dissatisfaction with the current political party.

This is also a key issue in the efforts to implement ASD (Alternate Service Delivery) in the public sector. In many cases, strategies include allowing the private sector to deliver public sector services in order to try and reduce costs. This was discussed earlier in the book as such changes create significant potential impacts to governance frameworks. Not least of these is the ability to again maintain effective client relationships between all the parties involved. While internally, effective governance by management will require implementation of tools such as service level agreements with measurable performance criteria, this should be supplemented by those setting policy (*i.e.*, the "intent" area of governance) having the ability to monitor whether the client relationships are improving or declining. Having such information is critical to the policy setting organization's ability to modify or change both policy and "directed" practice to ensure that the goals of lower costs delivery are being achieved without degradation to the relationships.

4. THREATS — NOT KNOWING WHAT YOU DON'T KNOW

Current reporting frameworks that underpin governance accountability represent organizational value and performance through principally accounting results. Typically, these results drive those responsible for action to initiate changes but, as has been quoted in the past, doing this is like "driving forward using the rear view mirror to determine your direction".

Positive client relationships should have a tangible benefit for any organization; declining or poor relationships will probably pose a threat. This will end up being manifested in several ways:

- loss of clients and declining revenues;

- greater turnover of clients (churn) resulting in higher sales, marketing, and promotional costs;
- loss of margins as markets no longer see a premium to the brand value;

- loss of investors/higher investment costs of reputations appear to increase investors' risk;
- shift from focusing scarce resources from building for the future to taking reactive responses to correct current problems ("fire fighting");
- political implications;
- higher cost base (for both increased client replacement identified above as well as increased customer service, support, and administrative costs).

All financial indicators will indicate these problems after they have occurred or started to occur. By the time corrective action can be taken, the decay is underway. Numerous examples can be provided of organizations that have failed to realize these problems were occurring and then had significant financial impacts afterwards by trying to correct them. Brand names such as Xerox, IBM, Kodak, and General Motors have all experienced such problems when their reporting systems failed to provide early warning of actions required to respond to a changing mood in the market place.

Management's response in these situations can be catastrophic; in the absence of good information about the trade off between fiscal performance, based on financial reporting and other key metrics such as client, employee, and process dimensions, managers will react by slashing costs. The cycle of declining customer satisfaction and employee morale, declining sales, and the continuing need to further reduce costs will have started. Failure to arrest such a process might well result in being profitable until the last client leaves.

5. ACCOUNTABILITY FOR CLIENT RELATIONSHIPS

Client relationships have value in both public and private sectors; the question then is how do shareholders, Board, directors, and managers become aware of the value of this intangible asset as well as monitor its increase or decrease as part of the governance accountability?

There are a number of ways that this can be addressed to add to the effectiveness of governance. Whatever approach is used, the separation of the valuing the "worth" of the relationships and determination approaches for increase or decrease in worth are both addressed. This reflects the earlier discussion that intangibles have both "balance sheet" and "earnings statement" implications. Approaches could include:

- values determined at a point in time by the market place as a part of "goodwill" in a purchase sales agreement and the conversion of such value into a metric that can be replicated at future dates to assess impairment;

- replacement cost assessments" based on the investment cost required to bring the intangible asset to fruition, coupled with a process to assess future impairment;
- "make versus buy" valuations (*e.g.*, what cost would be incurred through using one's own distribution channel versus going through a third party and reducing margins?);
- "net present value" (NPV) calculations of current benefits enjoyed by the existence of the intangible relationship;
- individual non-financial measures driven by areas such as client satisfaction ratings, and including other criteria such as turnover rates, repurchase intentions, market share, and others;
- integrated indicators such as the Skandia Customer Focus metrics.[4]

Organizations can develop a combination of both indicators and financial measures that deal with the status and trends within this area of intellectual capital. However, from a high level governance perspective, there need to be a few well defined and focused metrics.

6. CLIENT SURVEYS — AN INCOMPLETE TOOL

Many organizations will respond that they track client satisfaction through surveys. While this is the type of "leading indicator" that is needed, it must be used in a way that provides meaningful information and links with actions that an organization needs to take. Ensuring that an organization is nurturing its client base could be demonstrated through maintaining high scores on client surveys. However, to be effective they must meet the following criteria:

- there must be some level of consistency and continuity to the surveys (annual, bi-annual, or otherwise in today's market place do not provide adequate feedback);
- they must ask specific questions relative to the maintenance of the competitive advantage (as an example, organizations with an acknowledged reputation or "brand" must understand the key objective and subjective criteria that determine loyalty to the brand and ask questions that provide rankings on current performance of these aspects);
- they must ask questions that are client-based (external) rather than provider-based (internal); too many organizations kid themselves into thinking they have positive responses, but this only happens because they fail to ask the questions that would demonstrate a problem);
- questions asked must be capable of linkage to the organization's performance *i.e.*, what it does that is increasing or decreasing the observed

---

4 L. Edvinsson & M. Malone, *Intellectual Capital*, Chapter 6 "Real Worth: The Customer Focus" (HarperCollins Publishers, 1997).

outcome from the survey (otherwise how could a response be initiated?);
- responses should be, where possible, capable of being compared against benchmarks of either best practices or industry sectors.

The most important linkage is to connect wherever possible brand performance and client satisfaction with financial outcome. An example of how this could be achieved is outlined in the following hypothetical case. Effective client surveys can be an indicator of the level of intangible capital and of whether it is declining or increasing.

Example:

Garments Inc. has historically established its position as a brand leader. As a result, the company determined that consumers were willing to pay, and in fact were paying a premium for their products that amounted to approximately $10/garment. Based on this value and the volumes that the company was selling, this amounted to an annual margin premium of $100 million. The company had identified that the key drivers to brand preference were as follows:

- style among 21 to 26 year-olds in market place;
- variety of finishes and colours compared to competition;
- perception of wearability versus competitors;
- value for money of above versus competitors.

The company only carried out surveys every two years and focused on general aspects of client satisfaction. The Directors became increasingly concerned about financial performance. Margins were eroding due to frequently required discount programs, and volumes were deteriorating. Steps were taken to correct the financial performance through staff reductions including the marketing area and quality management. By the time it was realized that: the current buyers were no longer predominantly the 21 to 26 year-old age group; for the majority of current clients finish and colour was not a key issue; the perception was now that the competitors had improved their product to the degree there was little wearability advantage perceived; and the buying public no longer felt there was a value for money advantage, the company had already seen its brand premium deteriorate. In addition, expertise that could have responded to the shifting market place (marketing) had been lost as part of the actions required to cut costs in line with revenue declines. Had the Directors of the company aligned financial performance (brand premium) with customer capital, and been able to monitor client satisfaction with the brand drivers, then maybe earlier responses could have been taken to avoid the later significant losses.

7. CONNECTING VALUATION TO RELATIONSHIP

At any point in time an organization's external relationships have a value. This value can be computed by assessing the brand premium being generated, as in the last example, or through the impact that the existing base has on other cost areas in terms of lower selling costs.

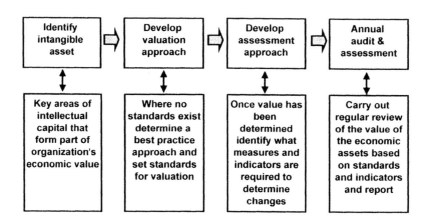

Determining the economic value of existing customer relationships will not be an exact science; what *is* important is to establish a set of "rules" that can be used to determine approximate values and then to support these with a series of indicators that complement the rules to determine whether there has been a probable increase or decrease in the value to the organization.

There will be no right or wrong approach at this stage. One of the challenges of moving to a framework for governance of a 21st century organization, whose major value is knowledge and other intangibles, will be that the approach will need time to evolve. Much work has already been done in the 1990s to try and value and measure knowledge; the challenge is that the way in which this needs to be done at the current time will probably be unique to every organization. There is no problem with this, as codification of best practice will come at a later date when a great deal more learning has been added through trial and error. As an example, we can use the following case study.

Example:

Big Feet Inc. is a footwear company that sells through retailers. Over the year, the organization has developed a loyal following of clients who, because of reputation and brand name, tend to repurchase the product. However, the company, through its research, knows that "intent to repurchase" decisions tend to relate to product satisfaction. Using a base case, the company determined the following facts:

- current satisfaction levels are poor (15%), fair (55%), good (25%), and excellent (5%);
- repurchase intentions reflect the following: poor (0%), fair (25%), good (65%) and excellent (90%);
- when clients re-buy, 10% will buy in year 1, 60% in year 2, and 30% in year 3;
- the company sells 20 million pairs of shoes a year and the margin per pair is $10.

Using the above information, the company knows that there is an inherent value of its existing customer base. Using the figures of satisfaction and re-purchase intent, the company can assess a value to the customer base. This equates to $69 million assuming that the value is only attributable to one re-purchase decision. This value can then be discounted to arrive at the net present value of the customer base. Now the company can measure customer satisfaction and re-purchase decisions and assess on a continuous basis whether the relationship "value" attributed has increased or decreased. (As an example, if the level of satisfaction was raised to 0% at poor, 15% at fair, 55% good and 30% excellent, and repurchase intent remained the same, the inherent value of the client base in future sales would have increased from $69 million to $133 million. (Customer satisfaction pays and can be measured!)

From this we can see that a) a value can be attributed to the existing relationship and, that b) indicators can be put in place that allow for a re-assessment of the implicit economic value of the relationship.

8. SUMMARY

Values drive relationships through which an organization's reputation is developed and maintained. The people within the organization can impact this reputation and, as such, can increase or decrease the organization's economic value particularly as it relates to client relationships. While the calculation of the economic value is not an absolute number, it can create indicators through which a Board (as well as management) can determine whether the long-term behaviour through the application — or lack thereof — of organizational values is increasing or decreasing organizational worth.

As Boards struggle to ensure the long-term viability and sustainability of their enterprise, information pertaining to client reputations as well as overall reputations as indicated by surveys and other feedback tools becomes an important aspect of determining whether the actions of management, to whom the Board has delegated day-to-day operations of the organization, are being conducted not only to produce the financial returns expected but to enhance the overall sustainability of the enterprise.

Checklist
Example of Client Effectiveness Governance

Item	Assessment	Result			
		Yes	No	NI	Action plan anticipated
1	Has the Board established policy criteria for client relationships?				
2	Is this policy linked to the values and other aspects of the enterprise?				
3	Has an economic value of client relationships been determined?				
4	Are there metrics in place to determine the economic value of client relationships?				
5	Are there performance criteria to assess any changes in client relationships based on economic value?				
6	Has a risk assessment been completed on aspects that might create negative impact in client economic value?				
7	Have "influencers" on client retention/value been identified and linked to key processes?				
8	Are process measures in place to monitor changes on client influencers?				

Item	Assessment	Result			
		Yes	No	NI	Action plan anticipated
9	Does the organization monitor changes in client's expectations on a regular basis and communicate to staff?				
10	Does the organization have best practice benchmarks against which client relationships are verified and used as a base for improvement?				

List of Typical "Capacity" and "Performance" Metrics for Client Relationships

Capacity/Balance Sheet Metrics	Performance/Earnings Metrics
• NPV of repurchase decisions based on loyalty rating; • satisfaction results; • customer turnover/retention percentage; • customer loyalty ratings; • customer satisfaction ratings • with company; • with products; • with people interaction; • with service/post service; • with channel of supply; • with access/help availability; • with problem resolution; • performance index on satisfaction relative to competitors/best practice benchmarks.	• number of new customers/turnover rates; • number of customer losses; • number of customer complaints (returns, recalls, replacements, etc.); • number of improvements in client-centered service/support capacity; • $ savings due to client suggestions; • number of product/service improvements based on client input.

9

ECONOMIC VALUE OF HUMAN CAPACITY

Organizations have identified their people as their "most important asset" for many years yet their behaviour towards these "assets", as well as the impacts that occur when this asset is poorly managed, has not reflected the stated importance. This is mainly because, from a traditional accounting perspective, labour costs are treated as "short-term expenses" and, in most cases, are considered the cost of generating today's revenues and services. Economic sustainability requires that a more enlightened and transparent view be taken of the human component of an organization's intangible value. It is humans, after all that create all other aspects of organizational value — but this asset can "walk out the door" at any time. Human capital needs to be identified and accounted for as part of the value that Boards and investors entrust to management. Short-term financial benefits can be generated and reported upon giving the impression that management is doing a good job — yet in fact actions being taken can be decimating the intangible value of the human capital base upon which future wealth is dependent.

1. HUMAN CAPACITY AND SHAREHOLDER EQUITY

For years, the phrase "people are our most important asset" has been used; yet, when many employees have the opportunity to respond to how they are treated by their organization, the reality is quite different. Much of the current concern over employee loyalty and changing attitudes can be traced back, through cause and effect analysis, to the way in which people have been treated as the organizations which employ them struggle to deal with a changing and more competitive economy. Humans are conditioned to respond to current events based on past experiences, therefore, if past experience shows that "you cannot trust the company because of broken promises", then that is the response that will be seen.

A major dilemma of Boards and managers is that of dealing with short-term survival and long-term sustainability, when faced with unplanned events. While one can suggest that poor planning on the part of the Board and management contributes to events arriving as a "surprise", there is no question that events outside the ability to plan or control do occur, and create repercussions for organizations. In addition, as corporate costs for employee expenses are typically one of the largest, financial problems result in across-the-board reductions in the work force "asset".

The importance of human capital as a core component of an organization's economic value cannot be understated. In advanced economies, it is becoming apparent that many jobs in the medium to lower skill levels (manufacturing, product assembly, call centres) are moving to countries where labour costs are lower. This can be equated to the loss of a need for manual labour in agriculture as automation significantly reduced the jobs available. If countries are not able to replace these jobs with "new economy" knowledge workers, then economic activity will slump, social unrest will increase, and standards of living will decline. (It is interesting to note that governments often reduce funding for education just at a time when education and the ability to develop and apply knowledge are becoming more critical to a country's economic survival).

The challenge is that, unlike unskilled and semi-skilled workers, knowledge workers have greater "thinking power" and mobility; this results in them having a higher expectation to be involved and participate in decision making and to "vote with their feet" if their needs are not satisfied by their current work situation. Demographic changes, including the aging population, make this a ticking time bomb. Not only will knowledge be lost from existing knowledge workers, but incoming workers will have less intent to surrender their independence to an employer and, in addition, there will be fewer of them to fill the position available. In effect, labour turns from a buyer's market to a seller's market. Organizations that fail to position themselves as being preferred environments within which to work and cling to the traditional models of human relations management will not be able to attract the human capital necessary to sustain their existence.

Thus from a governance perspective, Boards as well as management need to recognize, track, and monitor the value of human capital at a level equivalent to that afforded to financial capital.

In our governance model we can see that the "people focus" is a key element of the factors that management deploys in order to execute business plans; by definition, the competencies, skills, and experience of people can contribute not only to relationship building with clients but also to the quality, effectiveness, and continual improvement of the processes through which work is performed. Developing frameworks for integrated performance management, such as the "balanced scorecard",[1] include human aspects through the "learning and growth" dimension (this subject will be discussed in more depth as an "integrating" tool).

---

1   R.S. Kaplan & D.P. Norton, *The Balanced Scorecard: Translating Strategy Into Action* (Boston: Harvard Business School Press, 1997).

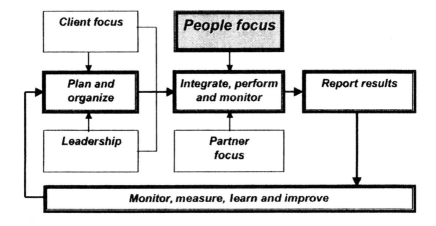

Shareholder equity, in terms of both "earned" equity (*i.e.*, the results of the organization over time in both earnings retained and paid out as dividends) as well as intangible equity (*i.e.*, the collection of other assets that have been brought together to generate the capacity to create these earnings and will contribute to the capacity to create earnings in the future), is what directors are accountable for ensuring is sustained and optimized. In addition, *managers have been given what may be called a contractual "sacred trust"* to use such assets in the most effective way possible to maximize the sustainability and earnings of the entity. Therefore, effective governance systems must include the ability to exercise accountability over such assets that have been placed in their care.

The situation is similar in the public sector although in this case there are no earnings *per se*; there are, in fact, tangible financial benefits that accrue from having a well-trained and skilled work force. Loss of such a work force or even some of its accumulated capacity to effectively perform the processes, activities, tasks, and projects that are assigned is a depletion of "value" within the organization; thus, public sector managers, wishing to exercise responsible stewardship of the resources under their care, must also ensure effective measures are in place through which the performance and status of such "assets" can be assessed on a regular basis.

Remember — great things can be achieved by an organization of average people who have learned to work effectively together. Human capital is probably the most critical of all intangible assets in that it is, essentially, the "enabler" of all others. Client relationships, innovation, teamwork, process development, product design and development, and applications of new technologies — *all* of these cannot take place unless the human "brain" acts to convert knowledge into applied action.

2. THE THREAT OF WHAT IS NOT KNOWN

Through the creation of the good governance model, we have established a process framework through which all of the elements required to ensure effective governance are integrated. In creating this approach, we have moved away from the traditional structural approach to management based on "planning, organizing, staffing, directing, and controlling" which, it could be argued, is the central core of the proposed model, following, to a framework that deals with the key relationship aspects of an organization. This is a necessary part of the evolution towards a knowledge-based society, one where controls are being decentralized as a result of globalization. This is, itself, in response to the required speed of action necessary to be competitive and agile (an issue which applies equally to government services supporting the economy within which its national enterprises operate).

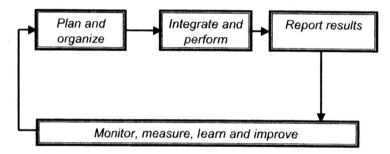

A major learning that, although identified and accepted and hard to deploy, is the reality that *values and ethics within the "people" of the organization are as critical for good governance as the processes with which they do the work and report the results.* This is the reason for the leadership, people, client, and partner areas of focus, in that they are *all* based on building not only solid processes but also the integration of the values through which the organization has committed to operate.

The type of problem that often exists, is that there is no linkage between what is communicated as being the vision and values of the organization and what the people within the organization see on a day-to-day basis. Good governance goes out of the window if there is no credibility or trust. This is probably *the* major issue in deployment of good governance models, especially as they apply to the effective ability of those in a governance role to be accountable for the intangible value of this resource. The type of tools that must be used to ensure that these relationship elements are balanced together with the traditional process based elements can include:

- ensuring that clear expectations and criteria are established for the recruitment of organization personnel prepared to commit to the organization's values;

130

- orientation programs for all employees that include values as well as clearly defining the organization's expectations of both its members and of its own conduct;[2]
- manager and supervisor training on how to deploy the values and to use listening and problem resolution skills to address gaps;
- surveys and feedback approaches where data is gathered from those involved in the relationships and acted upon in areas needing improvement;
- checklist for use whenever a new product, service, or process is introduced that asks questions about how the organization's values have been incorporated into the new approach;
- creation of the scorecard type reporting approach (integrated between both management and governing body) that measures actual relationship results;
- opportunities for those in the organization to raise issues and have them dealt with.

So, the inclusion of relationship aspects of governance becomes a critical issue for the long-term sustainability of the organization.

The problem is that those holding accountability often "don't know what they don't know". As a result, *assumptions are made* that whatever actions management is taking to "use" the human resources, these are in no way depleting the intangible worth of their accumulated value (assuming that what is being done is increasing the value and thus "putting money in the knowledge bank").

3. THE EMERGING ROLE OF HUMAN CAPITAL

Within an organization's intangible value, human capital — where much of the knowledge resides — is probably the most critical component. The challenge as we move to the 21st century, is that this element is growing rapidly as a driver of overall corporate value. Because of this, effective governance and sustainability of organizations' "knowledge capacity" becomes crucial.

Significant work has been done and articles written that deal with the need to retain key staff; in addition, it is a well-known fact that "knowledge workers"; especially in high technology industries, are critical to both sustainability and success. Articles in the *Economist* (as well as in *Fortune* and *Business Week*) have identified over the last ten years or more that mergers often fail to deliver the planned results and that these failures are relative to

---

2 Health Canada report on the linkage between wellness and work-related stress. See "The 2001 National Work-Life conflict study — Report One" by Dr. Linda Duxbury and Dr. Chris Haggard at www.hc-sc.gc.ca/pphb-dgspsp/publicat/work-travail/pdf/rprt_1_e.pdf

an increasing number of mergers and acquisitions between organizations whose wealth is composed of intellectual capital.

What is also important to recognize from an effective governance standpoint is that human capital is not just a key "element" of intangible worth but is the main force behind the creation of *all* other areas of intangible development.

- people drive and create innovation, through both development and application;
- people drive the building of relationships with customers and client;
- people drive the maintaining and growth of effective internal relationships;
- people drive the building and sustaining of key supplier relationships;
- people are a key repository of corporate knowledge that has not yet been codified;
- people create the intuitive connections between pockets of disconnected knowledge (although considerable efforts are underway to "systematize" this area);
- people provide both effective leadership as well as task management;
- people are the key force in creating an effective organizational learning capacity;
- people develop, design, and improve all business processes.

In cases where other intangibles are created, the driving force behind them all is the human dimension; without this, all others cease to occur. Thus, an organization that has created wealth in any one of these areas, needs to ensure that the ongoing capacity to maintain and develop this corporate asset is nurtured, protected, and enhanced.

4. ASPECTS OF MOTIVATION — PEOPLE AS PARTNERS VERSUS "RESOURCES"

A key shift in thinking is required, to move from seeing the cost of human capital as an *expense that needs to be minimized*, towards an *investment that needs to be optimized*. Traditional accounting for human capital worked effectively when such expense was either all incurred relative to current revenue, or where simple "high level" adjustments could be made to reflect the human cost of "work in process" in production (and also in the development stage of research and development). Both these are acceptable adjustments within existing accounting standards, that see current period financial expenses matched with current period revenues. In this scenario, human cost was just another part of production resources.

Two things have changed. First, in many organizations the old *"direct labour"* element of human cost has declined relative to the "indirect" portion; *i.e.*, the people doing the production work versus those doing activities that support this — accounting, purchasing, sales, marketing, *etc*. Traditional accounting, that smears overhead costs across production costs on some allocation basis such as direct labour hours or material costs, becomes increasingly inaccurate as the direct cost base declines and the indirect increases. Second, those costs are not treated as "overhead indirect" costs but considered SG&A (sales, general, and administrative) and have traditionally been treated as "period expense costs" assuming that they are all incurred in a particular financial reporting period and that all value coming from such expenses is in fact relative to that same reporting period. *These assumptions are increasingly inaccurate*, particularly for the purposes of effective governance:

- key production indirect costs often relate to ongoing future investment;
- sales and marketing costs are building future value;
- information technology costs are often being incurred for future benefit.

The historic assumptions upon which accounting principles were based can be considered less accurate than they were in the past to allow those accountable for governance to truly recognize the inherent value at the end of any particular fiscal period the human investment capital that exists in both building and sustaining future value.

Capability + motivation = results

ASSET	ENABLER	OUTCOME
Capability	**Motivation**	**Results**
• technical abilities	• turnover	• client satisfaction
• years of experience	• absenteeism	• new products
• industry knowledge	• survey results	• new service
• tenure in company	• pay levels	• growth
• level of learning	• benefit levels	• fast cycle time

What is the correlation for ROIC**?

**Return On *Intellectual* Capital

Second, as the nature of the work being done by the human element has changed, so must the attitude towards this "asset" change, by those responsible for governance both at Board and management levels. Human capital should no longer be seen as a "turn on/turn off" cost of production that can be increased or decreased at will; the impact of doing this is to create the exact results that have been seen of declining commitment and motivation. If human capital is a key element of future value, then this aspect of an organization's asset base should be treated more as a partner in future success than just an expense.

The impact of this is that measuring employee commitment and motivation becomes a key aspect of assessing increases or decreases in the intangible asset worth of an enterprise. Directors and Boards not aware of activity that is depleting this asset, are failing to exercise due diligence with the owners' economic capital.

Thus, the level of effective "partnering" with employees *plus* the assessment of the "stock" of human capital, are key measures for assessing the sustainability of the economic worth of the organization.

5. ENABLING HUMAN PERFORMANCE

Work environment is a key factor that either adds to or takes away from employee motivation. This is especially true as emerging knowledge workers look for a different level of "needs satisfaction" than in the past. Futurists have predicted that as technology builds alternative work capacity, human expectations will change. This is already being seen in aspects such as decisions not to take promotions, not to move to a new location, and to trade off more money for greater work flexibility and freedom. Failure to address these issues is creating increased mobility (less loyalty) and overall employee unrest.

What has to be recognized by those in governance capacities is that unlike the tangible assets of the organization, the intangibles are very portable. While an expensive piece of equipment cannot decide to get up and take its productive capacity elsewhere, a knowledge worker can and will if the environment does not fit their needs. Without responding to this, organizations will create a competitive disadvantage.

Organizations are trying to address the human resource sustainability issues, but few are achieving the results that are needed. "Continuing improvement" is a well-worn yet valid buzzword that is a key aspect of where human capital needs to be applied (organizations cannot improve without people creating and applying improved concepts, ideas, innovations, *etc.*). This is demonstrated in *First Break All the Rules*[3] by Buckingham and Coffman, who illustrate that key fundamentals of effective work environment issues must be addressed by any organization wishing to attain continual improvement commitment from its work force.

---

3 M. Buckingham & C. Coffman, *First Break All the Rules: What the World's Greatest Managers Do Differently* (New York: Simon & Schuster, 1999).

6. EMPLOYEE SURVEYS — USE AND ABUSE

Traditionally, employee surveys have been used as a key tool to assess the "state" of human capital. However, few organizations actually benchmark the results of surveys against the impact the results may have on their "store" of human capital. While surveys are one of a number of tools that can be used to determine the movement in the motivation of human capital and therefore indicate upcoming "depletion" or enhancement issues, they must be used in a way that adds value:

- there must be a short set of fundamental questions that are asked repeatedly in every survey to track trends;
- surveys must be conducted on a regular basis (*i.e.*, as a minimum annually);
- questions asked must be relative to, and determined by the "satisfiers" in terms of the motivational aspects of organizational behaviour (often the "tough" questions are not asked because of fear of the probable results);
- surveys must be capable of analysis by groupings that are impacted by differing stimulators (in particular by work areas, locations, supervisors, *etc.*);
- satisfiers must include the work, direction, supervision, involvement, work environment, tools, and equipment (including information systems), communications, recognition, perception of worth and other key personal issues that impact an individual's ability to become motivated. (Note that the best way to do this is to have employees contribute to the questions being raised.)

Additionally, surveys must result in a process of communication and feedback; through this the results can also be linked to the specific actions and issues that have created the actual or perceived level of satisfaction with the question being asked. This assists management and the Board to focus on the linkage between corporate direction and action and the effect that it is having on the store of human capital.

7. THE ROLE OF A LEARNING ORGANIZATION

Key to sustainability of the economic value of any organization is the ability of its employees to contribute ideas and innovation to move the organization forward. This may be through innovative product ideas, relationships that have been developed with key suppliers and clients, as well as coming up with ideas that contribute to more effective and efficient operations — leading to the ability of an organization to be cost effective. It has long been recognized, for example, that employees can make or break effective quality management systems. Yet quality is a key organizational strategy to reduce costs as well as to ensure client satisfaction through "capable" processes that are predictable and can deliver on promises such as shipment dates.

Many organizations have adopted the concept of a "learning organization" as being key to recognizing and integrating the human dimension to sustainable management — but many fail. In his book on learning organization, Andrew Forrest[4] starts with focusing on the accountability of directors to "walk the talk" in terms of creating an environment where "learning can flourish" (my words). Management and directors have a prime responsibility to create an environment where learning at the individual and group level can occur. This happens when employees feel part of an organization, are treated as an inclusive element of the organization's economic value, and are able to share in some way in its success.

Reporting on the effectiveness of a learning organization is a key component of future governance. If employees are not learning and innovating then the economic value of the organization must by definition be declining. Metrics that track aspects such as employee satisfaction, involvement in innovation and ideas, levels of competencies held by employees, and levels of learning taking place would all be valid examples of how this might be achieved.

8. MEASURING AND REPORTING THE HUMAN DIMENSION

To date, a great deal of work has been done in the area of intellectual capital as it relates to the human dimension that has focused on measures created to assess human capital. In particular, materials by Leif Edvinsson and Michael Malone and by Thomas Stewart, including extensive work on reporting systems by Skandia,[5] were developed in the late 1990s to assist the organization in managing its intangibles.

The challenge that exists is that having an asset and effectively using such an asset are two entirely different issues. Measurement of the economic value of human capital therefore, requires at least two separate dimensions.

Effective corporate governance comes from knowing both the worth of the asset (*i.e.*, traditional balance sheet expression of value) and the results of using the asset (the typical earnings statement view). Much of the work

---

4 A. Forrest, *Fifty Ways Towards a Learning Organization* (London: Industrial Society, 1999).

5 L. Edvinsson & M. Malone, *Intellectual Capital* (HarperCollins Publishers, 1997); T.A. Stewart, *Intellectual Capital: The New Wealth of Organizations* (Bantam Doubleday Dell, 1997). For more information, see readings for this chapter as well as http://www.skandia.com/en/index

on developing criteria for reporting human capital has focused on the "what we have" context. However, the greater challenge is answering the question "so what?"

HUMAN ASSETS *THE* *BALANCE SHEET*	HUMAN PERFORMANCE *THE EARNINGS* *STATEMENT*
ASSET	**OUTCOME**
Capability • technical abilities • years of experience • industry knowledge • tenure in company • level of learning	**Results** • client satisfaction • new products • new service • growth • fast cycle time

Unlike financial reporting where there are benchmarks of key performance criteria such as ROIC (Return on Invested Capital), there are few benchmarks on ROHC (Return on Human Capital) or ROIC (Return on Intellectual Capital). In addition, being able to clearly link the human assets available and the degree to which these actually drove other measurable performance criteria is fraught with difficulty.

(a) Human Capital

Boards need to know the status of the existing human capital base in the same way that they need to know the status of their financial capital (fixed assets and working capital). This requires a "balance sheet" approach to human capital that covers what the existing capital is. This can be defined in many ways and should be specific to the organization.

One important aspect of human capital assessment is to recognize that different values are probably ascribed to different types of employees. As an example, many organizations report overall turnover rates. Based on all employees this may be, say, 10 per cent per year; however, if the overall employee count is 1,000 and 100 of these are considered highly specialized and critical to the future developments and innovation of the organization, then a rate of 10 per cent a year may mask the reality that if 25 per cent of the losses were in this area alone then the key measure would be a 25 per cent turnover rate on critical resources.

- overall number of employees;
- employee data by category;
- average length of service within the organization;
- years of experience within the industry;
- "breadth index" identifying cross-training experience;
- demographic analysis (equivalent to "aging" of fixed capital?);
- succession summary of coverage in key areas;
- qualification index/criteria (internal and external);
- levels of development such as number completed orientation, trained in values system, team development, and other key criteria;
- self-awareness capacity (number completed self-assessment and feed-back

Therefore, reporting should mirror the various areas of human capital in terms of their relative levels of importance to the organization's sustainability.

(b) Enabling the Use of Human Capital

People perform best when they are interested in the work that they do, involved in decision making, clear on their expectations, and are accountable for work in an environment that provides them with a desire to contribute effectively. Boards need to have assurance that the human capital within the organization is in fact being *managed effectively* so that this key resource is not being depleted. In order to develop indicators that provide insight into the degree to which human capital is being optimized, the important factors need to be defined and tracked. Buckingham and Coffman[6] indicate that the most critical aspects of human contribution are being able to answer the following two questions at a 4/5 level on a scale of 1 to 5.

- Do I know what is expected of me at work?
- Do I have the materials and equipment I need to do my work right?

Indicators can be used for the motivation area in order to address the climate that exists for motivation. These can include:

- results on surveys (see notes related to effectiveness, though);
- levels of work related health/accident problems;
- overall statistics on use of HR advisory services (EAR/EAP);
- employees on health leave/work-related disability;
- turnover levels/results of exit interviews;
- absenteeism records;
- grievances filed/escalated/reinstatements; and

---

6 Above, note 3.

- re-investment/employee (education/training).

Combining the human capital in place (*i.e.*, the "balance sheet" measure) with a series of performance measures above, an organization can create an index for assessing increase or decrease in the intrinsic value of the human capital.

(c) Outcomes/Creating Value With Human Capital

The most challenging aspect of determining the value of human capital is to assess the actual performance outcomes that accrue to the organization as a result of a) having the human capital in place, and b) providing an environment that sustains and stimulates those individuals.

As a starting point, it may be well to reflect back on what aspects of an organization's overall intellectual capital are created through the enabling of human capital; in effect, feeding of the human capital should be the "top of the intellectual capital funnel" that, if managed effectively, will see measurable outcomes at the base of the funnel. What will these outcomes be? What is it that we expect a talented and high producing base of human capital to create? Past discussion indicates that the following are some key examples:

- sustaining and building reputation and branding;
- sustaining and building the customer capital;
- creating innovation in products and services;
- creating innovation in processes and application of improved methods of work execution (*e.g.*, the application of value-adding information technology);
- creating through communication and knowledge sharing a fast (agile) ability to analyze situations, resolve problems, and make decisions.

The challenge is to try and establish criteria where there is some degree of tangible link between the capacity of the human capital and the outcomes

---

- high scores on customer responses to survey questions related to employee knowledge, capacity, and support;
- analysis of customer loss data that reflects losses caused through employee issues;
- levels of complaints related to employee interactions;
- new product or service introductions;
- suggestions made and implemented with measurable performance improvements;
- speed of resolution of process or other problems;
- process problems and defect levels attributable to human issues (*e.g.*, training or performance issues);

- cost of waste generated through any type of process problems;
- percentage of new hires coming through internal references;
- high scoring on internal work relationships (*e.g.*, teamwork/support);
- existing interviews reveal low incidence of real HR issues;
- level of internal complaints/grievances filed.

related to these aspects of organizational capacity for performance. Some examples of indicators that can be used to assess these areas could include the items in the table above. These would be more akin to the "earnings statement" type of measures in that they look not at what "capacity" exists in human capital but what performance is being delivered by having that capacity in place.

One of the best measures of innovation is the example quoted of 3M who established a goal that "25% of revenues generated today come from products or services that did not exist 4 years ago." This, while possibly being a combination measure, nevertheless does provide insight into the human capacity to innovate as well as the effectiveness of the cycle time within the organization.

(d) Valuation of Human Capital

While it is difficult to develop pure financial measures for human capital, some work has been done in this area. In addition, there is some capability to actually capitalize on the financial statements of some areas of the results of human capital, in particular as this relates to research and development. In summary, general research and development (more the former) must be expensed as incurred in that it has no defined future benefit; however, once the work crystallizes around an anticipated outcome that can be defined, planned, and quantified in terms of expected future returns, then costs incurred between the beginning of what could be called "application development" and "production" can in fact be treated as an asset, the dollar value accumulated, and then amortized over the anticipated life of the product or service that it created. As in all cases of intangible assets, the value remaining at the end of each financial year has to be reassessed to ensure that the attributed value is still realistic based on the remaining life of the product or service.

Again, one of the challenges is that the "learning" that occurs and gets added to the "bank" of intellectual capital through this process still has a value. Failure in itself has a value — as we discussed in the segment related to a learning organization. Other potential approaches to establish a value for human capital could include the following:

- identifying the "cost of acquisition" of employees and then creating a notional capitalization of this value, that would be added to as re-investment in the employees, takes place through training and development. Then creating an "amortization reserve" against this amount based on a target turnover rate that is adjusted up or down annually depending upon higher or lower results.

- segregating payroll expenses by type of employee and then apportioning between "capital" (*i.e.*, in the intellectual capital asset account) those expenditures that relate to future work versus those processing today's transaction. Examples could be as follows:

Type of payroll expenses	Capital	Current
Marketing department	60%	40%
Sales department	80%	20%
Research and development	90%	10%
Accounting	0%	100%
Production control	5%	95%
Human Resources	70%	30%

Note that, typically, production workers would be treated as expenses and then traditional accounting (through GAAP Generally Accepted Accounting principles) would automatically adjust between the balance sheet and current expenses that portion of labour relative to unsold work in progress. What is important here is that at least an attempt is made to attribute a "capital" value to a traditionally intangible asset; the split can be decided, and can also reflect more than one year's salary. As an example, it may be determined that an effective marketing person in actual fact has an attributed capital value relative to what they create in the value of relationships and other outcomes, the equivalent of three years of salary as a going forward sum.

Two of the key issues that such indicators may start to address in terms of effective planning and Board oversight would be the relationship between creating short-term financial results and taking actions that deplete intellectual capital. Typically, it is hard to motivate sales staff to focus on new account development as this is an investment in the future "customer capital" but does not deliver current revenues (and probably does not deliver personal financial incentive to the sales person). Recognition for investment in the development of intangible assets with future benefit might highlight such issues. In addition, organizations often treat training as a "current expense" without consideration of the value that this contributes to the human capital investment bank. Again, identification of the increased value of human capital especially when this can be linked with measurable anticipated outcomes would assist in more strategic decision making.

Checklist
Example of Human Capital Effective Governance

Item	Assessment	Result			
		Yes	No	NI	Action plan anticipated
1	Is human capital considered a part of Board reporting?				
2	Does management monitor human capital?				
3	Is there linkage between Board policy towards human capital and accountability reporting?				
4	Have Board level metrics for human capital been developed?				
5	Are there metrics that identify human capacity (*e.g.*, qualifications, competencies)?				
6	Are there metrics that identify the outcomes from human capacity?				
7	Is the organization conducting and reporting regular satisfaction surveys?				
8	Do the employees believe that such survey results are acted upon?				
9	Is the participation rate in surveys tracked?				
10	Is manager/leadership performance tracked in a way that includes fostering and growing human capital?				
11	Are there metrics that track human capacity development relative to organizational strategic knowledge?				
12	Is effective team development and interpersonal relationship monitored?				
13	Is there alignment between management's HR metrics, Board metrics, and competitive advantage related to the human dimension?				
14	Is there trend data that indicates stability and/or growth in the retention of knowledge?				
15	Does the organization have metrics for knowledge transfer?				

List of Typical "Capacity" and "Performance" Metrics for Human Capital

Capacity/Balance Sheet Metrics	Performance/Earnings Metrics
• overall numbers of employees; • employee data by category; • average length of service within the organization; • years of experience within the industry; • "breadth index" identifying cross-training experience; • demographic analysis (equivalent to "aging" of fixed capital?); • succession summary of coverage in key areas; • qualification index/criteria (internal and external); • levels of development such as number of completed orientation, trained in values system, team development, and other key criteria; • self-awareness capacity (number of completed self-assessment and feedback); • number of employees completed ethics/values training.	• high scores on customer responses to survey questions related to employee knowledge, capacity, and support; • analysis of customer loss data that reflects losses caused through employee issues; • levels of complaints related to employee interactions; • new product or service introductions; • suggestions made and implemented with measurable performance improvements; • cost reductions implemented through work improvements initiated by employees; • speed of resolution of process or other problems; • process problems and defect levels attributable to human issues (*e.g.*, training or performance issues); • cost of waste generated through any type of process problems; • new hires percentage coming through internal references; • high scoring on internal work relationships (*e.g.*, teamwork/support); • existing interviews reveal low incidence of real HR issues; • level of internal complaints/grievances filed; • safety/lost time and other H&S measurements; • employee involvement (hours) in social/community contribution.

10

ECONOMIC VALUE OF THE CAPACITY TO EXECUTE EFFECTIVELY

In recent years, the issue of "execution" has become another area of organizational performance focus. This is not a new aspect of an organization's value. Many organizations invest substantial amounts in developing their capacity to execute. This is one of the factors of value that helps build relationships and generate brand reputation and client value. However, this capacity, unlike tangible assets, fails to appear anywhere on an organization's balance sheet — yet their past and future economic value depends to a great degree on their ability to not only sustain this capacity but to continue to use it as a competitive advantage. Effective governance requires that this capacity be considered, monitored, and measured as a key asset when determining the effectiveness of management's actions. This chapter identifies how current initiatives in this area can contribute towards creating greater transparency for this asset and also form a critical component of managing future financial performance through the effective optimization of resource consumption during work execution.

1. LINKING THESE ISSUES TO STAKEHOLDERS' EQUITY

A critical linkage for effective governance between the traditional route of financial reporting and the way ahead, is the recognition that effective management controls an organization's cost through effective *process management*. Every organization, whether profit or not-for-profit, consumes resources and the ability to reduce costs is a key success factor in maintaining competitive advantage and an organization's economic value. Shareholders clamour for organizations to reduce costs to improve profitability and put significant pressure on both Boards, CEOs, and management to make this happen; the results, traditionally, have been rounds of downsizing yet, in many cases, this fails to bring the desired result.

People continue to make up a significant portion of any organization's cost base so, as pressure mounts to reduce cost, this category of expense makes an obvious and easy target. Yet we need to remember the relationship between people and an organization's ability to sustain and grow economic value:

- people are needed to get work done;
- people have a significant impact on quality and through this process — cost;
- people are a key source of innovation and ideas;
- people build and maintain relationships — individually and collectively;
- people synthesize knowledge into application that adds value;
- people are key repositories of experience;
- people can learn — organizations depend on this for organizational growth.

In the later days of the industrial revolution, it was already becoming apparent that the old "direct labour" (that is, the human costs associated more often with unskilled work which allowed managers to easily substitute one supplier of labour for another) was already declining and being replaced by semi-skilled and skilled "indirect" workers.

An example would be the introduction of robotics into the automotive sector; this aimed at improving consistency and productivity and reducing labour costs through eliminating jobs. In this situation, several unskilled workers were often replaced by fewer skilled workers upon whom the effective application of the technology now rested. As this trend developed, some key factors emerged:

- mature cost management systems used to track direct costs, based on the Taylor approach to work breakdown, became applicable to fewer elements of the overall labour cost;
- increased indirect costs resulted in significant growth in "overheads" that by definition are bad and should be reduced, yet most organizations had ineffective cost analysis systems that link this resource to measured output for effective management;
- organizations sought (and continued to seek) reductions in labour cost by outsourcing and "off shoring" key activities, making logistics, supply chain, and process management even more critical; and
- the accounting profession failed to shift its focus from responsibility accounting (silo-based/command and control organizations) to process-based thinking.

All of these changes resulted in a significant shift of how work was performed and managed within organizations without any complementary changes in how Boards conducted insight into cost control or process effectiveness. Many Boards and management continued to drive "across the board" cost cutting that in many cases (even over 10 years ago), failed to deliver the long lasting improvements anticipated,[1] many articles in *Fortune* and *Business Week* carried headlines during this period such as:

---

1   Wyatt Company survey 1991-2 on 450 companies indicated that as a result of downsizing

- *"Wall Street Loves Layoffs"*
- *"Belt tightening the smart way"*
- *"Cost cutting — how to do it right"*
- *"Is this layoff necessary?*
- *"The pain of downsizing"*
- *"Getting beyond downsizing"*
- *"Managing the bottom line — what to do when there are no more costs to cut"*
- *"Anorexia — some companies cut too close to the bone?"*
- *"Weighing the costs and benefits of downsizing"*

Several articles of the period voiced concerns that this mania with cost reduction, which was aimed at improving competitive advantage through responding to lower prices as well as increasing earnings so as to attract more capital, was doing *long-term damage to organizations*. In fact, many voices were raised about the problems of the short-term thinking of the financial markets relative to their focus on quarterly results and a (possibly) non-sustainable level of corporate earnings. Some organizations either held on fiercely to their private status or took their organization private so that they could "get away" from this thinking.

The problem with all of this was, and remains that, as the world has changed, governance and accountability frameworks have not kept pace. Globally, one can point to a number of organizations that have, in fact, managed their cost cutting in a way that did not create other problems and issues. Examples would be S C Johnson and Wal-Mart — particularly Wal-Mart who appeared to *add* staff when the rest of the retail world was cutting staff — how could this be?

While many retailers addressed the shake-out in the industry through cutting costs at the front lines — where much of the labour cost was incurred — progressive organizations such as Wal-Mart looked at the business and decided that having people deal with customers was, in fact, a strategic imperative. Rather than cutting here they looked at their supplier relationships and "back office" processes and totally re-designed these to reduce costs. While customers were leaving other retailers (such as Eaton's and the Bay) in droves, Wal-Mart customers continued to be met with "greeters" and with staff to serve them. (As time has played out, it will be interesting to see whether potential treatment of employees as well as suppliers is sustainable in the longer term — assessing the impact through measures would be a key success factor!

The answer is that these organizations took a more holistic view of their business decisions including the inter-relationship between cost actions

---

only 60% of the organizations saw their costs actually go down and fewer than half improved profits.

impacting human resources and the spinoff side effects of such actions. Those who handled this aspect well enhanced shareholder equity; those who used traditional approaches very often negatively impacted or, in some cases, eliminated shareholder equity. How many businesses that existed twenty years ago no longer exist or have disappeared through mergers and acquisitions because their owners and managers failed to maintain their economic value because of the way that they addressed competitive problems?

If investors, boards, and managers have the wrong or, worse, misleading information, then they will be led to make wrong or misleading decisions about the future success and health of their organizations. There is plenty of blame to go around: professional advisors who continued to rely on traditional methods; legislators who continued to apply traditional governance approaches; managers who failed to heed the voice of people within the organization who saw much of this depletion of value taking place; and investors (this is "us" in many cases) who wanted ever increasing levels of non-sustainable returns.

In summary, cost management is a critical issue for those accountable for governance; the effectiveness with which management uses resources in terms of processes and activities within the organization will determine its ability to manage and continually reduce cost. Handled poorly, cost reduction will deplete the economic value of an organization and, because of this, should be a key consideration of any Board.

2. MANAGEMENT ACCOUNTABILITY — TURNING INTENT TO RESULTS

As discussed in the basic model of governance, Boards are responsible for setting policy and establishing "intent" in terms of what the organization under their stewardship is accountable for. We have discussed how this includes both performance criteria as well as behaviour — both what is done and how it is done. Writings about Board accountability typically focus heavily on the need to segregate the role of "directing" the enterprise versus "managing" it. Typically, there needs to be a clear line of delegated accountability through the CEO to the management team to manage the business affairs on a day-to-day basis for the benefits of the shareholders and other stakeholders. Legislation dealing with incorporation in most jurisdictions focuses on this *but* clearly defined the directors as retaining responsibility for "managing the business affairs" of the organization.

"Business" is not defined within the Act, but can be stated as the external relations between a corporation and those who deal with it as a business enterprise — its customers, suppliers, and employees — as well as relationships with government regulators and society as a whole.

"affairs" means the relationships among a corporation, its affiliates and the shareholders, directors and officers of such bodies corporate but does not include the business carried on by such bodies corporate;

. . .

102. (1) Subject to any unanimous shareholder agreement, the directors shall manage, or supervise the management of, the business and affairs of a corporation.[2]

. . .

When the Board delegates this authority, it must exercise due diligence so that management has the capacity to act. Typically, all of this accountability rests with financial measurement and adherence to standards. What does management have entrusted to it through which it delivers outcomes and results? The answer is a "system" that has been created, that has the capacity to deliver products and services to clients. The Board is responsible for setting the specifications for this system. These specifications focus on results in financial terms — however, digging below the surface it becomes apparent that there are many implied specifications that exist but are not clearly defined. Responsible Boards will identify several other key specifications. These will probably include:

- sustainability over the long term;
- good corporate reputation;
- satisfied customers and good relationships with suppliers;
- retention of key skills and knowledge as a competitive advantage;
- protection of the organization's innovation and know-how;
- "no surprises" in terms of compliance with applicable legislation.

These are all aspects that contribute to the accumulated economic value of an organization. It is, in fact, the value of the system that is in place that can deliver the required results. Thus, Boards need to ensure that, as management "executes" to deliver the planned results, the overall value and worth of the system is being maintained or increasing. Failure to achieve this will mean that management is delivering unsustainable results because key economic assets are being depleted.

A great deal of work has been undertaken to try and determine the components of this system through which management executes its delegated responsibility. We discussed earlier the various international management frameworks for excellence; in addition to this, the ISO 9004:2000 Guidelines for Continual Improvement (the "sister" publication to the Quality Management System standard ISO 9001:2000) sheds additional light. In that publication, the authors identify eight principles of an effective management system:

---

2   The above extract from the *Canada Business Corporations Act*, R.S.C. 1985, c. C-44, ss. 2, 102, is typical of this requirement.

The 8 Underlying Principles upon which ISO 9001:2000 is Founded	
• Customer Focus	• System approach to management
• Leadership	• Continual improvement
• Involvement of people	• Factual approach to decision making
• Process approach (to getting the job done)	• Mutually beneficial supplier relationships

Thus, as *"custodians of the enterprise"*, management has extensive flexibility to use all aspects of the "system" to deliver the results called for as part of the business plan. Management has already discovered that using just financial information to manage the system is no longer viable. Boards and shareholders need to become aligned with this thinking so that not only does management exercise accountability over all aspects of the system, but that they are held accountable by the Board for the protection and safekeeping of all aspects that contribute to the economic value of the entity that has been created and is being used. Relying on financial reporting no longer provides adequate insight into the sustainability of the enterprise.

3. THE THREAT OF WHAT WE DON'T KNOW

The old adage *"you don't know what you don't know"* is apt in this situation — and is extremely dangerous. Well-meaning managers and Board members make ongoing decisions with inadequate information about the cause and effect of such decisions and, as a result, may damage an organization's capacity to effectively execute its business strategies. Boards require transparency in ensuring the ongoing economic value of the enterprise through knowing answers to questions such as the following:

- Are the processes that form the basis of all cost and resource consumption operating effectively so as to minimize costs?
- Is the competitive value of the processes developed in the past being sustained?
- Are the relationships that have been invested in, being maintained and enhanced with suppliers, distributors, agents, and customers?
- Is the accumulated knowledge about our internal operations, held by our employees being retained, enhanced, and improved through development?
- When mistakes are made and problems occur are these being used as learning experiences that result in improved operational activity?
- Are the inherent risks in any of these management system capabilities being increased or decreased as a result of management actions?
- Are the organizational *outcomes in terms of client satisfaction* with the product or service at a satisfactory and/or improving level?

This type of questioning allows managers, as well as directors, to start dealing with the degree to which the system that has been created is being maintained so that the economic/organizational value is not depleted.

The following schematic places emphasis on the commercial nature of a "for profit" organization:

sales less costs = profits

Cost control is critical; however, it is the framework of the management system that drives the cost base and, in particular, the operating processes that consume the greatest portion of resources. In the case of manufacturing, the costs of the "supply chain" being both process as well as prices paid to suppliers drive the cost base.

Efforts to improve organizational financial performance through focusing on minimization of costs can only be effective if management and the Board are able to ensure that the integrity of the management model is not being adversely impacted as a result of actions taken.

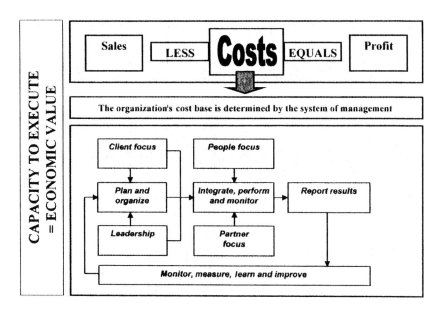

The major cost drivers in any organization are *the processes through which work is done — the central box in the management model.* This element *"consumes" key resources* in terms of the human dimension as well as the supplier dimension and thus forms the ready target for cost reduction. However, as will be discussed later, it is the *effectiveness of the process* that determines the level of consumption and this is the source of economic value depletion if not handled correctly. Actions that strive to cut cost, without addressing process or supplier improvement by definition, "disconnect" key elements in the management model creating unplanned side effects as a result.

4. PLANNING AND EXECUTION — THE PARTNERS IN PERFORMANCE

Planning, together with leadership and external focus including the client, are key components that link Board intent with management's capacity to execute. The business plan is, in effect, the "hand off" between the Board and those responsible for execution. This fact, combined with the reality that management is accountable for the responsible stewardship of the existing economic value of the organization, means that there must be integration between the aspects that make up the economic value and the aspect of planning and managing.

Without this integration and alignment, plans would fail to address policy and direction in key areas. This is where an effective management model fits into the framework — it becomes the vehicle through which accountability moves beyond financial aspects and deals with intangibles that contribute to capacity, sustainability, and economic valuation.

Using this concept, an effective framework for governance would create alignment between all the factors necessary to deliver ongoing results as well as addressing intangibles.

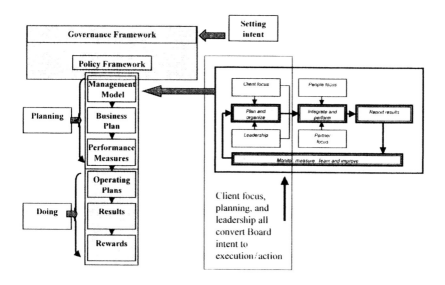

In the model shown above, the "management model" — containing the key aspects of converting intent to execution — forms the fundamental linkage in the governance chain. Starting with the Board's responsibility to set direction and establish a policy framework, the management model then becomes the vehicle for integrated and comprehensive planning, covering *all* of the economic aspects of an entities operation (*i.e.*, an Integrated Performance Measures System such as a Balanced Scorecard). Failure to use this approach results in many aspects of intent becoming lost in translation. As the management model then is used to convert intent into a business plan, a measures framework is also in place that allows management to monitor the broad base of economic activity as well as to serve as a potential conduit of broad-based economic value information back to the Board.

5. THE ROLE OF "PROCESS" IN BUILDING EQUITY AND VALUE

Traditional accounting and the presentation of an organization's value in terms of a balance sheet not only misstates but also misleads thinking in terms of economic value. Some years ago, AOL argued with the IRS that its losses accumulated as part of building its customer base were, in fact, a corporate asset and should be capitalized (they were not successful). However, the thinking is important. The shareholders of AOL contributed significant investment to fund the development of marketing and other activities through which AOL was able to create a significant channel to the market. This channel, by definition, had value — AOL argued that it was about US $750 million — the losses sustained in building the channel but, according to generally accepted accounting principles, treated as a loss and "expensed".

Here, then, we have a significant issue for 21st century economies from a governance perspective. There is no asset according to accounting balance sheet rules (allowing for a very simplified presentation without dealing with future recovery of income taxes on losses, *etc.*!).

Assets in $M		Liabilities in $M	
Cash	$0	Loans or contributed capital	$750
		Accumulated losses	-$750
Total assets	$0	Total investment & liabilities	$0
So — does accounting make sense in a 21st century economy?			

Therefore, according to accounting methods of treating certain expenses, losses are capital investments — marketing development, brand building, staff development, and supplier relationship and supply chain development. *All of these are written off as current expenses.* Yet, if these are not visible to the Board, the impact of not "nurturing them" can be a significant reduction in economic value and a future decline in earnings and equity.

From an economic perspective, the organization has an investment of $750 million which, from a governance perspective, needs to be protected, reviewed, and maintained. How does a Board deal with this, using traditional aspects of reporting and accountability? There are many other examples of intangible assets that, from an accounting perspective, do not exist but clearly have value from an economic perspective and need to be considered as part of governance and accountability. Examples could also include:

- the *value of* accumulated resources put into developing a *loyal customer base*;
- the accumulated resources spent in *developing capable processes* (in some organizations, such as FedEx, this is a *key* asset of the business!);
- the accumulated *value of learning* invested by the organization in training and developing the work force;
- the accumulated *value of internal systems and procedures* — in particular, information systems and technology (for example, a good website can clearly be a corporate asset);
- the accumulated *value of relationships* with key suppliers who have come to learn about our business;
- the accumulated *value of internal communications* structures through which problem solving occurs.

Intangible assets that form economic worth clearly need to be considered as part of future governance frameworks, as their value may increase or decrease. Another key aspect that needs to be considered, within the envelope of an organization's management model through which capability to execute is determined, is the issue of risk management and how directors and managers need to address every aspect of economic value as well as the core issues such as leadership and planning within an enterprise-wide and integrated approach.

Risk management and corporate governance use the same model to ensure accountability and comprehensiveness. An effective management model and governance framework ensures that all aspects of organizational risk are addressed and that *scarce resources are deployed to where the greatest risks to the economic value of the organization might exist.*

6. RISK MANAGEMENT WITHIN THE CAPABILITY MODEL

Much of the concern of a Board's capacity to manage, and its effectiveness in exercising its responsibility to shareholders and society, started with the scandals referred to in the 1980s that gave rise to Cadbury, COSO, CoCo and others. The example of Barings Bank can be used to illustrate the fact that the risk problem occurred within the management model of the organization's execution capacity. Traditionally, Boards have focused their attention on risk management towards internal controls that are dealt with as part of the annual audit.

Today, many organizations have moved beyond this to identify risks in many other areas — particularly, environmental and health and safety. In addition, an area such as succession planning for key positions is one that progressive Boards will address. However, much risk exists within all areas of an organization's activities and some have moved towards an integrated approach to risk management that is often referred to as an ERP or ERM (Enterprise Risk Program or Enterprise Risk Management), as well as CSA (Control Self-Assessment).

These approaches — developed in response to the risk management issues of the late 1980s — seek to position directors to identify and understand *all* of the aspects of corporate risk. The challenge is that internal controls might address process risks, but are often unable to deal with behavioural risks. If directors and managers have no information on the degree to which "softer" criteria have been deployed, then they will fail to address a key area of risk management. Establishing corporate values with no vehicle to assess and verify deployment is, in fact, a waste of time.

The breadth of risk assessment is complementary to the areas of governance that need to be addressed, thus they may be integrated with both the governance framework and the management model. As an example, risk exists in the "people" aspect of the management model that was discussed. Knowing this, the organization can create risk assessment checklists that can be used to review and assess the existence of risk within all the main components of the model — in fact all the main areas that management deals with in managing the day-to-day affairs of the business.

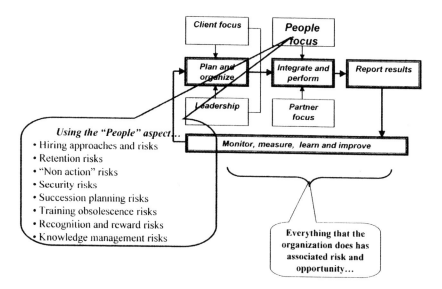

What is important from a governance aspect of integrating the behavioural risk management into the aspects of the model? For example, having a series of questions that deals with assessing whether the organization faces risks in employees execution of work may be critical in ensuring understanding of, and compliance with, an organization's values, code of ethics, and code of conduct.

Many recent lapses in effective governance can be tracked back to behavioural problems. No organization can ever write enough procedures and implement enough controls to ensure effective compliance with behavioural norms. Thus, ensuring that risk is minimized at the operational level in an organization through effective interviewing, screening, staff selection, testing, and other approaches, cannot be understated. Reliance on rules, policies, and standards alone will not solve the problem.

Several tools to assist in the implementation of an effective risk management program built around the management model are included as part of the appendices at the back of the book. These include:

Template/Chart	Purpose and linkage
Sample Risk Management Checklist	Used as a high level assessment to identify readiness and recognition for initiating a broad risk management program at the policy level.

Template/Chart	Purpose and linkage
Thinking about risk tolerance	Some specific examples as a basis for considering risks that may be inherent within each of the aspects of the management model (people, clients, processes, *etc.*).
Classifying the status of risk*	Examples of tables that will need to be developed to a) assess the status of current risk and b) determine the level of risk.
Summary of risk evaluation profile	Example of a checklist that could be developed and used when creating a risk assessment process for each of the key areas.
Types of actions to be taken	Typical criteria when dealing with results of a risk assessment — do nothing through to "get out of the business" or obtain insurance.
Risk evaluation and assessment — establishing weighted criteria	Example of the type of matrix that needs to be created to create a measured score for assessing the combination of probability of the risk occurring with the impact of it when it occurs (combination of the two creating the priority list for action planning).
Risk evaluation and assessment — assessing probability of existence of risk	Matrix to score the third dimension of risk assessment — that is the probability of detection using existing controls and procedures (note that probability of occurrence, probability of detection, and impact of occurrence are the three key rating criteria).
Detailed process mapping risk assessment	Example of a tool to carry out process level risk assessment looking at every step in a work process and assessing for each task what may go wrong, impact, probability, and possibility of detection; a very valuable tool for building effective processes and integrating risk management with internal controls.
Typical risk evaluation and self-assessment checklist — template	This template shows another example of how an assessment checklist could be prepared that would bring together three levels of impact, probability of occurrence, control, and detection.
Typical risk evaluation and self-assessment checklist — template	This builds on the above template providing a specific example of a completed sheet focusing on risks associated with Board self-management.

---

* Appendix H

Effective approaches to governance in the future will reflect a high degree of integration between the following key aspects:

- governance intent (and level of tolerance — driven by risk assessment) as defined by the Board;
- governance accountability during execution as managed by the CEO and management;
- a consistent framework for planning and managing that deals with financial and non-financial assets;
- comprehensive inclusion of economic aspects of organizational value;
- integration of risk management around a common governance and management model;
- a measurement, audit, and feedback system that pulls all these elements together.

This risk management in the future vision for governance becomes an integrated part of the framework built around the same common base.

7. QUALITY MANAGEMENT — A WINDOW ON PROCESS WASTE

Earlier we identified that processes within an organization consume the principle resources; in fact, this can be broadened to reflect three key aspects of resource consumption that form the overall basis of cost incurred.

Resources, and therefore the drivers of an organization's cost base (thus its competitive advantage that exists as an economic value), are composed of three core elements — processes through which ongoing work is done; projects through which specific initiatives and tasks are completed; and what we refer to as non-value added activities (these being the non-discretionary aspects of the cost base such as audit fees, taxes, and others that are driven by statute rather than discretionary management choice, generally).

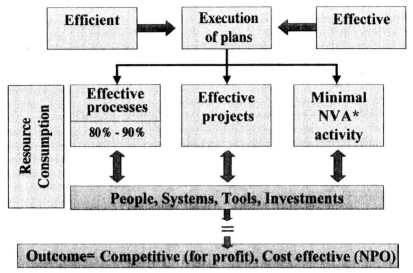

* NVA – Non-Value Added

A key competitive advantage (and economic value) of an established organization is that it has *learned how to do its work effectively*; one of the advantages of a free enterprise competitive system is that this learning must occur otherwise costs will be too high and the organization will go out of business.

In the case of the public sector, there is much less drive to reduce costs due to *competitive pressure* therefore it is critical that, from governance perspective, controls and measures are in place to focus on minimization of resource consumption through either projects or processes and to benchmark these against best practices and to strive for trends that show processes are operating more and more effectively. (This is a reason that ABC as well as modern comptrollership in the public sector is such a critical issue in obtaining control of government spending; without this, there is little ability to relate costs incurred to output generated. Management accounting still seeks to improve this analytical ability through other tools such as RCA (Resource Consumption Analysis or "German Cost Accounting").

If processes drive the consumption of resources, then a key accountability for management is to demonstrate the continued effectiveness and improvement of processes.

As a Board member I would want to know "is management using my resources effectively to optimize the shareholders' return on investment?" I can rely on the financial performance but I can also ask some other key questions to obtain insight into the effective use of resources, opportunity for improvements as well as stewardship of my intangible assets. These would include:

- Does the business process reflect best practice performance?
- What level of excess cost is being incurred due to process failure?
- Is my historic investment in process development providing ongoing savings or are process costs increasing driven by other problems?

Effective planning, leadership and communications, client understanding, employee performance and motivation, and supplier competitiveness and relationships significantly impact process effectiveness. These factors together with the processes themselves form the basis of an organization's economic value and intellectual capital. Because they are so interdependent, changes in one area can impact another.

Boards and managers, to exercise effective governance, need to ensure that the business processes that *use up the resources*, are being managed effectively. This requires that organizations include in reporting a degree of process-based accountability as well as addressing the sustainability of core processes through which work is done. Through this the risk of failures is minimized and actions in other areas are quickly identified where they start to negatively impact the overall value of the economic model.

For over 30 years, quality professionals have struggled to try and attract senior management attention to the fact that effective process quality translates into a lower cost of operation. The problem has been that while quality initiatives focus on the horizontal view of the organization, the accounting profession by and large remains mired in a world of responsibility accounting and reporting — focusing on who is spending the money rather than why the money is being spent. When senior managers start to realize the potential of these savings, considerable effort is made to harness the benefits. Mike Hari as a proponent of "6 Sigma" was very successful in making this an initiative of the executive suite, yet the concepts were not new — just very well presented.

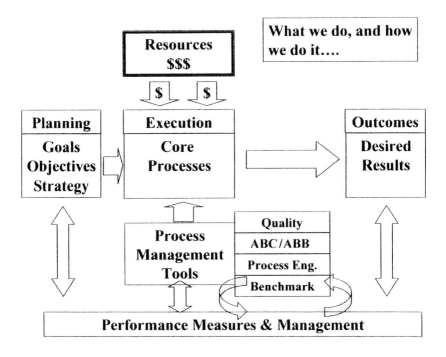

The above schematic shows how core processes are the enablers of business goals, objectives, and strategies and that effective process management tools such as Quality, ABC, and Process Engineering help address the need to maintain and grow economic value by improving processes so they consume less resources and create greater competitiveness (the cost of doing this currently is treated as a current period expense though!). Effective management (the management model) and measurements systems (the balanced scorecard) ensure that these improvements are identified and addressed.

Management, in order to deliver on the business plans (goals, objectives, and strategies), employ processes to "get the work done". Much effort has been expended to develop better process control internally as well as to develop better metrics to help management understand the linkage between resources and processes (such as ABC). Effective governance and accountability for responsible stewardship of corporate resources would move ahead by bounds if Boards had visibility into the effectiveness of resource usage rather than remaining focused on just results — which, while in the short term may deliver the returns required, may over the long term be depleting the economic basis of the enterprise and eliminating its ability to remain sustainable.

8. MEASURING AND REPORTING PROCESS PERFORMANCE

Effective future governance requires a process focus for three core reasons that will be critical in ensuring sustainability of the enterprise:

* visibility into the current effectiveness of process performance;
* visibility into strategic improvements in process performance for enhancing future competitiveness; and
* protection of historic value of the intangible processes assets as a core portion of intangible assets contributing to economic value.

As in the area of accountability for the human capital, process capital can be divided into a balance sheet type component and earnings type component. Examples of metrics for consideration are included in the table at the end of this section. What will be important is the development of the critical few at the Board level that can then be decomposed through the organization so that more detailed metrics are used where there is individual accountability for task, activity, or process performance.

Checklist
Example of Process Capital Effective Governance

Item	Assessment	Result			Action plan anticipated
		Yes	No	NI	
1	Is process capital considered a part of Board reporting?				
2	Are there any processes that form a critical part of the organization's competitive advantage?				
3	Is there an economic value related to internal processes that has been incurred and expensed in the past?				
4	Are there process metrics available that identify major areas of cost consumption? Are these monitored and tracked?				
5	Is there reporting of excess process costs due to failures?				
6	Are process audits being conducted and do the results support/complement other reporting metrics?				

Item	Assessment	Result			Action plan anticipated
		Yes	No	NI	
7	Are key business processes benchmarked against best practice and results/trends reported?				
8	Are process improvements tracked and monitored?				
9	Are internal metrics on key processes used as part of management (time, quality, cost, quantity)?				
10	Is there internal accountability for process performance (owners)?				
11	Is process risk tracked and monitored in terms of "failures"?				
12	Is management aware of process compliance and non-conformances?				
13	Are employees trained in process management and improvement?				
14	Are there measurable improvements and learnings from process improvements?				

List of Typical "Capacity" and "Performance" Metrics for Process Capital

Capacity/Balance Sheet Metrics	Performance/Earnings Metrics
• percentage of organizational cost under process management;	• cost of poor quality/waste by process;
• number of process outcomes directly linked and aligned with client "satisfiers";	• on-time delivery to core clients;
• percentage of core business processes benchmarked against best practice;	• product defects and returns;
• notional investment in core processes by process;	• warranty costs of products;
	• number of defects/unit shipped;
• number of PCs/employee;	• client satisfaction rating on new products;
• average age of PC technology.	• client satisfaction rating on post-sales support;
	• process cycle time;

Capacity/Balance Sheet Metrics	Performance/Earnings Metrics
	• number of process steps/process;
	• costs/process;
	• cost/unit/process;
	• defects by process;
	• rework by process;
	• renewal/reinvestment as percentage of process operating cost;
	• process down time/process.

11

ECONOMIC VALUE OF SUPPLY CHAIN RELATIONSHIPS AND PARTNERING

Supply chain management has become another concept for improved performance. Considerable investments are going into building supplier relationships and partnerships, through which an organization's ability to execute its work is further enhanced — creating a situation where key suppliers are seen as a critical extension of an organization's own capacity. While these investments have been made, they fail to appear on any balance sheet as having an economic value yet again they are critical when considering long-term performance. However, supplier management and relationships can in the future form a key component of accountability for both social and environmental performance. Signs already exist where social accountability is sought through the application of small business procurement policies and aboriginal commitments. As more organizations move to outsource key activities to suppliers, their own reputation and social accountability then extends to the behaviour and performance of these "partners".

1. SUPPLIER RELATIONSHIPS AND STAKEHOLDERS' EQUITY

Supplier management, and the overall supply chain system, has a direct impact on organizational sustainability, however, the level of impact varies by industry. The greater the level of supplier input to the creation of products and services, the greater the need for addressing the economic value of the supply chain.

Vendor or supplier management plays a key role in any organization's effectiveness. Good suppliers enhance economic value through supporting predictability of process management (*e.g.*, are able to deliver on time to the correct locations in the quantity and with the quality required). Through this, suppliers assist the buyer in building effective client relationships through predictable processes. Delivery of the final product or service is itself going to be provided both at the time promised and meeting expectations. In addition, if supplies are well managed they should be capable of translating their own management effectiveness into competitive pricing.

Poor supplier performance depletes economic value, as well as increases day-to-day costs. Buyers have to spend significant resources and add processes to expedite supplier deliveries and address "non-conformances" — be they late delivery, poor quality of the product or service, and administrative costs. Buyers, at the end of the day are paying the cost of delaing with poorly performing suppliers.

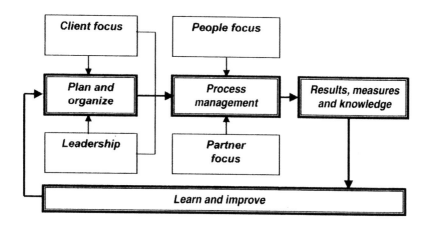

The management model created earlier shows suppliers as a key component of effective execution and one that directly links with organizational processes through which outcomes and results are generated. It therefore follows that processes that depend upon supplier participation are going to be impacted by the level of investment and development between buyer and seller.

In this section, we will explore the need for enhanced visibility, transparency, and governance attention that must be addressed in monitoring the economic value of relationships between an organization and its suppliers. The mistake is often made that this aspect relates more to manufacturing organizations but, again, as the economy and society changes, this is no longer as true. Examples of change include:

- the move to get back to basics and outsource non core (from a knowledge perspective) functions — including outsourcing and "off shoring";
- the moves to reduce costs by dealing with suppliers from other less developed countries (whose approach to business, social values, and work ethics may differ from the buying organization's environment);
- the *impact that technology suppliers now have on service organizations* and the impact that a loss of communications or technology can have on the service processes;
- the move towards ASD (alternative service delivery) in the public sector through which governments outsource to service providers (suppliers) the delivery of government services;
- the move towards elimination of any buffer inventories from suppliers,

resulting in supply chain integration between supplier, transportation services, and buyers (including both materials suppliers as well as parts and maintenance suppliers).

All of these shifts in the way that the business environment operates will generate shifts in how governance frameworks are structured but, in many cases, they have not kept pace. This becomes even more critical when aspects of enterprise risk management are assessed which reveal, as an example, that reducing costs through outsourcing has not only created new risks in the areas of supply management and process dependency, but has significant impact in areas such as social responsibility and employee ethics and codes of conduct.

The economic value of an organization includes the value of the relationships that have been created with key suppliers. Investment has been made to locate, evaluate, and develop the supplier base. Investment has been made in learning between the organizations in terms of integrating channels of supply, understanding production schedules and forecasts, and putting in place administrative support systems to enable administrative processing to take place between buyer and seller. In many organizations very significant investment has incurred in joint development of components and parts and, in many cases, the buyer has given up significant leverage with suppliers for the benefit of co-development, creating a far higher level of dependency. As a Board member, the issue of relationships with key suppliers, and the protection of the sunk costs that have been incurred in putting these in place, is part of the intangible equity that needs to be protected.

The costs to an organization that continually changes suppliers can be significantly higher than one that does not. In addition, to offset this, the risk to an organization that has made these investments but now is more dependent upon a limited number of key suppliers is also much higher. A responsible member of the Board would want to know about these aspects of the business. Changes that management makes to supplier relationships — especially key suppliers, can rapidly deplete an organization's economic value; inherent savings in cost due to lower administrative costs as well as integration of design activity resulting in the capacity for faster development process cycle times can be quickly lost if a CEO makes a short-term, financially driven decision to obtain a 5 per cent lower cost on certain products or materials.

2. THE THREAT OF WHAT WE DON'T KNOW

What inherent economic value exists due to supplier relationships? What existing competitive advantage does our organization have because of certain key supplier relationships? Are we able to be "first to market" with a new product because a key supplier has worked with us in developing one of their new products and, as a result, we have been able to incorporate this into our offerings before the competition? What is this worth? What would the impact be on our ability to innovate and meet market cycle time windows if we did not have these relationships?

No existing financial reporting and auditing standards can answer these questions; in most cases many Board members would not know that there is an issue or concern. Nor would they be able to ask insightful and probing questions of management as to what systems are in place to manage these risks and what metrics should be in place to assess whether the historic "expensed" investment made to develop these relationships are in fact being maintained and/or enhanced or are they being depleted through a "relationship deficit" that is developing?

The strange logic of accounting standards

Expenses incurred to create intangible assets such as processes, supplier relationships, customer relationships, and others are typically not capitalized as, under accounting rules, there is no clearly defined value of future benefit. Therefore, the costs involved are treated as expenses, either reducing profits or creating a loss.

Under accounting terms a financial loss may in fact represent an economic investment. The asset is not on the balance sheet, but the organization has expended the money to develop the capacity to execute through this particular factor or element.

Therefore Losses = Investments

The problem of not knowing the answers to these questions is that actions can be taken in other aspects of the management system such as changing processes without supplier participation of reducing costs through a combination of downsizing and supplier "rationalization" and these can, without notice, start to deplete the investment in the intangible asset that was created.

As a director, responsible for the protection of my shareholders' investment in this organization, one might start to wonder whether the right information exists, and is available, to provide effective direction. Directors must ask the right questions through which they can make informed decisions on policies and plans that relate to a key aspect of economic value.

3. SUPPLIERS AS SURROGATE EMPLOYEES

Supplier relationships, in many cases, rest heavily on the interaction between the buyers' representatives and the sellers' representatives. Thus, people once again play a key role.

Effective supplier relationships depend on a level of shared ethics, business conduct, and trust between buyers and sellers. Thus, in the same way that an organization would want to know about the level of this factor, in terms of the motivation of its own staff to participate fully for the benefit of the organization, so are the questions valid about "how do suppliers feel about areas such as communications, trust, feedback, shared values, demonstrated behaviour, *etc.*" Having supplier relationships in place has one level of economic value, but *having supplier relationships in place that are supported by innovative and active participation by the supplier is of a greater value.*

Suppliers should be thought of as extensions of an organization's human resource. The behaviour exhibited by an organization towards its suppliers should be fully consistent with its stated values as if it were dealing with its own employees.

4. CHALLENGES OF OUTSOURCING — PUBLIC AND PRIVATE SECTORS

Changes in sourcing decisions are impacting both public and private sectors. A significant portion of an organization's "expense" base can be incurred in developing and maintaining these relationships. In addition, as with the other factors within the integrated management model, changes in one area can impact others. From an effective governance perspective, the following types of problems will need to be considered:

- values and code of ethics may not be consistent between the buyer and seller;
- "norms" of social accountability between buyer and seller organizations may vary;
- significant support cost may be incurred in developing suppliers — how are these tracked and a hurdle ROI developed?;
- risk may shift through greater dependency on the buyer to fewer suppliers;
- ability to "hide" the impact of problems may be reduced (greater potential for problems between two organizations rather than all "in house");
- poor processes in the buyer organization may result in the supplier demanding additional costs (*e.g.*, poor ability to design and specify requirements, poor planning);

- sharing of information as a key component of partnering may result in third parties obtaining unauthorized access to information (including unauthorized release of confidential information, even privacy violations);
- greater dependency may make it harder to use price as the benchmark for "best value" requiring other performance metrics to be in place;
- understanding and communications may cause problems, especially when policy making is segregated from delivery capacity (a key public sector issue in ASD).

Overall, the emergence of supply chain management, creating greater inter-dependence between buyers and sellers as well as decisions to increase outsourcing and global supply channels, has created a need for greater diligence in governance in these areas.

5. EMERGING INTERNATIONAL STANDARDS

The use of suppliers from countries that may not have either the same social expectations or the same legislative controls, can give rise to significant problems that should be of concern to shareholders and directors, as well as senior managers. This has been a growing trend as organizations in high labour cost environments seek to outsource labour intensive activity to lower labour cost locations. In the mid 1990s, world attention was drawn to the issue of shoe production and, in particular, Nike was hit hard for "exploitation" of lowly paid workers in Asian countries (even though the trend to producing shoes in these areas was not limited to Nike alone[1]). One can surmise that the owners, Board, and individual directors were very happy that their brand was doing well and that costs were being held down through outsourcing; *however, one has to assume that the organization would not have openly condoned the practices that were taking place?*

Other examples of "western" companies exploiting workers in less developed areas are continually making press headlines — be it Sudan, Mexico, Asia, or other countries. The message though is clear — *beware* from a governance perspective as these *financially driven sourcing decisions* may create negative results that are *totally inconsistent with an organization's values, principles or codes of practice.*

Mainly as a result of the Nike case, a standard was developed by the ILO (International Labour Organization) that focused on setting a series of basics "best practice" standards for those organizations employing workers or using sub-contractors in less developed countries.

---

1 See website for more background details http://www.saigon.com/~nike/christian-aid.htm#just

SA - Social Accountability 8000

- ➢ Child labour
- ➢ Forced labour
- ➢ Health and safety
- ➢ Freedom of association
- ➢ Discrimination
- ➢ Disciplinary practices
- ➢ Working hours
- ➢ Compensation
- ➢ Management

This "standard" — SA 8000[2] — deals with a set of basic criteria that organizations can use for setting and assessing their suppliers and operations in other countries. In many cases, where no labour standards exist *per se*, voluntary compliance with an alternative set of guidelines becomes the best alternative. Organizations can have their operations certified against this standard as a base line for good practice. This approach should at least provide those with governance accountability some level of assurance that financially driven supply chain modifications are still maintaining compliance with corporate standards and values.

More recently, organizations have started to create voluntary "self declarations" of the conditions of work at sub-contractor facilities and some are, in fact, starting to publish full lists of the sub-contractors that they use together with the results of their assessments:

• *Local labour laws*	• *Child labour*
• *Environmental*	• *Wage and hour requirements*
• *Discrimination*	• *Working conditions*
• *Forced labour*	• *Freedom of association*

For example, GAP Inc. produced its 2003 Social Responsibility Report, that creates full disclosure of work practices and conditions across its supply chain. GAP uses a code of vendor conduct as a basis for its assessment that is very similar to the SA8000 standard.

Other organizations have similar commitments to effective social responsibility and provide a greater or lesser degree of transparency into the

---

2 For more information see D. Leipziger, *SA8000: The Definitive Guide to the New Social Standard* (Financial Times/Prentice Hall, 2002).

actual results against these commitments. For example, Levi Strauss has posted a very clear set of principles to social responsibility on its website. This type of practice supports the call for more effective governance as complements the directions generally identified in *The Naked Corporation*.

6. PROCESS DEPENDENCIES ON SUPPLY CHAIN RELATIONSHIPS

As the management model has identified, there is a close "integrated nature" of relationships between vendor/supplier activities and effectiveness and internal control of process management. Organizations that have invested in the supply chain between themselves and their suppliers have created significant equity in cost effective operations. Examples would include:

- lower cost of administrative operations through joint process improvement activities;
- investment in establishing supply chain and third party support (*e.g.*, transportation, clearing);
- faster cycle times from concept to delivery of new products;
- eliminated of (or significant reduction in) defects and quality problems, yet again lowering operating costs;
- shared knowledge between employees in both buyer and seller of the other's operations;
- shared learning — through joint training of each other's products and services.

This list could go on — but again it illustrates the fact that a) significant sunk costs in terms of investment in the relationships have been created, and b) flow-through benefits in lower process costs exist due to such investments. Decisions to change suppliers to reduce product costs, if taken without due consideration of the sunk costs of the process savings in place, might eliminate the accumulated equity as well as actually increase operating costs in other areas.

As a practical example, consider an organization that invests $500K in developing a particular supplier including costs such as identification, evaluation, assessment, training, joint process development, troubleshooting and others. This cost is treated as an expense and written off. Another supplier purchases a $500K piece of equipment that is placed on the balance sheet as a capital asset and depreciated over its anticipated useful life of 10 years. Two years into the relationship, the company realizes that it can save $100K annually by moving to another supplier, but is not aware that this move will add $50K/year in additional process costs. Two observations can be made. First, deciding to write off the capital asset after two years would result in a clearly identified write-off of $400K — very visible. Second, the decision to save $100K/year would probably be taken without realizing that there remains a sunk cost of $400K using the same anticipated life of the relationship with the supplier, as well as an offset $50K/year increase in other process costs. What we have is a net saving of $50K/year over the next eight years that from an economic equity perspective would not create any saving at all. Either the saving needs to be greater or the decision should be reconsidered (or the decision to spend the $500K in supplier development in the first case was incorrect?).

The problem is that the management metrics to make decisions related to intangible assets are not well developed. From an economic perspective, such decisions need to be made but current accounting and reporting approaches do not address management accountability in a true sense. As a final point, this is one of the inherent conflicts built into some quality management standards such as the automotive standard that requires buyers to support their Tier 1 suppliers through helping them improve their operational cost and quality performance to ensure longer term benefits in the supply partnership. Yet the buying company has to take a short-term financial loss to make this investment — mixed messages indeed. With a market focused heavily on short-term financial results, this is not necessarily a direction that is going to be embraced or be made in the mutual best interests of both parties. Supplier partnering is a good line — but practice to date falls quite short of the potential opportunities to exploit such situations. Another opportunity for improvement is governance at both Board and management levels.

Checklist
Example of Supplier Capital Effective Governance

Item	Assessment	Result			Action plan anticipated
		Yes	No	NI	
1	Are aspects of supplier relationships considered a part of governance?				
2	Is there an historic investment in building supplier equity as part of intangible capital?				
3	Are there metrics to assess the continued stability of growth of supplier equity?				
4	Have key suppliers been identified where there is a critical dependability?				
5	Are relationships with key suppliers assessed and monitored?				
6	Does supplier assessment extend beyond price and delivery?				
7	Has the organization integrated its values into its supply management strategy? If so, how?				
8	Do strategies include the continued development of vendor/supplier participation in competitiveness?				
9	Are offshore suppliers used?				
10	Are there clear guidelines on the selection of offshore suppliers?				
11	Is the performance of offshore suppliers assessed and evaluated on a continuing basis?				
12	Are problems and issues escalated and dealt with including deselection of non-compliant suppliers?				
13	Does the organization publish its social accountability related to supplier relationships?				
14	Are key suppliers included in planning activities?				

List of Typical "Capacity" and "Performance" Metrics for Supplier Capital

Capacity/Balance Sheet Metrics	Performance/Earnings Metrics
• percentage of cost base assigned to third parties; • percentage of third party cost base covered by partnership performance agreements; • percentage of suppliers offshore; • percentage of suppliers in minority or equivalent status.	• supplier partnership driven cost savings; • on-time supplier delivery; • defect level/returns from suppliers; • number of key supplier assessments completed — local; • number of supplier assessments completed — offshore; • number of non-conformances with supplier principles; • overdue non-resolved supplier values issues.

12

THE ECONOMIC VALUE OF LEADERSHIP AND THE NEED FOR INDIVIDUAL ACCOUNTABILITY

Of all the components required for effective governance and accountability, none is greater in the knowledge-based economy than effective leadership. First, we discuss how the CEO or equivalent position is the only connector between the policy intent of the Board and the organization's ability to execute. But further, this chapter discusses the importance of leadership at every level of the organization. This capacity to have in place an intangible asset of human capital that embodies leadership capability becomes key to creating an organization that embodies the required values and principles, but yet can demonstrate agility in a rapidly changing organizational environment.

1. DEFINING LEADERSHIP

Effective leadership is a key success factor for any model of governance. However, before going further we need to define what we mean in this context by leadership. Although there are many definitions and contexts within which the word is used (just do a web search on "definitions of leadership" and see how many come up!), the following is an effective definition:

> A leader is one who conducts and guides; leadership is the ability to gain the confidence of others and to motivate, inspire and guide their actions to the achievement of a desired outcome.

Leadership is exercised throughout an organization and our definition here does not just include the CEO. Leadership is a quality that needs to exist right through any organization in the following context:

Exercise of Leadership	Demonstrated "belief in action"
Leadership as exercised by shareholders	The ability to set themselves apart by requiring their organizations to adopt best practices over and above statutory minimums for governance.
Leadership as exercised by Boards	The ability to work as one, to the collective benefit of all key stakeholders, and to establish self-management criteria through which they are held accountable.
Leadership as exercised by individual directors	The ability to work as a team to drive for consensus, but also to ask probing questions of management to ensure effective accountability while having a personal code of principles that is consistent with the organization being represented.
Leadership as exercised by the CEO	The ability to work as the key "lynch pin" between the Board and the organization to hold the same principles and to demonstrate those principles in the behaviour of leadership in communicating commitments, values, mission, goals, and direction to the organization.
Leadership as exercised by managers	The ability to hold and manage through principles that are consistent with the organizations that they represent and to motivate, lead, and direct those under their responsibility to achieve the specific plans and actions required to ensure the organization delivers on its commitments to the Board.
Leadership as exercised by individuals	The ability to understand and commit to the organizational principles of the entity they represent as well as to take personal accountability for performing the tasks and activities required to deliver on their personal commitment for the organization's performance.

This may seem to many an idealistic interpretation, but in the 21st century economy leadership and motivation of people towards the achievement of a shared organizational set of goals and objectives is critical. Having people in positions is no longer adequate — leadership requires having the right people in the right positions. This aspect of effective organizational performance is covered well in the book *First, Break All the Rules*.[1]

---

1 M. Buckingham & C. Coffman, *First, Break All the Rules: What the World's Greatest Managers Do Differently* (New York: Simon & Schuster, 1999).

2. THE CEO ROLE AS A LEADER

Leadership links to sustaining shareholder equity through all of the linkages identified above; however, the key one is the role of the CEO. This is the one position that is represented at both the Board level and at the management level. The CEO alone carries the dubious role of communicating the expectations of the Board down through the organization. In effect, the CEO "owns" the contract that is developed between the Board and management, that allows management access to the accumulated wealth

Governance - direction

and resources of the organization, in a position of trust; to take these and use them in a way that delivers a series of results back to the shareholders or stakeholders that sustains and perpetuates the organization's existence and well-being. In very direct and simple terms, a poor CEO will guarantee effective governance problems. Managers at all levels have some level of leadership as part of their responsibilities and this varies at the level of management.

The above schematic demonstrates that the CEO (or equivalent position) forms the critical "lynch pin" in converting intent to execution. Clear alignment with the Board's intent as well as belief systems based on the organization's values and commitment to key stakeholders is paramount.

What is most important, especially at the senior level, is the message that is communicated about corporate behaviour. This provides the context within which all other management activities are to be performed. Some examples of how this might relate to the way in which work is performed could include: how clients are to be involved; consideration for the environment; consideration for the community; involvement of people within the organization in decision-making; and innovation. This "context setting" is the only way in which stated values and principles established by the Board can be translated into internal and external behaviour. This has been a key governance problem either because

- the Board has failed to state the expectations clearly, or
- the CEO has diluted or ignored the Board's intent, or
- the CEO has done a poor job of communicating and embodying the principles and values into the way in which work is to be done.

GE is often cited as a traditional organization that transformed itself and created success under the leadership of Jack Welch. The role of leadership in this transformation is included as a key element through which this transformation took place.[2] Successful long-term organizations sustain themselves by ensuring that a common set of principles guide what they do. In effect, leadership is the candle that lights the way. Values driven leadership is cited as a key to success in the book *Discovering the Soul of Service* in which nine drivers of sustainable success are identified.[3] The more recent works of James Collins[4] have also shed light on the importance of effective leadership. *Managing Service Companies: Strategies for Success*,[5] published in the early 1990s, also dealt specifically with the role of leadership. Note that some of the earlier works focused on leadership in service organizations *i.e.*, those organizations at the leading edge of the new economy.

3. MANAGEMENT AND LEADERSHIP

While the CEO links the Board's intent to execution, managers and supervisors become the disciples of "spreading the word". Nowhere is this more important than in embracing and demonstrating the belief systems and values of the organization. Their leadership ensures the effective deployment of such stated behavioural aspects of an organization's culture and policies.

---

2 R. Slater, *The GE Way Fieldbook: Jack Welch's Battle Plan for Corporate Revolution* (McGraw-Hill, 2000).
3 L.L. Berry, *Discovering the Soul of Service: The Nine Drivers of Sustainable Business Success* (The Free Press, 1999).
4 J.C. Collins & J.I. Porras, *Built to Last: Successful Habits of Visionary Companies* (HarperBusiness, 1994), as well as J. Collins, *Good to Great: Why Some Companies Make the Leap . . . and Others Don't* (HarperCollins, 2001).
5 K. Irons, *Managing Service Companies: Strategies for Success* (Addison Wesley Publishing Company (EIU), 1993).

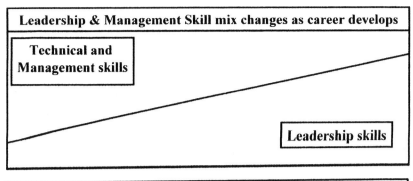

The challenge is that many managers have never been either selected for or trained in aspects of leadership; this is not a role that comes naturally to many or is automatically included in management skills. Managers and supervisors are typically hired or promoted for their management or specialty skills rather than for leadership. As an individual's career progresses, they tend to move away from technical and management skills and spend more time on leadership.

The hiring and promotion of individuals to such positions must include assessment of leadership components. For effective governance, such processes should be in place but employee surveys and other tools should be used by senior managers as well as by a Board. Each needs to be able to determine whether key managers and supervisors are demonstrating such behavioural norms; not just achieving the goals but doing it in a manner consistent with the organization's professed values.

4. THE THREAT OF WHAT WE DON'T KNOW

If leadership is so critical for both sustainability as well as the achievement of organizational expectations, how does a Board know whether it is being performed effectively? Even more importantly, how does management know whether it is being executed effectively throughout the organization?

In the current business environment of rapid change, and continued challenges and changes for survival, it is extremely difficult to exercise consistent leadership, in fact, there is a great temptation to revert back to "command and control" management as discussed in the GE *Fieldbook*. The problem is that while this "directive" approach may deliver the short-term results required, it will eat away at the accumulated equity that has developed between the organization and its people and through that will diminish the economic value that was discussed in Chapter 7. Boards may be obtaining the desired results but at what price? Is the longer term sustainability of the organization being impaired because of poor leadership either at the CEO level or elsewhere in the organization? *Effective managers are not always effective leaders — and an organization needs to know the difference and deal with it to maintain its economic value.*

5. THE CRITICAL ROLE OF THE CEO IN BROAD-BASED PERFORMANCE

The CEO has a pervasive impact on every aspect of the organization's activities — as spokesperson, figurehead, public "face", and internal leader and communicator. Every person that comes into contact with, or receives direction from the leader will be impacted in terms of how the leader portrays his or her commitment to the principles of the organization — not just in what they say but in what they do. In today's sceptical society, employees, customers and suppliers (as well as investors and other third parties) are indicating that it is not the words that carry weight anymore — it is the demonstration of the principles and values through the actions that are taken. Frank Feather — a leading futurist who has published on aspects of future societal activities and whose work creates a good underpinning for the societal forces re-shaping the economy — gave an interview to the Schulich School of Business at York University in Toronto in 2002 and made the following comments on leadership that focus on the importance of the role. Leadership is an active role — not a passive one.

Executives need to learn how to lead rather than manage. They need to learn far more about the future. True leaders are geo-strategic futurists who gaze across time and make extraordinary things happen. Just as China's leaders did, true business leaders literally breathe new life, direction and an exciting sense of purpose into moribund, meandering organizations. In today's world, corporate orthodoxy is far more dangerous than even the toughest competition. Leaders break from the past, challenge conventional wisdom and open up new avenues. In their mind's eye, they imagine or dream a clear and simple vision of a reinvented future for their organizations. Leaders are pioneers who venture out to a future they and those around them can clearly envision; they come to "know" and to "own" that future. Serving as the nerve center of their organizations, leaders are strategic visionaries who consistently and persistently lead their organizations into a new and better future. They live in a simultaneous time continuum, with one eye on today and tomorrow and another eye on the far horizon. Always ready to act and to change course, they use real-time planning and decision-making to steer their organizations through the fast-changing tides of time. They spot trends and act on them before competitors even realize there is a trend challenging them. That's what executives need to learn.

Schulich School of Business, Division of Executive Development Newsletter, Spring 2003, Interview with Frank Feather — futurist and author of G-Force Re-Inventing the World *(Summerhill Press, 1989).*

A key concern in North American business at the beginning of the 21st century is the degree to which the entry to the CEO office has become a revolving door — with average tenure slipping from almost 10 years a decade ago to about three years. Leadership is about trust: how can a leader, especially in a large far-flung enterprise, hope to establish leadership, an effective culture, and a sense of values in such a short time? This problem is especially critical in government where political leadership changes continually impact the culture and values of the public service. This makes the role of any manager and leader in the public sector a completely unenviable one in this day and age.

6. ENGAGING MANAGERS AS EVANGELISTS — DEPLOYMENT OF LEADERSHIP

Leadership means and includes "spreading a message"; making sure that followers understand as well as commit to the direction of the organization. A leader who cannot create "followers" is not a leader and cannot function as such. Communication, therefore, is one of the key expectations of those in leadership positions; spreading the corporate gospel.

Books such as *Jesus CEO: Using Ancient Wisdom for Visionary Leadership*,[6] by Laurie Beth Jones (while dismissed by some), do deal with some of the key success factors of organizational leadership. Leaders must believe in the message that they are delivering and be committed to the tasks that are required to meet the organization's plans and directions. Sincerity, trust, and openness are key attributes that must be in place. Leaders can only do this if the following types of systems are in place:

- clearly defined expectations from Board to CEO;
- clearly defined conversion from high level principles to "what does this mean to me in my job" at all levels (code of conduct based on relevant vignettes of organizational situations is a good approach);
- linkage between behaviour and beliefs and other parts of the organizational management model (as an example, integrated with HR management systems — reviews and expectations, design of products and services, delivery of products and services, sales and post-sales strategies, and all aspects of process design, *etc.*);
- assessment metrics that allow feedback on consistency of the message between "what we say and what we do".

To have a sustainable set of values, leadership must constantly reinforce these principles every day, in every aspect of the organization's activity — a long-term commitment.

---

6 Published by Hyperion, 1995.

7. LEADERSHIP AS A SHARED ROLE AMONG ALL

Leadership is everyone's responsibility. No organization can effectively deploy a set of behavioural criteria unless application is consistent. This is the role of leaders and managers; however, accountability for compliance rests with every single individual within an organization. Tightening legislation and applying more rules cannot achieve effective governance in the 21st century economy. What is needed is the embodiment of expectations in the basic culture of the organization. Every single person must know what is expected of them, and be supported by their managers and leaders in what they need to perform. Only then can accountability be expected at the individual level.

8. CRITICAL ROLE OF COMMUNICATIONS IN SETTING A BASE FOR ACCOUNTABILITY

Much has been written about the effective application of change management; organizations entering the 21st century already know that change is no longer an event but a continual journey of renewal. People are uncomfortable when change occurs and the only way they can become more comfortable is to be offered the opportunity to understand and participate in the way in which changes are being addressed. Leaders are the key conduits through which the need for such change is constantly communicated to those within the organization. "Agile" organizations that continually evolve and change to reflect their place within society, as well as remain competitive, will have, as part of their economic value, a framework of effective leadership.

Established and successful organizations have a cohesion of values and direction that only comes from effective leadership; thus, the economic value of a "well led" organization exceeds that of one where there has been little development of an accepted corporate culture. This, in many cases, explains the demise of many mergers and acquisitions in the "service" sector where successful organizations seem to become ineffective (and their goodwill disappears) when they are subsumed by another entity. Understanding and maintaining corporate culture are critical to maintaining economic value.

In the 21st century economy, the average employee is no longer an unskilled individual who will blindly follow orders. Many are well-educated and experienced and expect, as a basic condition of employment, that they will be offered the opportunity to express their views and provide input to decision making. The ability of an organization to motivate employees depends upon this approach.

Managers must be the prime communicators of expectations as well as coaches, helping individuals respond to these changing situations. However, many organizations provide woefully inadequate support, education, and training to those that they put in management and leadership positions. The result is poor or inconsistent messages, varied interpretations, or no message in some cases. In these situations the "bush telegraph" runs rampant and staff spend more time "filling in the blanks" than using their skills to further the work goals of the organization.

Managers are the setters of expectations all through the organization and trying to by-pass the management chain of command is going to spell disaster — even though it may be perceived as being faster. In fact, in many situations the managers are perceived as the blockage in getting the corporate message out. The solution is not then to go around them, as doing this will only further confuse the work force. The only solution is to deal with the management problem head on.

Organizational goals and objectives set by the Board (that define "what" an organization wants to achieve — *i.e.*, intent) must be converted into strategies that form the basis of delivering outcomes and results (*i.e.*, "how" the anticipated outcomes will be achieved — who will do what, where when, and how).

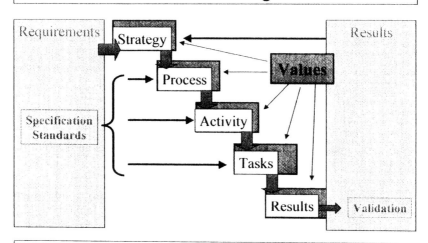

185

Strategies must be executed through core business processes and may also involve projects. Each of these involves executing plans and actions to perform the desired work and generate the planned results.

Organizational resources are all consumed in this effort — this is what people in the organization get paid to do; this is where they practise their competencies and skills. However, the "what" must always be carried out in the context of the desired behavioural standards *i.e.*, the values of the organization. The principles and values that stand behind every step in the process and which must form part of the manager's communication to employees as plans and reviews are being conducted are, in effect, a parallel universe or shadow behind every step in the execution process (see the graphic below).

An organization must provide people with the training they need and ensure the right people are in place and then, if the managers disagree with or cannot arrive at consensus on the corporate direction and are therefore not enforcing it, *it is the management problems that will need to be addressed.* You cannot spread the gospel through non-believers!

9. ACCOUNTABILITY AGREEMENTS AND OTHER PERFORMANCE MANAGEMENT TOOLS

A key challenge in many organizations is that there appears to be a process of corporate "osmosis" in play. Individuals are somehow expected to know and act in a certain way — yet nowhere has this expectation been codified as a set of employee orientation or assessment criteria. When they fail to meet expectations — whatever these are, if they have not been documented — then they are chastised. This creates negative morale as people start wondering where all these rules come from. This then undermines the whole viability and sustainability of the organization as individuals operate based on their own interpretation, values, and context.

The challenge is striking the right balance, and the only way this will happen is if expectations are clearly defined right up front and then consistently applied in all practical situations. Will there be exceptions? Naturally, but the key is that people can always track decisions made back to a sense of underlying principles around which the organization operates.

Karl Albrecht[7] in his books in the early 1990s that dealt with the (then topical) issue of service quality referred in a number of situations to the values of the organization and to providing value to customers. One of the points he made that is relevant to the issue of corporate governance is that every organization, in dealings between individuals (be it service provider/

---

7 K. Albrecht, *Service Within: Solving the Middle Management Leadership Crisis* (Homewood: Dow Jones-Irwin, 1990), and K. Albrecht & L. J. Bradford, *The Service Advantage: How to Identify and Fulfill Customer Needs* (Homewood: Dow Jones-Irwin, 1990).

client or between individuals internally), has what he calls *"moments of truth"* and it is at these times that the organization's ability to have embedded a sense of values towards common commitments and goals is demonstrated. No amount of writing procedures that determine how things are supposed to operate is going to deal with the unanticipated situations that occur and it is then, where an individual will ask themselves, *"So what do I do? How do I respond?"*, that the inculcation of corporate values shines through. Either they have a set of touchstone principles that can be applied or they do not. Without these, they will fall back to policies and procedures which in most cases will, in dealing with an unplanned problem, prove completely futile and, in fact, in many situations, will make matters worse. What is worse and what makes the corporate governance problem more of a challenge is that, in the absence of corporately defined expectations, *the individual will fall back on their own sense of values*. If these are not aligned with the organization's expectations, then problems cannot fail to occur.

> If you hire innovative and creative sales staff, don't be surprised if they start acting innovatively and creatively. Just be sure that you have defined where the boundaries are and what type of behaviour is accepted and what is not acceptable.

Many governance and risk management problems in the past twenty years can be tracked back to this problem. Be it the creation of "special purpose entities" to finance "off balance sheet" financing at Enron or a complete disregard for investors funds in situations such as the Michael Holoday story,[8] the actions of individuals, acting outside of corporate boundaries, reverberate around the corporate world and continue to change the public's perception of the integrity of corporate entities.

10. MEASURING AND TRACKING THE EFFECTIVENESS OF LEADERSHIP

Effective leadership is hard to assess let alone measure — however, in many cases, good or bad leadership can be identified through the degree to which surveys of both employees and clients reflect a high or low degree of consistency or commitment within the organization. Planned outcomes and results at the Board level may indicate that in the short term, leadership is being exercised but again it is only through time that an organization may begin to realize that the results being obtained are, in fact, being achieved in such a way that economic capital is diluted. Effective leadership not only "builds the brand", as discussed earlier but builds the overall capacity of

---

8 J.L. Reynolds, *Free Rider: How a Bay Street Whiz Kid Stole and Spent $20 Million* (McArthur & Company, 2002).

the organization to execute the goals and objectives set by the Board. What is needed is a portfolio of inputs that allows a Board to know that their CEO and senior managers are providing the requisite leadership, but also internal assessments that satisfy the CEO and senior managers that their message is also being deployed in a consistent way.

Much work has been done in recent years to try and quantify and measure the essence of leadership. In the area of EI — Emotional Intelligence — significant progress has been made[9] in identifying leadership traits of an individual that create effective "followership". Another excellent and somewhat lighter reading that deals with leadership as part of the "art of learning to give, take and use instructions" is the *Yellow Brick Road.*[10]

In most cases, the effectiveness of leadership, because the main role stems from being the "inspiration" that links the Board and the intent to execution by management, will come from an assessment of organizational performance in all other key areas, including feedback from employees, clients, suppliers, the public, the Board itself, and other sources.

Checklist
Example of Leadership Effectiveness Governance

Item	Assessment	Result			
		Yes	No	NI	Action plan anticipated
1	Is there a statement of performance expectations for the CEO that incorporates behavioural aspects?				
2	Are there stated performance expectations for senior managers that incorporate behavioural aspects?				
3	Does the Board use extensive profiling to ensure consistency of values between key staff and expectations?				
4	Does management use selection profiling to ensure required skills and beliefs at all management levels?				
5	Have leadership expectations been incorporated into all aspects of the management model and process?				

---

9 D. Goleman, *Emotional Intelligence: Why It Can Matter More Than IQ* (Bantam Books, 1995) and also R.K. Cooper & A. Sawaf, *Executive EQ* (Grosset/Putnam, 1996).

10 R.S. Wurman, *Follow the Yellow Brick Road: Learning to Give, Take, and Use Instructions* (Bantam Books, 1992), in particular chapter 15 on Leadership.

Item	Assessment	Result			Action plan anticipated
		Yes	No	NI	
6	Is leadership education and training provided to all managers and supervisory staff?				
7	Are leadership metrics in place to assess qualities, perceptions, and reality to expectations?				
8	Are there metrics that assess leadership in terms of others in the organization?				
9	Has the Board conducted a risk assessment as it relates to the leadership of the CEO in terms of "fit" for the position and has it acted on the results?				
10	Does the CEO demonstrate by action the vision for the organization established by the Board?				

List of Typical "Capacity" and "Performance" Metrics for Leadership

Capacity/Balance Sheet Metrics	Performance/Earnings Metrics
• number of managers who have completed leadership profiling; • number of managers who have received coaching on leadership improvement skills; • number of managers completed leadership training; • number of managers rated 5/5 as "effective leaders" on point scale survey (with subset data such as communications, problem resolution, *etc.*); • number of managers with completed EQ assessments (Emotional Quotient — measure of Emotional Intelligence); • high — 4/5 and 5 point scale — "trust" rating between employees and management within the organization; • tenure of CEO; • tenure of managers; • promotions/growth from within; • leadership capacity based on 360° assessment results.	• number of grievances/staff problems related to leadership skill based issues; • number of suggestions for improvement from employees supported/championed by managers and supervisors; • leadership time allocation by managers and supervisors (MBWA, *etc.*); • number of internal recognition situations and awards involving managers on teams; • number of hours managers/supervisors spend on group/team interaction/ development activity; • hours spent by managers/supervisors/year communicating plans and organizational vision.

13

MEASUREMENT SYSTEMS — DEVELOPING A NEW MODEL

This chapter starts to bring the aspects of performance together with a vehicle to collect and report the required information. In particular, the parallel aspects of models for enterprise risk management and comprehensive frameworks for governance and accountability are shown. This is complemented with a discussion of the emerging multiplicity of audit and verification approaches that already exist within many organizations, but which have only received limited attention as components of potential Board level accountability or, in their value to investors and other stakeholders, as providing insight into behaviour and performance on both tangible as well as intangible assets. Finally, the chapter identifies how newly emerging performance reporting models such as GRI are starting to build enhanced accountability that should be reviewed and adopted by all key members of the governance structure.

1. LINKING THE MEASUREMENT ISSUE TO STAKEHOLDERS' EQUITY

In its traditional, simplest sense, a system of measurement is a feedback mechanism that allows those setting goals and objectives to determine whether these expectations are being achieved.

Historically, the major common denominator for reporting back to shareholders was money. First, this allows all other activities to be converted to a common denominator, but second because the most important aspect of a shareholder's capital *was, in fact, the money* that had been invested and then accumulated as retained earnings. In the past, an investor enjoyed the benefits of good governance through receiving regular dividends from their investment and from seeing their equity grow through a certain level of re-investment of earnings, created by the effective and judicious use of corporate assets to earn revenue, control costs, and generate an acceptable level of returns.

However, as we enter the 21st century, we see significant changes occurring; among these being the hidden value of organizations created when their economic value exceeds their book value. In this era of knowledge management and intellectual capital developing as one of the most important aspects, the reliance on financial reporting alone is inadequate.

In order to protect stakeholders, including shareholders' accumulated investment, better criteria are required to track organizational performance.

In addition, traditional risk management systems usually revolved principally around aspects of *fiscal control*, and so performance standards and audit criteria by definition tended to also rely upon financial reporting and accountability. The last twenty years have seen an emerging problem of corporate non-compliance; in some cases, because financial criteria and standards have not kept pace with the business environment or have created unexpected results (such as the use of "off balance sheet" financing and stock options). Situations have occurred that relate more to the sets of values and principles that underpin an organization's activities: the ineffectiveness of Boards to control management; Boards that take a passive role in setting performance criteria; or management taking actions to improve financial performance with unacceptable consequences such as the use of child labour.

Together, these issues tend to indicate that Boards today no longer have the measures or the tools to do the job. Inherent accumulated wealth, built up as intangible assets, is being placed in danger by management, either by overt or covert actions which focus on delivery of financial performance without paying due attention to the offsetting economic impacts on the organization as a whole.

2. TRANSPARENCY, ACCOUNTABILITY, AND RISK ASSESSMENT

Boards need to clean up their own act so that there are clear and openly shared expectations between shareholders (or stakeholders in not-for-profit, government agency, or other organizations) and Board members. They also need to have processes in place which allow them to function in an effective oversight mode and to exercise the control that their mandate requires.

The problem rests then with the tools that they are provided to do the job, *e.g.*, if one cannot see where one is going, it remains difficult to drive — even if one has purchased a bright new shiny car with lots of new features attached. Like the Board, one would still be "managing in the dark".

What is needed, to complement the broader perspective of economic capital that has been discussed in this book, is a performance measurement system that complements the breadth of issues for which a Board, as well as senior management, holds accountability. One cannot blame a Board or directors for lack of oversight if the framework for knowledge is not available.

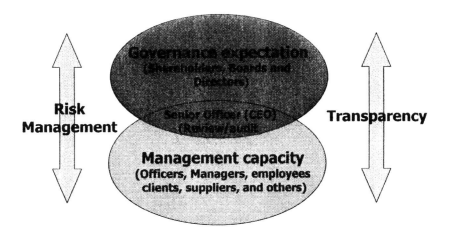

A Board's mandate, as well as management's responsibility for execution, includes four key aspects that any measurement system must address:

- measures to monitor management's accountability for sustaining the ongoing value of the enterprise;
- measures that report upon current business plan performance;
- measures to assess organizational risk management and response; and
- measures to demonstrate externally (perceived) transparency.

The challenge is to develop a system of measures that is consistent with the reality of four key users — *external agencies* (those making external assessments of the organization's performance), *shareholders* (those who actually have an investment and interest in the organization), *Boards* (who need visibility at a higher level of analysis), and *management* (who needs their own portfolio of measures, ranging from high levels that parallel the Board down to detailed operating levels for those who are managing the day-to-day tasks, processes, and actions through which work is done). The types of measures developed, need to be broad enough to meet both the traditional financial requirements, and to complement these with information that adds value but does not give away aspects of competitive advantage. One can portray this challenge in the following way:

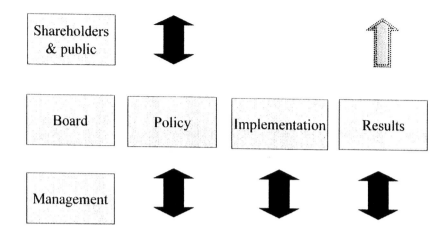

The Board must link both internal and external interests in order to execute the mandate it wants to set policies, implement business plans, and monitor results. The measures that it uses to assess compliance with policies and plans should be driven by those policies and plans; however, the problem is "to what level does an organization want to disclose externally its achievement or lack of achievement with these intentions?" While the goal might be a set of consistent, even the same measures for all users, this is clearly impractical.

There is no option for Boards when reporting against mandated requirements — including the requirement to have such reports assessed according to mandated standards by external and independent bodies. The problem comes when one moves outside the mandatory area and starts to consider disclosure of other information. The "hawks" of the corporate world still consider that meeting the minimum requirements is all that should be done — anything else is a waste of corporate resources. Meanwhile, the (progressive?) "doves" are already listening to the bush telegraph and realizing that the day of secrecy in conducting corporate affairs is fast disappearing. They are beginning to see greater disclosure as a competitive advantage and one that should be judiciously approached.

It is interesting to note that Henry Ford stated, in 1926, "business must run at a profit, else it will die. But when anyone attempts to run a business solely for profit and thinks not at all of the service to the community, then also must the business die, for it no longer has a reason for existence." How does this compare with the statement "a corporation's social responsibility is to make a profit", attributed to Milton Friedman? The fact is that there remains disagreement between the two schools of thought yet, increasingly, organizations are seeing the need to demonstrate greater transparency through broader and more comprehensive reporting.

3. HOW THE NEW ACCOUNTABILITY MODEL PROVIDES A BASE FOR MEASUREMENT

The range of opportunities is wide — from mandatory requirements, including some level of MD&A (management discussion and analysis). Various jurisdictions also have varied levels of supplementary requirements — in particular if one compares the securities reporting requirements of the SEC to the various Canadian standards, and then with other international bodies in Europe and elsewhere. However, leaving this aside as the base for whatever model is adopted, an organization can move forward and start internally by looking for measures, including assessment tools, that can provide visibility into a broader set of performance criteria.

What is critical is to build a basis for measurement that accommodates and uses the many evolving types of assessment and compliance tracking. The chart below illustrates this issue. In many organizations, there is already a proliferation of audits and assessments taking place. These include financial as well as many other operational aspects and should be considered as key first components of enhanced management and Board visibility.

Enhanced reporting and governance accountability can also start with building a framework around the key aspects of the management model and accountability framework that this book has discussed.

This would provide a clear basis going beyond the traditional and mandated requirements, and would complement the work already done by many management groups in moving towards organizational criteria for excellence such as Baldrige, Canada Awards, European Award, and others. *All* these have a specific linkage between the key aspects of "elements" being managed and the measures required in the results category through which feedback is generated.

Using the following table, we can see that, in most situations, there are a variety of possible metrics that can be developed to both assess the current performance of a particular aspect of management as well as to assess the "intangible balance sheet" which would represent the economic value of the intangibles created over time by the organization but not represented as part of traditional reporting.

Areas of performance to be addressed, including tangible and/or intangible elements	Possible categories of metrics						
	Financial	Audit/ assessment	Volume	Speed	Satisfaction/ survey	Quality/ defects	Time-liness
Planning		X		X	X	X	X
Leadership		X			X		
Client focus	X	X	X	X	X	X	X
Process management	X	X	X	X	X	X	X
People/HR management	X	X			X		
Supplier management	X	X		X	X	X	X
Overall results and outcomes	X	X	X	X	X	X	X

4. TYPES OF MEASUREMENT

In addition to the various categories of metrics discussed above, consideration needs to be given to the types of information a measure is to produce. One consistent criticism of the continued focus on financial measures is that it reflects "driving ahead while looking at the rearview mirror." It is important to remember, though, that this was the purpose for which financial reporting was developed — to report the results for a past period of time as well as the status of the shareholders' investment at a particular point in time.

Current thinking of performance measurement continues to evolve in line with the speed with which decisions have to be taken. For years, managers have sought new and better ways of monitoring performance that allows them the ability to take action more quickly. Metrics today have different characteristics that need to be considered when looking at a "best fit" for a broader governance capacity. Alternatives include:

- Is it a measure or an indicator?
- Is the measure financial or non-financial?
- Is it objective versus subjective (is the response definitive or subject to variation and interpretation)?
- Is it a lagging or leading indicator (is this providing past information or information that indicates potential future events)?

In addition, the choice of metrics needs to take into account whether the issue is critical or non-critical and also, assuming an item is a critical measure (*i.e.*, it links directly to the organization's key success factors or current objectives), then is it capable of being decomposed into incomplete measures that, when assembled together, provide a valid metric for overall performance?

5. OBJECTIVE AND SUBJECTIVE MEASURES — DEALING WITH THE SOFT STUFF

Managers, especially accountants, like "hard" measures — the tangibles versus intangibles and, typically, the lagging versus leading types. Producing numbers and reports that are "plus or minus 5%" is not an output that accounting reports are expected to deliver, yet this is the reality of some of the areas where accountability metrics to support improved governance will, in fact, reside. In addition, performance will be most important over time rather than at any particular point in time.

Of more concern are the challenges related to assessing "judgment" criteria where results are likely to be subjective. This is particularly true when dealing with survey data used for performance in areas such as leadership, people performance, suppliers, and customers. The fact that this data is open to greater interpretation before it can be considered "actionable" information should not be allowed to take away from the importance of collecting it; it should lead users to a) choose the questions carefully and after consultation with those being surveyed, and b) validate data received through a review and feedback session where responses are analyzed and interpreted by groups of those responding to the survey, based on results obtained. Many of these sources of information should be considered as indicators rather than absolute results.

An example of how such indicators might provide leading information is a client survey that focuses on the organization's performance on key "satisfiers" that are directly linked to a customer's buying decision which might indicate a reduction in economic equity through a depletion of client goodwill, and may also be a source of predicting future reductions in revenue. In fact, studies have been done, for example in the footwear industry where levels of current satisfaction have been linked to repurchase decisions, that can then be used to assess the inherent intangible value of the customer base in terms of anticipated future revenues and margins. Reductions in satisfaction can be calculated specifically to arrive at a reduction in future profitability.

6. SERVICE STANDARDS — INTERNALLY AND EXTERNALLY

One aspect of performance measurement that must be incorporated in a broad-based system, especially as it relates to process effectiveness, is the aspect of service standards (often referred to as SLAs or service level agreements).

Organizations who create products and services do so through a series of interlocking and interdependent processes; however, at some point, an "end of process" will deliver a final outcome specific to a client's expectations. The key to effective process design is building processes around clearly defined performance criteria. Starting at this end point, and then using this to build back through the supporting internal processes, a series of measurable performance criteria can be established that determine measurable standards against which the actual results of all supporting processes (including the requirements that are fulfilled by third parties) can be assessed. SLAs are the outcome of such an activity, and they form the specifications against which managers, supervisors, and process owners can be monitored.

Effective process management will be demonstrated by SLAs being met or exceeded so that an organization is performing at or above standard. An organization that has built effective processes that are "capable" of delivering to specified requirements will have created an intangible asset that has a key value.

For example, FedEx supports its whole branding position through committing to a specific time frame within which packages will be delivered. This requires a capable process that then provides "brand confidence" which, in turn, drives revenues. Tracking of process performance will provide both an early warning indicator of dissatisfied clients as well as the beginning of depletion of the economic value of this intangible asset, combined with predicting potential loss of revenues at some point in the future. In addition, because poor process performance drives up operating costs, it will also start to indicate cost pressures.

Thus, SLAs can play an important role in a measures framework that provides greater transparency into operating conditions and economic value of an organization. Not only are they important for management to "run the business", they should also become part of key Board metrics.

7. INTEGRATING WITH A BALANCED SCORECARD APPROACH

While concerns over governance have been developing over the past twenty years, management and, to some degree Boards have been struggling with how to effectively run their organizations. Several approaches and initiatives have developed, all aimed at providing managers with better tools to manage the day-to-day activities of their organization. These initiatives, some of which have already been discussed, include:

- frameworks and awards for organizational management excellence (Baldrige, *etc.*);
- international standards for quality and environment (ISO 9001/14001);
- standards for global operations in less developed countries (SA8000);
- TQM — total quality management;
- ABM/ABC (activity-based management/activity-based costing);
- ZBB (zero-based budgeting);
- EVA[1]/MVA (economic value added/market value added);
- supply chain management/integrated logistics management;
- ERM/ERP (enterprise resource management/planning);
- IPMS (integrated performance measurement systems);
- BSC (balanced scorecard).

While many of these issues have been addressed within this book as providing a particular part of a new model for governance at both Board and management levels, the last one (the balanced scorecard)[2] provides a key set of concepts that can be utilized to build an integrated approach to performance measurement that accommodates much of the discussion relative to enhanced governance. While it does not try to address the aspects of economic value of the enterprise, it does a good job of creating a framework for a broad-based set of metrics that are required in 21st century organizations to assist them in converting strategy into action and, through that, to delivery of the performance expectations desired.

8. USING SUSTAINABILITY REPORTING MODELS

Parallel to the work in improving governance, extensive activity has been taking place to develop and apply other approaches to corporate reporting. Chapter 4 discussed some examples that organizations are beginning to use to enhance their reporting criteria. The accounting profession, as well as business groups, are beginning to recognize and embrace such

---

1 EVA is a copyright term of Stearn Stewart and Company.
2 R.S. Kaplan & D.P. Norton, *The Balanced Scorecard: Translating Strategy Into Action* (Boston: Harvard Business School Press, 1996).

frameworks as a way of dealing with supplemental reporting information through which greater corporate transparency can be achieved, yet without requiring major changes to the existing mainstream of compliance with statutory standards and legislation.

The three main examples that were discussed include:

- the guidelines developed by the World Business Council on sustainable development;
- the GRI — global reporting initiative; and
- the SIGMA guidelines developed in the United Kingdom with the participation of the Department of Industry and the Association of Chartered Certified Accountants.

The Ford Motor Company can be shown as an example of leading edge application of the GRI framework. In its 2002 "Corporate Citizenship Report", which received a commendation for sustainability reporting at the CERES[3]–ACCA[4] North American Awards for Sustainability Reporting, presented in Toronto in April 2004, Ford provides information on some of the key aspects of "non-financial" information including the following:

Products and customers	– Statistics on product quality, customer satisfaction, loyalty, and new buyers;
Environment	– Fuel consumption and emissions/vehicle; facility emissions total and per vehicle equivalents and energy and water consumption;
Safety	– Workplace and product safety statistics;
Community	– Involvement and giving;
Relationships	– Employee satisfaction and minority purchasing;
Financial health	– Overall returns to shareholder and income levels.

In addition, Ford links its own reporting back to the GRI framework as a basis for representation of progress towards, and compliance with, an internationally developing framework. Organizations whose corporate reporting was "short-listed" for these same awards included:

---

3 See CERES at www.ceres.org.
4 See ACCA at www.accaglobal.com/sustainability.

• AMD: Advanced Micro Devices	• Interface Research Corporation
• Barrick Gold Corporation	• Kinko's, Inc
• Baxter International Inc.	• Royal Bank of Canada
• BC Hydro	• Shell Canada
• Ben & Jerry's Homemade Inc.	• Suncor Energy Inc.
• Dell Inc.	• VanCity Savings Credit Union
• Dofasco Inc.	• Weyerhaeuser Company
• Énergie NB Power	• Wisconsin Energy Corporation
• First Environment, Inc.	• Xerox Corporation
• Ford Motor Company	• YSI Incorporated
• Hydro-Québec	

The SIGMA guidelines developed in the United Kingdom also have a string pedigree of support and corporate users who participated in the "pilot trials" activity in selected areas of the model, as the framework was being developed. These participants included:

• BAA Heathrow	• Jaguar
• Boots Group PLC	• Marks & Spencer
• Bovince	• Northumbrian Water
• Co-operative Bank	• PowerGen
• CIS	• RMC
• Innogy	• Vauxhall Motors
• Land Rover	• Waltham Forest
	• Wessex Water

While this framework is at an earlier stage, its strength is its ability to build on, and integrate with, other frameworks such as management and social accountability standards, as well as accommodating organizational "capital" in both the traditional financial terms as well as the economic areas that have been discussed here.

9. IMPLEMENTING A MEASUREMENT SYSTEM TO IMPROVE ACCOUNTABILITY

No one system will be the correct answer for any organization, but there are enough examples in place that Boards and management can start to build a broader more transparent base with which to set policies and track compliance. Resistance to change will exist especially among those who consider such changes and greater transparency anathema to the world of corporate accountability. Key to success will be building on what work is already taking place within the organization, in the area of broader performance management metrics combined with high level governance criteria, that Boards deem appropriate to support their aims of improved governance and accountability. There are enough leading edge organizations who have started down this path, which should convince others that these changes are more than a passing fad.

10. STRUCTURING AN EFFECTIVE REPORTING FRAMEWORK

Economic value of an enterprise can be defined by using the following criteria that must form part of any reporting framework and of a Board's assessment of management performance and their own accountability:

- tangible financial values based on GAAP (generally accepted accounting principles);
- intangible economic values based on core criteria being:

    - the human dimension — the entrenched value of the organization's "people" assets in terms of both competencies and learning plus motivation;
    - client/customer relationships, including brand values and protection of market position, channels of distribution, agencies, and others;
    - capacity to execute being the organization's process values and quality of process performance criteria;

- societal impact of the organization in areas such as environmental performance as well as contribution to the community within which the organization operates.

In addition, a Board must carry out its own assessment in terms of adding value to the enterprise through assessing their contribution to organizational activity and direction.

Checklist
Example of Measurement Effectiveness Governance

Item	Assessment	Result			Action plan anticipated
		Yes	No	NI	
1	Has the Board established metrics and/or a process to self-assess Board performance?				
2	Has the Board identified and developed approaches to assess and protect intellectual capital?				
3	Has this intellectual capital been linked to the intangible economic value of the organization and to a set of assessment tools?				
4	Does the Board establish business plans and measures for non-financial performance?				
5	Is there a framework for risk management that aligns measurement of risk and business activities?				
6	Is there a framework for performance management that aligns vertically from execution back to organizational objectives for Board review?				
7	Is there alignment between internal and external measures?				
8	Do the key performance measures focus on areas of strategic importance (*e.g.*, both financial and client, process, people, *etc.*)?				
9	Are performance measures in place to support individual areas of outcome accountability?				
10	Is there a mix of objective/ subjective, tangible, and intangible measures for a balanced view?				
11	Do senior management and the Board have lagging and leading indicators?				
12	Have leading indicators been linked with intangible value and/or forecasted outcomes of results?				

Item	Assessment	Result			Action plan anticipated
		Yes	No	NI	
13	Are processes in place to ensure regular discussion of all metrics with employees at all levels?				
14	Has a measurement risks assessment been conducted that assesses visibility of performance deviation or protection using current measures?				
15	Is the system of performance measures embedded and used as a key resource in building a learning organization?				
16	Do measures systems extend to assessing and improving relationships with third parties e.g., suppliers, consultants, temporary staff, contract personnel, etc.?				
17	Are there measures that assess both "what is done" in terms of outcomes, and how it is done in terms of behaviour?				
18	Does the measures framework provide a realistic combination of short, medium, and long-term measures?				
19	Is there a clear identification between the use of indicators versus measures and the use of each?				
20	In areas where trends are important, do key measures reflect consistency in the base of measurement and/or assessment (e.g., client/ employee surveys, etc.)?				

List of Typical "Capacity" and "Performance" Metrics for Measurement Systems

Capacity/Balance Sheet Metrics	Performance/Earnings Metrics
• number of aspects of organizational performance covered by measures; • index of compliance with a global standard of sustainable measurement; • investor/community assessment or survey of governance and accountability (*i.e.*, by independent rating agencies); • value of notional goodwill and percentage covered by intangible value monitors; • number of employees with specific performance measurement criteria assigned.	• number of unplanned performance deviations identified without existing metrics (*i.e.*, "surprises"); • timeliness of availability of measures data; • number of revisions to initially published data; • number of audit observations related to incorrect data presented; • cost avoidance related to action based on predictive indicators; • managers/employees rating of effectiveness of measures systems.

PART 4

GETTING STARTED

Transitioning between the existing approaches and the proposed frame-work will be a complex and sensitive challenge yet one which is starting to be demanded from organizations representing shareholder interests such as pension boards, shareholder rights organizations, and others. Initially, disclosure can be based on existing measures and reporting in other "compliance" areas — such as international management standards, health and safety audits, product compliance testing by regulatory boards and standards associations, and others. In addition, certain other areas may be seen to represent minimal exposure to the organization such as corporate commitments to the community, charitable works, *etc.*

The greater challenge will start when accountability for more sensitive areas is reached. These might include client satisfaction reporting, brand value movements, and employee satisfaction ratings. Decisions might start with developing these as internal metrics for discussion between management and the Board; only at some later date might these be made public.

Any shift of this magnitude brings with it risk to the organization. Disclosure of "good news" carries no penalty while problem areas might tend to be obscured — exactly why a new framework is needed.

14

BRINGING IT TOGETHER — HOW TO MAKE THE EFFECTIVE TRANSITION

Having identified each of the areas of organizational performance that contribute to sustainability, this chapter now moves towards creating a basis for implementation. Challenges exist in any initiative for change from entrenched interests. The new approach must start with a changed vision that extends to include both internal and shareholder accountability to one that deals with societal expectations. The negative short-term impacts of moving to a new paradigm will need to be explored. The accounting profession will need to re-invest itself to deal with the new economy.

1. WHAT WOULD MAKE A GREAT SYSTEM FOR ACCOUNTABILITY?

Expectations for responsible governance will continue to evolve as society develops, but there is no question that the traditional approaches are going to change. Dependence on financial reporting is not going to be adequate in an era when much of the accumulated wealth of an organization and its shareholders and other stakeholders is not financially quantified. Nor can society rely on the accounting profession to "fix these problems" with governance. Accounting is *not* accountability.

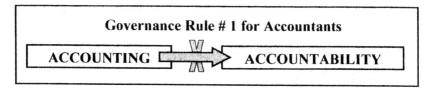

Governance Rule # 1 for Accountants

ACCOUNTING ⟹ ACCOUNTABILITY

Accountability rests on a belief system through which organizations, represented by their Boards and management, believe in the need to act in a different manner and then put in place systems and processes where they can establish policies in areas such as social accountability and economic sustainability, and then hold management accountable for as well as report on the effectiveness with which their enterprise meets these expectations.

A "great" system for accountability then, will be one that combines the best aspects of statutory compliance with a broader set of accountabilities that deal with the organization's behaviour in the way in which it does its work and operates within the society or societies within which it has activities. These, plus a focus on the retention, protection, and enhancement of economic value through the recognition, nurturing, and monitoring of economic value through intellectual capital and related intangible assets, will provide a base from which future generations can assess the corporate world as a member of society.

2. AN ACTION PLAN FOR MOVING TOWARDS SOCIAL COMPLIANCE

Developing such an approach will start with the acceptance that corporate entities can no longer ignore the impact that they have on the society within which they operate. Clearly, this has been an aim and principle of the environmental movement over the year.

Today the desire for change has moved beyond just addressing the societal impact on the natural resources to where sustainability of all other aspects of an organization's resource base is key. In this area, an organization's social value extends to the impact it has on society, through the way in which it manages its economic value.

History shows a number of examples of good and bad behaviour on both economic and social performance. Mining companies and other resource organizations have been faced with working with an asset base that is depleting; however, while environmentalists worry more about the restoration of the natural elements of production, social activists have identified and been concerned with the community aspects. Good corporate citizenship in these organizations has traditionally included aspects such as:

- living conditions of the work force in remote communities ensuring effective sanitation and other services;
- handling the relocation of work forces when the community is no longer viable;
- bringing in secondary businesses and supporting them in order to broaden employment opportunities;
- ensuring a level of local hiring and purchasing takes place to develop economic value within the community — again, growing its core business.

Why did the good organizations do this? Because it was "just good business" and they knew that their reputation in the business community, as well as their welcome in new areas, would reflect their reputation. Even at that time, corporate citizenship extended beyond the minimum necessary, though there were, and remain a few operators who create a bad reputation for business as a whole through acting irresponsibly. The only difference today is that "community" has a broader context. No longer can an organization be concerned just about each remote location in which it operates; business today is an integrated part of the whole social and economic framework. National barriers mean less, brands are global in nature, and reputations move at the speed of light. In approaching a broader framework for accountability, work must start at the Board level.

Organizational oversight and leadership
Representing investors and protecting their interests

Board behaviour	Compliance	Performance
Effective self-management of Board activities	Establishing and monitoring statutory and discretionary policies	Protecting and optimizing the investors' interests

No system of broader accountability will move ahead unless it is backed by policies at the investor and Board level; this group represents the prime oversight and leadership. Governance renewal starts with addressing not just policies on social accountability, but also Board reform and clear alignment of business plans and actions between the Board and management and between financial performance and all other aspects of organizational economic value.

3. CHANGE MANAGEMENT AND THE BARRIERS TO EFFECTIVE DEPLOYMENT

The "mechanics" of deploying a new basis for governance, accountability, and risk management may become the smaller part of the challenge. Change management techniques will need to be used to ensure that such approaches are not just "yet another corporate fad" but do in fact change the way that an organization is managed and controlled on a permanent and sustainable basis.

As far back as the 1970s and into the 1980s, when the North American automotive industry was re-inventing itself to deal with the rapid increase in imports and the need for more fuel-efficient vehicles, the CEO "leading the charge" at Ford was Don Peterson. His book[1] covering those years identified the breadth of behavioural changes that were needed by management to bring about a focus on quality. These included recognizing the value in corporate communications with employees. Initially, the major detractor from change was the financial community who focused on the lost level of overhead recovery when a plant was "down" for communications. The benefit, of course, was not quantifiable in traditional financial terms. Many other aspects had to change: relationships with staff and union; involvement of employees, changed attitudes of managers and specialists; changed measures that include quality levels and defects, cycle times, client satisfaction, and financial value of process improvements; and many more. Unless the attitudes can be changed from top to bottom (*i.e.*, from investors and Boards down through to front line workers (and not just words but actions that demonstrate such commitments to change), then deployment will fail.

The results that people generate are defined by their actions and, traditionally, through "command and control" systems management has often instructed people to act differently on the basis that they will follow the rules and do what they are told. This is a fallacy. Behavioural science tells us that peoples' actions are basically conditioned by their experience and this leads them to generate a set of personal rules and decisions through which they live their life. Unless efforts are made to alter and/or align belief systems with those required to implement the values, principles, and behaviours that an organization desires to live by, then any change will fall short. This need for "behaviour modification" is a long-term commitment that requires unswerving adherence to principles such as open and honest communications with employees, effective leadership skills by all levels of management, and the development of trust. Resolving the lack of trust that now exists between the general public and all corporate entities, both public and private, will not be a short-term fix. It will require changes to the way organizations are controlled and directed, as well as a willingness to change the current accountability to embrace those areas that have become increasingly important to the society within which all operations conduct their day-to-day business.

---

1   D.E. Peterson & J. Hillkirk, *A Better Idea: Redefining the Way America Works* (Boston: Houghton Mifflin & Company, 1991).

4. THE NEED FOR A CHANGED ROLE FOR THE ACCOUNTING PROFESSION

The accounting profession itself is at a watershed; tangible assets, while still important, are gradually diminishing to a smaller percentage of an organization's value, while at the same time intangible assets and the accumulated wealth created by effective management of such intangibles is increasing. While the profession may be able to use goodwill accounting as the catch-all to represent the premium paid when intangibles change hands for a greater than book value, this will not address the governance challenges that Boards and management deal with.

There is and continues to be a role for compliance accounting. This will continue to be a challenging and developing field as organizations and the profession continue to globalize. However, in this area of the profession value needs to be generated by looking at incorporating approaches such as comprehensive auditing and at ways to help the profession better connect.

The area that must develop and become more mainstream is the role of management accounting. For a long time viewed as a supporting analytical tool, this area has already started to look at and develop tools to better handle economic value through approaches to partnering with suppliers, implementing ABC and process-based management, and addressing intellectual capital. This type of approach and information can start to focus management on a broader based set of metrics, managed by those with analytical skills, as well as starting to build a base of non-compliance but support-based information for Boards and investors.

One challenge that the profession will need to address, both in the way that members handle these changes as well as the public's perception of accounting being responsible for accountability, is through education of the public. This is a major undertaking as the need for better governance moves forward. Investors need to be better educated to start asking the right questions. Boards need to be better educated to understand the implications of non-financial organizational worth and the linkage between this and the accountability of management performance. Managers and employees need to be better educated about how organizations are, in fact, an integrated "whole" of different economic aspects that need to be managed as a system not as individual components.

If the profession wants to have a role in governance for the 21st century, it will need to be seen to play an active role in these challenges; however, even within the profession itself, the focus and desire for absolute or near absolute accuracy will need to change to recognize that economic value has a degree of uncertainty associated with it; however, having some idea of what economic value is and whether it is increasing or decreasing with a plus or minus level of accuracy is surely better than ignoring the aspects completely?

One accounting organization that seems to be engaged in both the dialogue for change as well as in new approaches is the ACCA (Association of Chartered Certified Accountants) based in the United Kingdom. Although the organization's base, and significant membership is in the United Kingdom, the organization has for several years had in place a world council with representatives from many of the 160 countries in which the organization has members. This move recognizes and embraces the fact that accounting is a global profession and changes are taking place, including adoption of international standards that will make the Association a truly representative body where skills sets are becoming more global in nature. However, the organization is actively involved in moving beyond traditional accounting issues to become involved in activities such as the development of the broad-based SIGMA model for corporate governance reporting that has been discussed earlier.

5. PROBLEMS WITH TRANSPARENCY AND ACCOUNTABILITY

A key decision that organizations will need to make is the perceived competitive advantage or disadvantage that such moves to greater transparency and accountability will bring. With more and more shareholder representation organizations advising corporate investors on the conduct of various large publicly traded organizations, there is no question that providing added demonstrated leading edge accountability can be seen as a good thing. The challenge will be to move at the right speed to allow learning to occur while at the same time staying ahead of the average organizations, and putting in place frameworks that can enhance the value of the overall governance systems to increase awareness and improve decision making.

15

INTEGRATING RISK MANAGEMENT

The new economy will see the increased integration of new models for corporate governance and frameworks for risk management. Boards will need to ensure that models for addressing risks take into account all aspects of the system's economic wealth and the potential dilution of that value. This will be achieved through the development of risk management frameworks where the elements of risk assessed align and integrate with the framework for governance. Risks assessments can then be conducted using checklists to assess gaps and set actions. While Sarbanes-Oxley addresses some aspects of this approach, the use of the COSO model needs to be extended from just process to behavioural aspects both internally and externally.

1. INTERDEPENDENCY AND INTEGRATION

Risk management was identified as one of the early issues in the warning signs for governance renewal. In addition, management of risk is a common thread that weaves its way all through every aspect of an organization's decision-making and activities. Therefore, when Boards make decisions as to the deployment of a broader range of accountability, they will need to consider as an integrated issue what the risk aspects of such an area are going to be. In order to effectively deploy risk management, there must be three core aspects:

1. establishing policies that identify the organization's intent on risk management, including key areas of acceptable risk and tolerance;
2. conversion of risk policies into operating practices and procedures through which the key tools for risk management are actually put in place; and
3. an assessment capability that reviews on a regular basis both the compliance of the systems with the processes put in place to manage risk as well as to assess whether risk exposure has changed in any way.

Using this approach, effective risk management can and must be built around and integrated fully with an organization's governance framework.

2. ALIGNING RISK AND GOVERNANCE MODELS

Risk exists across every aspect of an organization's activity. The proposed model for effective governance also spans all aspects of an organization's activity, therefore the two can be fully aligned. Key areas of risk management attention will therefore include:

- board level risk management related to effective governance of the enterprise — this would include all aspects of stakeholder recognition, as well as Board constitution, operations, clarity of direction and leadership along with comprehensiveness of vision, mission, values, and policies that ensure clarity of both direction and behaviour (*i.e.*, aspects of risk management that deal with "intent" of the organization that must also include mandatory — legal — compliance as well as discretionary areas);

- management level risk management related to conversion of policies into execution including the effective protection of an organization's tangible and intangible assets, adherence to both results-based and behavioural expectations, and the effectiveness of reporting and accountability that provides transparency back to the Board.

Both levels of risk management need to build upon a framework that ensures a comprehensive approach. Board models must be built around effective legal compliance as well as incorporating best practices such as those outlined by shareholder activists as well as by progressive regulators. Management risk as well as the linkage between management and the Board (*i.e.*, conversion of policy to execution through effective planning and leadership) can be addressed through building a framework including assessment checklists that use the same management model as that used for planning and execution.

3. USING THE MANAGEMENT MODEL TO ADDRESS RISK

The management model discussed as a basis for assessing the areas of "economic value" also forms the basis for risk assessment as risk exists in all aspects of what management "does" to execute a business plan — converting "intent" to action and results. Thus, risk assessment needs to look at the areas of planning, leadership, client relationships and input, employee relationships and involvement, supplier input and involvement, process management (including quality), performance reporting systems (that identify and feedback results against intent), and the organization's ability to "act" upon such information to continually learn and improve what is being carried out.

This approach forms the basis of creating a self-assessment program which, combined with Board level risk assessment, should provide a comprehensive benchmark against which risk management policies can be formulated and scarce resources assigned and/or re-assigned to areas of critical importance based on the probability and risk to the overall organization (rather than leaving such decisions either un-addressed or dealt with on a departmental and individual basis).

4. MOVING AHEAD TO ALIGN RISK ASSESSMENT AND ACTION

The steps in integrating an enterprise-wide risk management approach include the following steps:

Step/Phase	Purpose
1. Development of a comprehensive framework for risk management	Need to establish a basis against which policy can be formulated and accountabilities defined. The governance and management models provide this as an approach.
2. Develop an enterprise risk assessment approach	Carries out an initial audit of risks across all aspects of the frameworks in order to identify all the types of risk that could occur.
3. Carry out and "score" the enterprise assessment	Creates a numeric evaluation of levels of risk both in occurrence, impact, and probability of detection given current controls
4. Tabulate and review results with the Board	Provides Board insight on risk areas as well as creates a base to establish a corporate policy on risk management.
5. Review results of assessment against policies and identify high risk/gap areas	Creates a strategic approach to deploying corporate resources for most effective protection against risk
6. Create and resource risk management improvement plan that addresses key areas and aspects	Ensures that limited corporate resources are deployed where greatest risk exists. A key issue here is the shift of accountability for risk management from a management silo-based approach to a corporate driven organizational approach
7. Re-assess and monitor through audits and evaluations changes and improvements in risk management activity	Ensures a continual improvement loop is put in place so that as business changes so do responses to risk management.

Such an approach would take into account all areas of governance including addressing aspects such as:

- Board relationships with shareholders and wider stakeholders;
- Board relationship and sustainability in itself and effectiveness of value provided to the organization;
- Board's compliance with all statutory requirements of legislation;
- Board's consideration, setting of policy and accountability for all aspects of corporate activity (intellectual capital aspects, accumulated economic, and financial values);
- Board's ability to monitor compliance with all aspects of accountability through feedback audits and complementary reporting;
- management's capacity to manage and sustain all aspects of the operation contained in the economic model;
- management's ability to identify and control core behavioural aspects of economic elements of the management model consistent with stated values and policies;
- Board's ability to align its visibility of management activity through effective and comprehensive reporting;
- management's ability to sustain and protect the accumulated economic value of the enterprise that is in place and entrusted as the factors of production within the economic model.

Many organizations have created policy statements in all sorts of areas including risk management; however, in many cases their ability to deploy such policy into actual operating activities, such as incorporating effective risk management techniques to the development and deployment of effective work process design, development, training, monitoring, and control, is not yet well developed.

5. CONVERTING ASSESSMENT TO ACTION

Once an assessment has been completed, levels of risk may be assigned numeric values through which priorities can be set (see calculation sheets in the Appendix). These criteria will address such issues as probability of occurrence, nature of impact, as well as relevance to the tolerance of risk established by the Board consistent with the values and other policies that may have been established.

Once all risks have been identified and areas of exposure evaluated, an action plan can be set in place that will start to reduce the risk profile of the organization; this will include steps to eliminate the risk (changing processes, changing business focus, *etc.*); minimize the risk (taking actions to increase internal controls), and finally, where required, seeking sharing of the risk either internally (through group self-insurance) or by paying a third party, such as an insurance company, a premium through which the impact of risks that are considered critical are shared.

6. *SARBANES-OXLEY* AND RISK MANAGEMENT

An example of how this approach to integration has already started is the inclusion of the COSO criteria initially developed by the Treadway Commission as a process to provide integrity in ensuring that directors and management have in place an effective system of internal controls. Auditing Standard #2 of the Public Company Accounting Oversight Board identifies the mandatory application of the COSO framework as the model against which this capacity should be assessed and reported.

This framework identified as the basis of auditing both management responsibility and management evaluation of internal controls looks at the five components of internal control being:

- the Control Environment (see following extract of what the definition covers as outlined by the Appendix of the initial report of the Treadway Commission);
- conducting a Risk Assessment against this framework (similar to the approach outlined in this chapter);
- establishing Control Activities (*i.e.*, based on risk assessment, determining which areas are most critical);
- establishing information and communications (*i.e.*, the need to support the controls that are put in place with an information infrastructure that affects management's ability to know what is happening);
- monitoring — being the ongoing capacity (required by effective governance and accountability) to continually monitor and assess the capacity of the controls to identify and allow transparency into what activity is actually occurring.

Each of these areas is then addressed in terms of operational activity, financial reporting, and compliance requirements at each of the levels of activity within the organization.

The company's control environment is the corporate atmosphere in which the accounting controls exist and the financial statements are prepared. A strong control environment reflects management's consciousness of and commitment to an effective system of internal control. While a strong control environment does not guarantee the absence of fraudulent financial reporting, it reduces the chance that management will override internal accounting controls. On the other hand, a weak control environment undermines the effectiveness of a company's internal accounting controls and may reflect a predisposition toward misrepresentations in the financial statements.

(continued)

> A company's control environment consists of its organizational philosophy and operating style, organizational structure, methods of communicating and enforcing the assignment of authority and responsibility, organizational control methods, and personnel management methods. (This description of the control environment is based in large part on the discussion in the Auditing Standards Board's proposed Statement on Auditing Standards on Control Risk.)
>
> A company's organizational philosophy and operating style encompass a broad range of characteristics, such as (1) management's and the board of directors' attitudes and actions toward financial reporting, ethics, and business risks, (2) management's emphasis on meeting budget, profit, or other financial or operating goals, (3) management's preference for centralized or decentralized administration and operations, and (4) the extent to which one or a few individuals dominate management. A company's philosophy and operating style are often the most important parts of the control environment.
>
> An effective organizational structure gives the company an overall framework for planning, directing, and controlling its operations. It considers such matters as (1) the form, nature, and reporting relationships of an entity's organizational units and management positions, and (2) the assignment of authority and responsibility to these units and positions and the constraints established over their functioning. A key part of an effective organizational structure is a vigilant, informed, and effective audit committee.
>
> Effective methods of communicating and enforcing the assignment of authority and responsibility clarify the understanding of, and improve compliance with, the organization's policies and objectives. These methods consider such matters as: (1) the delegation of authority and responsibility for matters such as organizational goals and objectives, operating functions, and regulatory requirements, (2) the policies regarding acceptable business practices and conflicts of interest, and (3) employee job descriptions delineating specific duties, responsibilities, and constraints. A key method of communicating employee responsibility is through a written code of corporate conduct.
>
> *As identified in the Treadway Commission Report and Recommendations 1987*

While this approach deals with many of the aspects of an integrated and holistic framework, it fails to address the behavioural issues other than through the initial assessment of the "Control Environment". What is needed

— and partly addressed through the *Sarbanes-Oxley* requirements for the CEO and CFO to certify on ethics within their organization as well as a "true and fair representation of the organization's activities" — is a broad enough based accountability process that includes the intangible elements entrusted to management that have been discussed in this book. Interpretation of the application of COSO, when applied by those in the auditing profession, will potentially continue to focus on tangibles.

One associate, in a senior position with a leading blue chip U.S. public company, made the comment that the more the organization looked at the requirements to meet *Sarbanes-Oxley* reporting requirements, the more they realized that efforts to put in place effective process and quality management (such as ISO 9001) as well as environmental management (ISO 14001) and adoption of management best practices (such as NQI or Baldrige), the more they realized that these were all components that had already created an effective accountability and control environment. This, in essence, confirms the overall approach that this book proposes!

16

IMPROVING GOVERNANCE — MOVING FROM ASSESSMENT TO ACTION

In this chapter we identify how an organization should start to move ahead with the transition from historical approaches to governance and accountability towards the type of frameworks and model covered in this book. Starting with building the Board's understanding and capacity, the approach then moves to building an integrated model for accountability and governance which provides the framework for developing critical areas of sustainability measurements as well as serving as a basis for conducting a risk assessment to determine areas of control and, through this, critical reporting. Existing models such as "modern comptrollership" and "frameworks for accountability", published by government, can form the basis for the public sector while models for excellence and reporting frameworks such as GRI and SIGMA can form the basis for the private sector. This can then be used as the basis to start moving forward by identifying gaps between the current and desired positions.

1. WHERE TO START FOR BUILDING A PLAN OF GOOD GOVERNANCE

As in any journey, the first few steps are critical. Leadership in the creation of a new good governance model must start from the top of the organization. This must then be supported by, and complemented through, the creation of a good governance capacity within the operational area of the organization.

(a) Step # 1 — Start With the Board

The first step must be taken by the Board through carrying out a strengths and "areas for improvement" assessment against a best practice. Suggested approaches for this would include using an example developed in one of the texts identified in this paper.[1] Non-profit organizations can use similar tools as can other public sector organizations. A particular source

---

1   D. Leighton & D. Thain, *Making Boards Work* (McGraw-Hill Ryerson, 1997), specifically using Chapter 8 onwards, in particular the key success factors for an effective Board on p. 142 and the explanation that follows.

of current thinking for the public sector is available through the CCAF-FCVI.[2] In addition, other sources exist from which a Board can create its own customized assessment framework against which it can build a strategy for improvement.[3]

The Board should work with an external facilitator who would craft the vision that the Board wishes to create to effect good governance. This would incorporate the selected best practices as a goal and a current position statement would then be created against which an improvement action plan would be created. This will then form the basis against which the Board tracks and monitors its own improvement and, in fact, can report to key stakeholders against improvement actions underway. The CEO, as a critical member of this Board, would participate in the discussions with a particular focus on how the desires of the governing body will need to be reflected in his conversion accountability between high level Board aspirations and activity that is to take place operationally within the organization.

Additional recommendations that Boards should consider would include the use of international/best practice standards, and the approach to be used to performance management and monitoring (*i.e.*, bringing Board reporting in line with an aligned and holistic approach such as the balanced scorecard). Consideration must also include close attention to the way in which the Boards structure committees to ensure an independent view of third party reporting such as the audit; in particular, the selection of auditors with no, or very limited exposure to internal affairs of the organization should be selected, and consideration should be given by the Board to move the budgeting for and payment of audit fees as a Board-managed expense rather than one that forms part of management's cost base. (The purpose being to head off situations where the independence and thoroughness of the audit as a key third party assessment is impaired by the desire that the audit should add value to management — this is NOT the primary purpose of the audit). Finally, the Board should also consider strategically how it will approach the planning and monitoring of aspects of wealth creation that are currently not seen until they show up as a declining financial performance.

---

2 www.ccaf-fcvi.com — was the Canadian Comprehensive Auditing Foundation. Those interested can pay a small sum and have complete access to proceedings, papers, and reports that identify many best practice areas.

3 Such as OECD guidelines at www.oecd.org (OECD Principles for Corporate Governance); the CICA/TSE study www.jointcomgov.com; the Commonwealth Association for Corporate Governance — Final Version December 1999 available at www.cacg-inc.com, and many other targeted practices available through websites internationally.

(b) Step # 2 — Create an Integrated Model for Governance

First comes the high level model that identifies "intent" and "execution" accountabilities and sets the framework for the Board's linkage internally and externally.

Supporting this will be the management model that determines the economic aspects of the organization's resources.

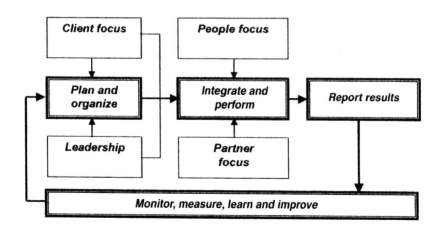

These two models provide context for an overall governance framework. The first model provides a high level linkage map that forms the basis for understanding the flow of accountability. The second model serves to identify the core "content" components that will need to be present to ensure accountability for both day-to-day operations as well as protection of economic value and management of risk.

Management's capacity to deliver

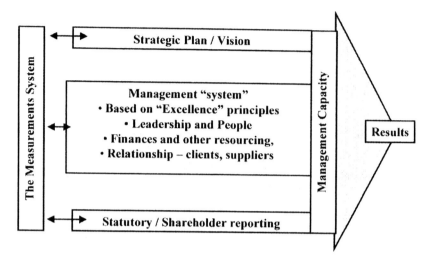

Underpinning both models is the framework for the capacity of the management system to a) clearly understand policies, b) understand plans and expectations (including *all* aspects of organizational performance), c) ensure that there is a deployment model for all aspects, d) establish a framework for internal results management and performance reporting to ensure that management is exercising control over all aspects; and e) ensure alignment between management reporting and accountability and the framework for transmitting such information back up to the Board to ensure transparency and accountability.

Once the Board has set direction, management must ensure that there is a holistic framework within which it can plan, deploy, and manage all of the key factors of capacity to deliver on its contractual commitments to the stakeholders, through the direction of the Board.

Some organizations in the private sector have been carrying out this work in the past through adoption of management models for excellence; these can form a good base for a broad approach, but the danger is that they can be driven as an event to gain an award and recognition rather than by the need to establish a new management framework upon which all of the aspects of planning, performing, monitoring, and reporting are built. This approach does provide a good start, but the good governance "context' is critical as in several cases organizations still see these models as "quality award models" and as a result they are relegated to just addressing process quality issues. In fact, all of them are enterprise-wide models that can form a key part of how any organization creates a framework through which it carries out all of its work and structures its reporting (see figure, below).

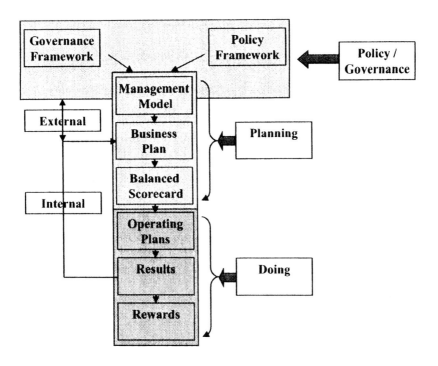

In this example, we can see that both policy, and other aspects of the governance framework and direction setting, drive into the organization's capacity to execute through the "management model" filter — *i.e.*, the way in which all of the governance expectations are deployed — is through the comprehensive approach that incorporates each of the various aspects of operational activity. From this, *all* of planning, reporting, and work execution flows.

The public sector also has several examples of integrated and holistic frameworks for managing operational activity — from policy interpretation and development through to service delivery. Good examples are the Ontario government's "cornerstones" model that most ministries either have, or are in the process of adopting, and the modern comptrollership activity in the federal government, driven through the Treasury Board, as well as provincial efforts in areas such as British Columbia and Ontario. However, one of the potential shortfalls of these approaches is that they are implemented in a way that adds to, rather than updates and replaces current practices.

In order to start down this path, first the management team should adopt a framework that is consistent with the organizational reality of today; moving as far as organizations like Skandia, discussed earlier, may be a little ambitious, but putting in place a common management context upon which *all* work initiatives and improvements are based and linked is a powerful context through which to explain to the people within the organization how all the changes do, in fact, fit together and contribute towards an eventual goal.

Once a model is adopted, a series of "best practice" statements can be developed, based on international research, that depict what levels of demonstrated performance can exist from a minimum compliance standard level to a "world class level". Examples of this could be from the original Treasury Board examples used in the capacity checklist for modern comptrollership as follows:

| 1.4 Linkage to strategic planning | Business plans are developed independently of strategic plan. Little or no effort is made to reconcile the two. | Strategic and business plans are prepared by independent groups. Some effort is nevertheless made to ensure consistency between business plans and strategic plan. Anomalies are raised with senior organizational heads (e.g., Sector/ Regional ADMs). | Strategic priorities are stated and ranked in business plans. Business plan objectives are linked to strategic priorities. Organizational strategies are reflected in operational/ work plans. Results achieved in business plan are monitored against strategic priorities. | Resources and performance targets in business plan reflect strategic priorities and key success factors. Assumptions are periodically challenged to ensure continued relevance. Results achieved are monitored on a trend basis against strategic priorities, and resources modified accordingly. | Program outcomes are reported regularly against both strategic and business plans on a trend basis. Perceived to be single highly integrated plan and process. |

The example shows the five levels of possible linkage between the strategic plan and the business plans used for execution. In addition, examples can be taken from the various assessment checklists that are used in evaluating organizations against the various models for excellence. An example from the Canadian National Award for Excellence follows as an extract from how client satisfaction (within the "clients" element of the model) may be assessed:

- Does the organization have a method in place to measure customer perception of our organization, our services and/or our products? Do we analyze reasons for these perceptions?
- Can we quickly adapt to changing customer expectations at our customer service areas?
- Are customer evaluations used in the development of our improvement strategies?
- What kind of measurement and dialogue do we have between the various functional areas of the organization to ensure that we consistently meet customer needs?

Establishing a set of evaluation criteria against which the organization can set its improvement goals and objectives creates both a base for action as well as one against which to report improvement progress.

In order to make such a framework for good governance effective, several other features must be in place:

- The performance management and measurement systems must be fully integrated with the model (*i.e.*, measures linked to all aspects of the framework, and integrated throughout the organization right down, and into individual performance agreements.
- Planning and reporting of results upward and downward throughout the organization must be based on this consistent measurement approach.
- A significant level of education, training and development will be required to bring all participants to a common understanding of the direction to be taken.
- Surveys of employees, clients, and others must not only be linked to key strategic aspects of the organization's activity but responses must be capable of being linked to a process or processes that can be changed to modify the current response (*i.e.*, to effect change).
- A clear framework for accountability and responsibility *must* be defined as a part of the planning and organizing aspects.

Such an approach is capable of creating a major strategic shift in an organization's performance as well as making good governance an integrated approach between those responsible for guiding the organization as well as those taking the actions that generate the results.

(c) Step # 3 — Find Out Where You Stand Today

Once we have created an improved framework for Board governance as well as management governance, the next step is to carry out a self-assessment in order to determine the areas of current risk as well as to set priorities as to what areas must be addressed.

In the case of the governing "board", we have already discussed many of the possible sources of existing checklists; what is important is to ensure that the criteria for good Board governance have been created and from this a checklist can then be developed. This can be reviewed with the Board and then a plan put in place. As an example, we can choose the organizational "values" element of good governance, within which we could develop a checklist that included questions such as:

#	Item assessed	Assessment				Comments/Actions
		A	NI	NA	NR	
1	Does the organization have a statement of values upon which it is founded?					
1.1	Does the values statement reflect the history upon which the organization is founded?					
1.2	Is the statement still relevant to today's organization?					
1.3	Are the stated values consistent with the organization's mission and direction?					
1.4	Are the values consistent with the social/societal commitments of the Board?					
1.5	Does the Board have a feedback mechanism in place to assess whether the values are being applied in practice?					
1.6	Does the Board ensure that deployment of values is a continual part of the business plan?					
1.7	Does the CEO represent these values and provide ongoing leadership in their deployment?					

Note that in the examples given, the assessment values can be A (Acceptable), NI (Needs Improvement), NA (Not Acceptable), or NR (Not Required). Once the assessment is completed, the action plan can then be developed. "Values" is a relevant example as this is typically an area where "what is said" and "what is demonstrated" on a day-to-day basis are often not consistent, causing both a governance risk as well as a credibility risk.

In the case of the deployment part of governance, the model for assessment is similar to that discussed above. Again we can create an example, although in this area the assessment checklists that already exist in many "models for management excellence" have already started to create the basis for an internal assessment document. In this case, we can review "leadership" as a category, as both the CEOs themselves as well as the Board should have an interest in how this key element is being deployed.

#	Item assessed	Assessment				Comments/Actions
		A	NI	NA	NR	
1.	Has the Board defined the leadership traits and behaviours that it expects from the CEO?					
1.1	Is there an assessment process through which this is evaluated?					
1.2	Is there a process in place through which the leadership traits of the CEO are then deployed through all levels of the organization, especially management and supervision?					
1.3	Is there a process through which the required behaviours for leadership are part of the personnel evaluation and selection process?					
1.4	Is leadership training part of the ongoing HR development framework?					
1.5	Is there consistency between the values and ethics of the organization and leadership?					
1.6	Does the CEO clearly demonstrate effective leadership communications through deployment of the business plan expectations?					

For more information, see the table of the Canadian NQI "leadership" checklist in the Appendixes. Note that this focuses on *quality* as the assessable element of leadership, but equally the approach can be amended and improved to align with the Board level criteria as well as holistic issues relative to the practice of leadership within the organization.

The results of a complete organizational assessment start with our top level "Board" governance assessment through to the elements of organizational deployment *including* results. Measurements and continual learning can now be used not only to develop an improvement action plan but to ensure that the relevant risks to the organization by having, or not having, certain key areas fully covered, may be determined and priorities set. In this way, enterprise risk management becomes a wholly integrated part of the governance framework, and is fully linked to the practice of management.

2. BUILDING IN CONTINUAL IMPROVEMENT

(a) Making the Organization a Truly Learning Enterprise

The final stage of this whole process is to ensure that the organization not only has a "no surprises" framework for good governance, but that it is also able to use this to move forward to ensure continuity as well as competitiveness. Many aspects of an organization's activity are continually changing and these must be incorporated into the assessment of good governance practice. There are three key ways that this needs to be maintained.

(b) The Measures Framework

First, as discussed earlier, the measurement needs of today's organization must grow beyond the heavy bias towards financial indicators. While financial performance remains key to survival, it is more of an outcome of effectiveness in all of the other areas that include:

- how well the strategy reflects and links with reality;
- how well relationships are managed with clients, suppliers, and employees;
- how well the leadership skills of those managing the relationships are developed;
- how well the other intangible assets are being used and leveraged — such as brands, market channels, patents, trademarks, business processes, and others.

If an enterprise is not "balancing" its financial measures with indicators that link to these elements that enable the financial results, then the likely outcome is a reactive response to past problems showing up late in the day, through the financial results.

In order to be effective and promote continual development and learning, the measures framework must be based on the governance framework. This means that measures must be linked — for example — to all of the elements of the new management model — leadership, processes, employees, and others. But more than this, the types of measures *must* be developed in a way that provides clear linkage between cause and effect. As an example, in cases where surveys are used for relationship assessment, it is no good asking a number of subjective questions that provide feedback, if this feedback cannot be linked to something that management is able to act on and change in order to alter the current score from the measure.

(c) Continual Assessment Against the Evaluation Checklists

Second, in order to ensure continual good governance, the audit process must extend fully beyond compliance with financial/accounting standards to include all other areas where good governance is required. In order to do this, there are both some professional practice changes that need to be made in the use and application of standards (that are beyond this discussion) but there are also some practices that can be put in place immediately.[4]

Organizations that develop their governance frameworks in line with the discussions in this paper will have a base for the development of an assessment tool. This tool that encompasses both Board level governance as well as management issues should be used on a regular basis to check progress against improvement goals as well as the currency of the infrastructure that has been put in place. An example of the need for this is the evolving global trend and interest in sustainable development, through which the whole framework within which enterprises operate, is being reviewed and evolving to a new level. Scores and results from the checklists can also be used as an input into the framework for balanced measures discussed above.

(d) The Ability to Create True Learning

The third key to moving forward is to create a "learning organization". While much is talked about in the creation of a learning organization, few in fact achieve the goal. Creating such an organization is not a technology issue, although this is a key part of the toolbox; it is, in fact, rooted in the cultural and behavioural norms of the organization. Learning in a human sense comes from experiencing; if the culture of the organization is risk averse and/or discourages the taking of risks and making of mistakes, then learning will creep forward at a slow rate. We have seen this in the past, in the public sector as the organizations were built to be risk averse to ensure "no surprises" — especially for politicians. The result used to be that experience came very slowly through gradual and controlled progression through the ranks.

This is not to say unfettered risk-taking is also wise! What is needed is balance. The types of tools that organizations must be encouraged to learn and develop include areas such as:

---

4 It can be suggested that the public sector is probably more advanced in this area than the private sector, through the development of comprehensive audit and the use of tools such as program evaluations.

- inclusive reviews of audits and assessments;
- commitment to education, training, and broad-based development including cross-training on a broad basis;
- post-mortem discussion on past experiences, be they projects, process improvements, use of new tools, launch of new products, and others;
- feedback mechanisms that allow learnings from such post-mortems to feed back into structured process improvements for the future;
- involvement of "partners" in post-mortems including suppliers, contractors, temporary staff, and consultants;
- investments in knowledge tools (not just coffee machines, water fountains, and areas to "chat") but also broad-based approaches;[5]
- creation of a management culture that encourages people to communicate with one another and share experiences.

Technology is a key tool and can be used in repositories of information as well as enabling people from distant parts of the globe to work together (evidenced already by many of the technology and consultancy companies who operate this way).

However, in addition to technology, people management approaches will be key. Learning must be supported and encouraged through the type of management culture that is used (participative, team based supportive, inclusive) as well as the reward and recognition systems that are in place. Organization cannot improve — only people can. With new ideas and the ability to share them and use them, innovation and creativity will be realized. A good governance framework, that links all of this to acceptable values will ensure that the balance between creativity and control remain a cornerstone of an organization that weathers the storms of change effectively yet maintains its integrity.

---

5 A good example of this is the integrated approach to organizational knowledge tools that are becoming available based on "intuitive" search where materials such as policies, procedures, training manuals, instruction books, project reports, project team post-mortems and *all* other sources of data can be searched in order to find "knowledge".

PART 5

APPENDIXES

Appendix A

Further Readings on Intellectual Capital

Becker, B.E., et al., *The HR Scorecard: Linking People, Strategy, and Performance* (President and Fellows of Harvard College, 2001).

Blair, M.M., *Ownership and Control: Rethinking Corporate Governance for the Twenty-First Century* (Brookings Institution Press, 1995).

Brooking, A., *Corporate Memory: Strategies for Knowledge Management* (Thomson Business Press, 1999).

Brooking, A., *Intellectual Capital: Core Asset for the Third Millennium Enterprise* (Thomson Business Press, 1996).

Davenport, T.H. & L. Prusak, *Working Knowledge: How Organizations Manage What They Know* (Harvard Business School Press, 1998).

Davidson, M., *The Transformation of Management* (Butterworth-Heinemann, 1996).

Drucker, P., *Post-Capitalist Society* (HarperBusiness, 1993).

Edvinsson, L. & M.S. Malone, *Intellectual Capital: Realizing Your Company's True Value by Finding the Hidden Brainpower* (HarperCollins Publishers, Inc., 1997).

Ehin, C., *Unleashing Intellectual Capital* (Butterworth-Heinemann, 2000).

Fitz-Enz, J., *The ROI of Human Capital: Measuring the Economic Value of Employee Performance* (Amacom, 2000).

Freidman, B., et al., *Delivering on the Promise: How to Attract, Manage and Retain Human Capital* (The Free Press, 1998).

Fusaro, P.C. & R.M. Miller, *What Went Wrong at Enron: Everyone's Guide to the Largest Bankruptcy in U.S. History* (John Wiley & Sons, Inc., 2002).

Harvard Business Review on Corporate Governance, published articles from 1992-20002 (Harvard Business Press, 2000).

Harvard Business Review on Knowledge Management (Harvard Business Review Series) (President and Fellows of Harvard College, 1999).

Harvey, E.B. & J. Blakely, *Re-thinking HR Management: strategies for success in an era of change* (Toronto: CCH Canadian, 1999).

Homer-Dixon, T., *The Ingenuity Gap: Facing the Economic, Environmental, and Other Challenges of an Increasingly Complex and Unpredictable World* (Vantage Canada, 2001).

Jaques, E. & K. Carson, *Human Capability: A Study of Individual Potential and Its Application* (Cason Hall & Co. Publishers, 1994).

Klein, D.A., *The Strategic Management of Intellectual Capital* (Butterworth-Heinemann, 1998).

Nevitte, N., ed., *Value Change and Governance in Canada* (University of Toronto Press, 2002).

Nofsinger, J. & K. Kim, *Infectious Greed: Restoring Confidence in America's Companies* (Financial Times, Prentice Hall, 2003).

Stewart, T.A., *Intellectual Capital: The New Wealth of Organizations* (Currency/ Doubleday, 1997).

Sullivan, P.H., *Value Driven Intellectual Capital: How to Convert Intangible Corporate Assets Into Market Value* (John Wiley & Sons, Inc., 2000).

Sveiby, K.E., *The New Organizational Wealth: Managing & Measuring Knowledge-Based Assets* (Berrett-Koehler Publishers, Inc., 1997).

Weiss, D.S., *High Performance HR: Leveraging Human Resources for Competitive Advantage* (John Wiley & Sons Canada Ltd., 2000).

Appendix B

Monthly Key Performance Measures Report

(i) Summary Report

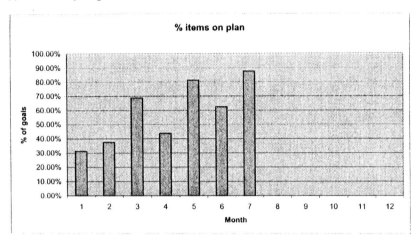

Measure	Goal	Actual	Last	YTD	High	Low	Prior
# of new accounts							
Unit trust market share							
% growth in gross income							
# new products introduced							
# partnerships with third party institutions							
Client Survey (service and timeliness)							
Customer services interventions							

Measure	Goal	Actual	Last	YTD	High	Low	Prior
Meet regulatory filing deadlines on time							
Process efficiency measures — see separate schedule (ii)							
Turnover rate of employees							
Cost of poor quality							
Profitability in first quartile of industry							
Yield % pt spread vs. money market							

(ii) Process efficiency measures

(example from Strategic Plan)

Measure	Goal	Actual	Last	YTD	High	Low	Prior
Monthly statements # days after month end	5						
Confirmation notes # days after placements	5						
Welcome letters to new customers # days after signed up	2						
Unit Trust Certificate list to Registrar days after purchase	14						
Unit Certificates to unit holders – days after purchase	30						
Unit Trust encashments – days after requests	10						
Redemption cheques for Unit Trust days after request	10						

(iii) Customer satisfaction measures

(example from Draft CS survey)

Measure	Goal	Actual	%	Wt	#	YTD	High	Low	Prior
Helpful service Reps.	90%	85%	94%	20	18.6%				
Statement timeliness	80%	60%	75%	30	22.5%				
Query satisfaction	95%	100%	105%	15	21.0%				
Wait % over 10 minutes	98%	100%	100%						
Call transfers	90%			15					
Confidentiality level	98%			5					
Corporate image level	90%			5					
Overall efficiency level	90%			10					
Total									

See work sheets attached for calculation of annual goals (example)

(iv) Calculation sheet for goals of satisfaction

#	Summary	Best	Average	Low	Poor	% in best and average combined
2	Helpful service Reps.	80	10	6	4	90%
3	Statement timeliness	60	20	10	10	80%
4	Query satisfaction	90	5	3	2	95%
6	Wait % over 10 minutes	95	3	2	0	98%
7	Call transfers	80	10	5	0	90%
8	Confidentiality level	90	8	2	0	98%
9	Corporate image level	80	10	10	0	90%
10	Overall efficiency level	85	5	5	5	90%

Appendix C

Original TSE/OSC Draft Guidelines for Board's Role and Responsibility

The Guidelines summarized	The method of response
1. The Board of Directors should explicitly assume responsibility for Stewardship, specifically for: • the strategic planning process, • identification of risks and risk management systems, • succession planning, • communications policy, • internal control, and • management information systems.	
2. The Board of Directors should be constituted with a majority of unrelated directors.	
3. Firms should disclose annually whether a majority of directors are unrelated.	
4. Firms should have a committee of directors for nominating new directors and assessing directors on an ongoing basis; members of this committee should all be non-management.	
5. Firms should implement a process for assessing the effectiveness of the board, its committees, and individual directors.	
6. An orientation and education program should be provided to new board members.	
7. The board should consider its size and potential for reduction.	
8. The board should review the adequacy and form of the directors' compensation.	
9. Committee members should be outside directors, a majority of whom are unrelated.	
10. Firms should have a committee with responsibility for governance issues.	

The Guidelines summarized	The method of response
11. Position descriptions for Board and CEO should be developed; corporate objectives should be approved/developed by the Board.	
12. Firms should have structures and procedures so the Board can function independently of management.	
13. The audit committee should: • be composed of outside directors, • have its responsibilities specifically defined, • have direct communication channels with internal and external auditors, and • have oversight responsibility for the system of internal control.	
14. A system should exist to permit individual directors to engage outside advisors at the expense of the corporation in appropriate circumstances.	

Appendix D

Simple Risk Management Checklist

Question	Response		Action planned
	Yes	No	
1. Have you identified the potential business risks for the organization?			
2. Have you assessed the likelihood and consequences of the significant risks being realized?			
3. Have you assessed the risks that could: • Damage your reputation? • Affect your market position? • Result in prosecution?			
4. Have you established controls to manage the significant business risks?			
5. Have you established a positive culture for controlling risks?			
6. Have you established a contingency plan to mitigate disaster?			
7. Have you established continuity management arrangements in the event of a disaster?			
8. Do you regularly audit compliance with control arrangements?			
9. Do you regularly review these arrangements with respect to their adequacy and effectiveness?			
10. Do you report annually on your risk control measures?			

Appendix E

Good Internet Links
for Research and Reference

www.ex.ac.uk/~RDavies/arian/scandals/classic.html
Great website that lists many illegal and fraud issues and links to articles written about these areas.

www.citizenworks.org/admin/press/corpreforms.php
U.S. site of Citizen works — advocacy group for change in social responsibility or corporations as well as government.

web.idrc.ca
International Development Research Centre — Ottawa site that has good reference materials on role of Boards and governance.

www.osc.gov.on.ca
Ontario Securities Commission — provides good insight into some of the changes that regulators are working on.

www.socialsciences.uottawa.ca/governance/eng
Ottawa University Centre on Governance — where a lot of work is being done especially as it relates to public sector governance.

www.sec.gov
Home site of the U.S. Security and Exchange Commission (SEC) who are at the centre of many of the changes taking place on corporate governance in the United States.

www.iisd.org/default.asp
International Institute of Sustainable Development, which is a good resource site that identifies many of the social forces driving change.

www.ccaf-fcvi.com/english
Canadian Comprehensive Auditing Foundation — much early work was done by CCAF in the area of improved transparency and disclosure.

www.wbcsd.ch/templates/TemplateWBCSD4/layout.asp?MenuID=1
World Business Council on Sustainable Development site that complements the other site but is based on representation of business interests. Good source for looking at comparative corporate reporting of non-traditional performance information; includes a number of Canadian organizations.

www.corpgov.net/forums/conversation/blair.html
Good source of background materials on corporate governance. In particular features the recent book by Margaret Blair (see reading list).

www.spartacus.schoolnet.co.uk/TUgeneral.htm
For the history buffs who want to look at some of the background that we have touched on relating to timescales of both regulations as well as social events such as Union organizations.

www.corporate-governance-code.de/eng/kodex/1.html
English language site that covers the recent changes (and the differences) in the German approach to corporate governance where Boards have a very different role and participation is shared through representation of the work force.

http://iog.ca
Institute on Governance who focus a great deal on public sector issues but also cover emerging issues on the broader spectrum.

www.worldbank.org/html/fpd/privatesector/cg/codes.htm
World Bank site on Corporate Governance best practices.

www.oecd.org/home
Home page of the OECD (Organization for Economic Cooperation and Development) based in Paris — that published "OECD Principles of Corporate Governance" in 1999.

Appendix F

The Principles of Quality Management

The eight underlying Principles upon which ISO 9001:2000 is founded	
• Customer Focus • Leadership • Involvement of people • Process approach (to getting the job done)	• System approach to management • Continual improvement • Factual approach to decision making • Mutually beneficial supplier relationships

The following principles are identified in ISO 9004-2000 "Quality Management Systems — Guidelines for Performance Improvements." They serve as a base for both the creation of the ISO 9001 standard but, more importantly, as a basis for management to focus its strategic thinking and decision making in their leadership role in creating an effective environment to ensure that the quality system forms the basis for continual improvement and thus delivers value to the organization.

a) **Customer focus**

Organizations depend on their customers and therefore should understand current and future customer needs and should meet customer requirements and strive to exceed customer expectations.

b) **Leadership**

Leaders establish unity of purpose and direction of the organization. They should create and maintain the internal environment in which people can become fully involved in achieving the organization's objectives.

c) **Involvement of people**

People at all levels are the essence of an organization and their full involvement enables their abilities to be used for the organization's benefit.

d) **Process approach**

A desired result is achieved more efficiently when activities and related resources are managed as a process.

e) **System approach to management**

Identifying, understanding, and managing interrelated processes as a system contributes to the organization's effectiveness and efficiency in achieving its objectives.

f) **Continual improvement**

Continual improvement of the organization's overall performance should be a permanent objective of the organization.

g) **Factual approach to decision making**

Effective decisions are based on the analysis of data and information.

h) **Mutually beneficial supplier relationships**

An organization and its suppliers are interdependent and a mutually beneficial relationship enhances the ability of both to create value. Successful use of the eight management principles by an organization will result in benefits to interested parties, such as improved monetary returns, the creation of value, and increased stability.

Appendix G

Thinking about Risk Tolerance

Risk profile element	Decision to be taken
Market risk profile — customer focus	What level of market risk is acceptable — for example drugs and pharmaceuticals would be close to zero tolerance, whereas automotive can accept some level of recall.
Market risk — employees and general public	What level of reputation does the organization wish to accept? Is it critical that it has a "best company to work for" profile or are the types of employees required not that critical?

What about environmental risk and reputation — is there an acceptable level of risk? |
Financial profile	What level of financial risk in terms of $ losses by event, annually, and/or over time are acceptable?
Safety risk profile	What level of accidents (major or minor) is acceptable over a given time period?
Human resource profile	What level of layoff to staff on an interim basis is acceptable? Is there a potential problem with laying off staff? What is the impact of any actual or potential union exposure?
Combination risk	Defined levels of project success on new markets/new ventures within an acceptable financial envelope (*e.g.*, 2 of 5 new services initiated come to market with a loss on failures — 3 of 5 not to exceed $200K per year.)

Appendix H

Classifying the Status of Risks

A	Acceptable	No issue with this question — appears there is no exposure at this time to risk or that this area is not applicable within the assessed organization. No action probably required.
NI	Needs improvement	There is a risk and based on the current situation some action will be required to reduce the risk.
NA	Not acceptable	There appears to be a significant risk in this item and action must be taken to deal with it.

Level 1	Greatest risk	Likely to occur and the impact would be significant.
Level 2	Significant risk	Not as likely to occur but risk would be considerable to the organization.
Level 3	Some risk exists	Likely to occur but the impact would not be as high to the organization.
Level 4	Low level risk	Low likelihood of occurrence and if it happened the impact would be low.

Appendix I

Summary Risk Evaluation Profile

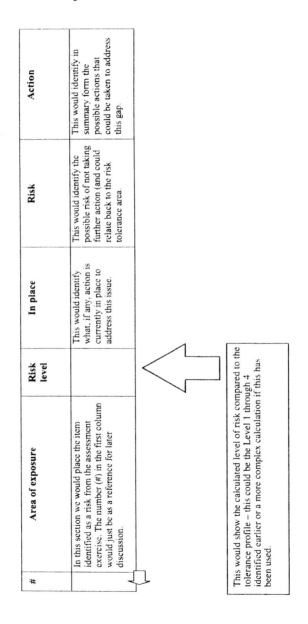

#	Area of exposure	Risk level	In place	Risk	Action
	In this section we would place the item identified as a risk from the assessment exercise. The number (#) in the first column would just be as a reference for later discussion.		This would identify what, if any, action is currently in place to address this issue.	This would identify the possible risk of not taking further action (and could relate back to the risk tolerance area.	This would identify in summary form the possible actions that could be taken to address this gap.

This would show the calculated level of risk compared to the tolerance profile – this could be the Level 1 through 4 identified earlier or a more complex calculation if this has been used.

Appendix J

Some of the Types of Actions that Need to be Taken

Internal action to reduce exposure. Risk avoidance and/ or Risk control methods.	Examples may include training of staff, investment in equipment or safety items, changing of work practices. It may also include re-engineering processes or activities as well as changing suppliers and/or materials. It could also include setting up items such as Health and Safety audits, and implementing systems such as ISO14000 (Environmental Management) ISO9000 (Quality/Process Management) and looking into Health and Safety programs (such as Canadian NQI Healthy Workplace framework). Improved internal controls and internal audits may also be applicable.
External actions to reduce exposure. Risk removal.	In some cases, the decision could be to cease carrying out a particular area of operation or activity. Eliminating the work through substitution, sub-contracting or even dropping the business area. In addition, risk sharing with suppliers could be addressed — vendor owned inventory as an example.
Sharing risk with a third party. Insurance.	In cases where risks remain and the organization is unable to take on the risk itself, the action plan would include a third party insurance organization assuming a portion — or all — of the risk for consideration of an annual fee or premium. Organizations can also vary the levels of deductibles with insurers so as to manage the risk down to an acceptable level while still optimizing the level of insurance premium. This may also include expansion to or revision of existing coverage.
Do nothing option — self-insure.	As a final choice, management or the owners may find it acceptable to assume the risk that has been defined. If this is the case, then the process will, as a minimum, have clearly identified the risk that is being taken and how it relates to the tolerance, as well as the implications to the organization.

Appendix K

Risk Evaluation and Assessment

(i) Establishing weighted rating criteria

Consequence Level and impact if event happens		Frequency of Occurrence if it happens				
Level		1	2	3	4	5
		Never	Rare	Occurs	Repeated	Often
1	Almost no impact	1	2	3	4	5
2	Minor impact	2	4	6	8	10
3	Average impact — not critical	3	6	9	12	15
4	Measurable and visible impact	4	8	12	16	20
5	Major impact	5	10	15	20	25

Appendix L

Risk Evaluation and Assessment: Probability of Knowing Situation Exists

Consequence Level and Impact	Organization has identified as an area of risk				
	1	2	3	4	5
	Actioned	Known	Aware	Some idea	No idea
Rating of risk being known	1	2	3	4	5

Appendix M
Detailed Process Mapping and Risk Identification Chart

PROCESS PERFORMANCE AND RISK ANALYSIS (PPRA)

ABC Service Organization

Service Process		Responsibility		PPRA #	
Location of Process / Activity		Supervisor		Prepared by	
Work Team involved				Date & Revision #	

For S (Severity), F (Frequency), V (volume) and D (Likelihood of detection) see the separate tables of how to assign scores from 1 - 10. Also use the S times F times V times D to determine overall risk level and assign score in SFVD.

SUB PROCESS / ACTIVITY / TASK STEP				POTENTIAL PROBLEM AND CURRENT CONTROLS						IMPROVEMENT ACTION PLAN		RESULTS				
Activity	Potential Failure	Potential impact	S	Potential Cause / Process Variable	F	V	Current Process Control	D	SFVD	Recommended Action	Who / Date	Results of action	S	F	V	D

Appendix N
Typical Risk Evaluation and Self-Assessment Checklist Template

#	Area of Assessment	Issue?		A. Probability			B. Impact			C. Degree of control			Total risk	Action Plan
		Y	N	1	2	3	1	2	3	1	2	3	AXBXC	

Note scoring based on multiples of three categories with maximum risk assessment of 27. Criteria should be established as standards for assessment such as political, economic, reputation, etc.

Appendix O

Typical Risk Evaluation and Self-Assessment Checklist — Example

#	Area of Assessment	Issue? Y	Issue? N	A. Probability 1	A. Probability 2	A. Probability 3	B. Impact 1	B. Impact 2	B. Impact 3	C. Degree of control 1	C. Degree of control 2	C. Degree of control 3	Total risk AxBxC	Action Plan
B1	The Board selects new candidates based on the method prescribed by the TSE guidelines.													
B2	Board guidelines are in place based on best practise with TSE as a minimum requirement													
B3	There is a Board orientation and training program and current Board members have all completed the program.													
B4	The Board participates actively in the strategic business planning process together with senior management													
B5	The Board's Terms of Reference are clear and understood.													
C1	Sales in Foreign Currency													
C2	Purchases in foreign currency													
C3	Employees handling cash transaction													

Appendix P

Leadership Assessment (from the Canadian Quality Criteria for Public Sector)

(i) Strategic Direction

☐ A mission and mandate statement is in place and has been communicated to all levels of the organization.

☐ Key success factors and priorities have been determined and are linked to strategic direction, for example, the accountability framework for the organization.

☐ Strategic planning incorporates ambitious objectives necessary to achieve the mission and mandate and is communicated to all levels of the organization.

☐ Implementation of strategic planning is monitored and reviewed.

(ii) Leadership Involvement

☐ The senior management team demonstrates a commitment to quality improvement for example through direct involvement in improvement initiatives.

☐ The senior management team works together to reduce barriers between functions, and promote teamwork and open communications.

☐ Responsibility, accountability, and leadership for improvement are shared throughout the organization.

☐ Reward and recognition for senior management are linked to quality principles.

☐ Responsibility to society in general is considered in the decision making process.

☐ Ideas and practices on quality improvement are shared internally, with other public sector service organizations and sectors.

(iii) Results of Leadership Action

☐ Indicators of effectiveness are setting strategic direction and demonstrating leadership in quality principles (are in place).*

☐ Indicators of the level of understanding in the organization, of the mission, mandate, and strategic direction (are in place).

☐ Extent of direct involvement by senior management in the implementation of quality principles and in improvement initiatives (are in place).

---

* Note "are in place" has been added to the NQI text for clarity.

□ Extent of senior management involvement of sharing ideas and quality practices internally, and with other public service organizations and sectors *(are evident)*.

(iv) Continuous Improvement

□ The organization evaluates and works at improving its approach to leadership.

Appendix Q

Building a Template for Transparency and Accountability

In Part 3 of the book, a number of different areas for governance focus were discussed as a basis around which a new model can be constructed. The following framework illustrates how this might then be incorporated into an effective holistic and integrated reporting tool for an organization.

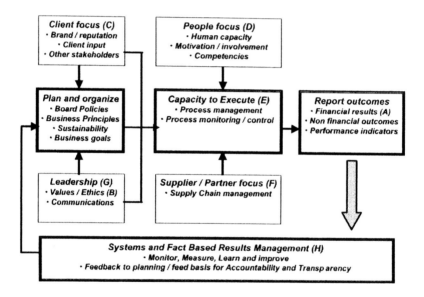

The topics that were identified include the following areas; for each the key components and cross-references to an integrated schematic model have been shown.

Ref	Criteria	Aspects of coverage
A	Financial Results	This remains a core component of "outcome" reporting to meet statutory reporting requirements, including compliance with regulatory rules and financial standards.

Ref	Criteria	Aspects of coverage
B	Values and Ethics	Values and Ethics are demonstrated through Leadership although the foundation for what these are come from Board direction.
C	Client Focus	Organizations exist to meet a need — whether market or societal (legislative) based. Focusing on this need is a core component of sustainability.
D	People Focus	Human capacity is the core component that enables execution but also contributes to most other areas of sustainable capability.
E	Capacity to Execute	Effective processes minimize costs and ensure a focus is maintained on delivering against planned requirements.
F	Supplier/Partner focus	Suppliers are key to the ability to execute in many organizations and effective relationships contribute towards economic sustainability.
G	Leadership	In addition to demonstrating behaviour consistent with values and ethics, leadership plays a key role in converting intent to execution.
H	Results Management	Using "fact based" input from outcome reporting and process reporting that addresses all aspects of the factors above, organizations can learn, improve, and attain transparency to the desired level.

Reporting must follow the core aspects of organizational accountability; if each component is required to present a broad-based picture of the organization's performance, then each must form part of the report. (Note that existing models already discussed in this book such as SIGMA and GRI, as well as "best practice" examples from organizations such as Ford, ALCAN, the GAP, Sun Life, and many others can also be used as templates).

Appendix R

Performance Highlights

SUMMARY REPORT — PERIOD ENDED XXX

Measure/Indicator	2004	Trend	2003	2002
Part 1 — Economic Sustainability				
Financial outcomes				
Shareholder return %				
Return on Equity				
Cash Flow generated				
Capital re-investment				
Values and Ethics				
% employee response on ethical conduct				
% employees trained on Code of Conduct				
# ethical complaints and investigations				
Client Focus				
Average rating (of 5) on client surveys				
# client complaints registered				
$ value of warranty claims				
% brand positive recognition				
% clients planning re-purchase				
People Focus				
Average rating on employee surveys				
Overall turnover rate %				
Average tenure of staffing				
% staff at defined competency level				
# lost time incidents/100 employees				
# Health and Safety critical observations				

Capacity to Execute				
# facilities maintaining ISO registration				
Average process defects/internal audit				
% cost base attributed to poor quality				
# process improvement suggestions made				
% suggestions implemented				
% process at/above target cycle times				
Overall on time delivery to commitment				

Supplier/Partner relationships				
% input costs covered by supply partnerships				
Average tenure of supply partnerships				
% satisfaction response on supplier surveys				

Leadership				
% Managers with Leadership training				
% employee rating on supervisory leadership				
% employees able to state values/vision				
% client response on company ethics				
% community response on citizenship				

Learning, Growth, and Improvement				
5 year average % revenue from new products				
$ invested in employee learning				
Average learning time/employee				

Part 2 — Societal sustainability				

Stakeholder participation				
Community charitable giving				
Community educational giving				
# employee hours donated to community				
# employees on secondment				
$ purchases from small business suppliers				

Part 3 — Environmental sustainability				

Environmental performance				
Waste generated/unit output				
% of product with recycle capacity				
Energy use/unit produced				
% value recycled material inputs				
Energy conversion ratio (Input/Output)				

One of the critical issues that any reporting must address is to achieve a balance between confidentiality (revealing information that might impact competitive advantages) and achieving transparency.

Reporting such as the above should be driven first by the information that the Board requires from management and only then should be considered for external exposure.

Appendix S

Simple Checklist for Transparency and Sustainability

The following simple checklist can be used as a basis for further developing a questionnaire that can be used to explore the level of reporting transparency actually being delivered by a reporting entity.

#	Question	Yes	No	Observations
1	Does the organization indicate application of Board Best Practices and its evaluation against these?			
2	Does the organization indicate that the Board is active in mandating statutory compliance as well as establishing discretionary performance and behavioural policies?			
3	Does the organization present both financial and non-financial performance information?			
4	Is the impact of intangible assets in the organization's performance discussed?			
5	Is the impact of the organization's involvement in community activities discussed?			
6	Does the organization identify and/or discuss key stakeholders other than investors?			

265

#	Question	Yes	No	Observations
7	Does the organization indicate that other stakeholders impact planning and strategy?			
8	Does the organization indicate it has a commitment to corporate values and ethics?			
9	Does the organization indicate that it tracks actual performance against values and ethics?			
10	Does the organization address its commitment to leadership among its managers?			
11	Does the organization present performance data on leadership practices?			
12	Does the organization present customer and market-focused performance data?			
13	Does the organization indicate the use of impartial validation of market loyalty, brand, or perception information?			
14	Is trend data presented to assess consistent measurement of client-focused performance?			
15	Is information presented that indicates the organization's relationship to industry associations and other external stakeholders?			

#	Question	Yes	No	Observations
16	Does the organization position its place in the market including both positive and negative aspects?			
17	Does the organization address measures or indicators that support sustainability of the work force?			
18	Do reports indicate both the attributes of the work force as well as the effectiveness with which they are being managed (*e.g.*, motivation/moral/turnover)?			
19	Does the organization indicate a commitment to effective process management?			
20	Does the organization discuss or measure its commitment to process sustainability and enhancement?			
21	Does the organization indicate commitments to third party assessments of its process capability?			
22	Does the organization indicate that it continually measures its own process operations against external best practice to ensure effectiveness and improvement?			

#	Question	Yes	No	Observations
23	Does the organization indicate that it tracks, monitors, and manages through the use of process performance indicators?			
24	Does the organization indicate that it uses client requirements to design work processes and track and measure actual performance against agreed standards?			
25	Does the organization indicate that it has partnering type (interdependent) relationships with key third party suppliers?			
26	Does the organization indicate that it tracks, monitors, and continually improves its supplier relationships?			
27	Does the organization indicate that it uses effective supply chain management approaches to build mutually beneficial supplier relationships?			
28	Does the organization track and monitor employee responses to leadership performance?			

#	Question	Yes	No	Observations
29	Does the organization indicate that it monitors and measures employee awareness of key policies (including compliance) such as values, ethics, and other Board level behavioural policies?			
30	Does the organization indicate that it has a process that supports innovation and creativity?			
31	Does the organization indicate measurable results from its innovation efforts?			
32	Does the organization commit to investing a portion of resources in education and development to support innovation?			
33	Does the organization indicate performance measures related to environmental sustainability?			
34	Does the organization track and report key environmental performance data relative to the industry?			

Appendix T

Progressive Canadian Organizations Involved in New Approaches

Rather than list organizations that are currently involved in activities of emerging governance renewal and enhanced reporting, the following websites can provide excellent research resources:

www.corporateregister.com

This site provides an excellent and comprehensive search capability on an international basis across a wide range of sectors. Resources are then shown either as downloadable reports or as access links to sites where information is made available.

www.globalreporting.org

This website, the home of the GRI or Global Reporting Initiative, provides a list of all those organizations who are known to be developing accountability and reporting frameworks using the GRI criteria.

www.wbcsd.ch

The World Business Council on Sustainable Development lists a number of case studies where organizations who are involved in this initiative have developed and implemented new strategies.

In addition to the above, many of the accounting bodies who support awards for sustainable development also publish case studies and provide access to added information.

Glossary

Terminology	Our interpretation and use
actions	The specific activity usually assigned to an individual or group of individuals who are accountable and responsible for making the plans happen.
goals	Those long-term high level directional statements that provide overall direction to an enterprise's activity (see also mission).
governance	Governance is the framework through which the affairs of enterprises are directed and controlled. Good governance ensures that the rights and responsibilties of all stakeholders are identified, recognized and protected. There is clear agreement of organizational principles and values and a process exists through which the enterprise's goals and objectives are executed, performance is monitored, and results delivered.
mission	A statement that defines the organization's "play box" — that definition that delineates for all those involved the areas within which the organization will operate.
objectives	Measurable milestones that are established along the journey to achievement of the goals, the mission, and the vision. The "what an organization will achieve".
outcomes	Essentially the same as objectives — they define the results of pursuing the various strategies in terms of what will be the end results.
plans	Specific steps along the way of implementing a strategy — usually defines who does what, by when, what resources are required, and what the specific measurable results will be.
strategies	The way in which the organization chooses to approach the deployment of achieving its goals and objectives. The "how to" ways in which objectives will be achieved.
values	The fundamental beliefs upon which the organization is founded and which (should) permeate every decision and action that the organization takes.
vision	Similar to "goal" — a high level general statement that provides a long-term view of what the organization is "forever" striving to become.

Index

Corporate Social Responsibility (CSR), 59

Dey report, 49, 53

Directors
Accountability, 66
Creation of, 68-69
Effectiveness, 65-68

Dot com crash, 9

Economic Value Added (EVA), 80

Effective Execution, economic value of
Checklist, 162-163
Linking issues to stakeholders' equity, 145-148
Management accountability, 148-150
Measuring and reporting process performance, 162-164
Planning and, 152-153
Quality management, 158-162
Risk management within capability model, 1555-158
Role of process, 153-155
Threat of what we don't know, 150-152
Typical capacity and performance metrics, 163-164

Enron, 91, 94, 101, 102

Enterprise Risk Management (ERM), 84, 155

Environmental management, 21

Ethical behaviour
Defined, 36

Excess costs, 72-73

FedEx, 198

Financial performance measurement, 92-93

Financial reporting, 97-99
Measures vs. indicators, 99-100

Ford, Henry, 194

Ford Motor Company, 200, 212